MIGUEL INDURAIN

A LIFE ON WHEELS

MIGUEL INDURAIN

A Life on Wheels

Pablo Muñoz

Translated by

Adrian Bell

To Jone, María and Ane,
the best companions I could have
in the stage-race which is life.

Aitatxo

First published in Great Britain in 1998
by Mousehold Press,
Victoria Cottage, Constitution Opening
Norwich, NR3 4BD

English language translation © Adrian Bell, 1998

Originally published in Spanish as
Miguel Induráin: y el mito se hizo hombre
Copyright © Pablo Muñoz, 1996

Published by Editorial Prensa Ibérica, S.A.
Camps i Fabrés, 3–11, 4°, 08006, Barcelona

Cover design: Patrick Loan
Cover photograph: Micael Löfgren

ISBN 1 874739 10 2

Printed by Watkiss Studios Ltd, Biggleswade

CONTENTS

FOREWORD

Miguel Induráin will always be remembered as the King of July, having spent his birthday of July 16th astride his bicycle doing what he did best — winning the Tour de France. Yet, until 1991 when he raced to the top of Val Lourens to claim his first race-leader's *maillot jaune*, there was nothing to distinguish the tall, good-looking Navarais from any of the other competitors in the greatest race in the world.

Many people are shocked to learn that Big Mig, as we eventually came to know him, rode himself into anonymity in his first two Tours. He didn't finish either of them. Then, as he matured, he became known as a strong rider able to help in the mountains when his captain, and the real Spanish star of the time, Pedro Delgado, demanded it. Delgado, the Tour winner in 1988, was an idol back home and Induráin's introverted character made sure that he stayed very much one step behind.

But strength will out and, by 1991, with discussion abounding as to who would lead the Spanish Banesto team into the Tour, the decision was taken that the best man would continue the fight for the final yellow jersey in Paris. Induráin left no one in any doubt as to who that was: after a long breakaway with the Italian Claudio Chiappucci, he earned that right. Not until 1996 would he ever again be challenged.

This beautiful book by Pablo Muñoz traces the life and career of one of the greatest cyclists ever to have lived. He was a private man who changed his character each July to challenge the roads of France which held many fears for him, and he delivered back to his small village in Spain the biggest sporting prize of all.

Any lingering doubts as to how great Induráin was, were dispelled in 1996 when he rode *La Grande Boucle* for the last time. It was the year the Tour would go past his house; the year all of Spain had waited for; and the year that Miguel Induráin could no longer discover the magic to win the race for a record sixth time.

As riders much less talented than he hurt the Spaniard like never before, he slowly slipped away from contention. No longer looking like a winner, Induráin had every opportunity to retire from the race he once dominated. Champions find it difficult to accept defeat and, since 1991, he had known only good times, but now he was being dragged across the Alps and the Pyrenees by the seat of his pants, and every bump in the road hurt – hurt very much.

This was the year when Miguel Induráin, a champion athlete, also became the people's champion. He did not retire: instead, he suffered like everyone else and, on what should have been a great moment, he raced past his house on the long stage through the Pyrenees, not in the lead group, and without a glance towards the makeshift grandstand outside it. The race finished in Pamplona, a few kilometres from his home, but Induráin showed no thoughts of retirement and, eventually, he reached Paris in eleventh place.

The Induráin period was over, but his refusal to leave the race by the back door made Bjarne Riis from Denmark look a proud new champion, and it endeared him to the hearts of all. He didn't need to win the Tour de France again: he had shown the world that he was simply the best.

Phil Liggett
May 1998

Miguel Induráin in the 1991 Tour de France

VILLAVA IS NO LONGER WHAT
IT USED TO BE

Only four kilometres away from the Plaza del Castillo, in the very heart of Pamplona, lies the village of Villava or, as the road sign in Basque indicates, Atarrabia. In the 1960s it was a small village, clean and opening on to cornfields, its centre crammed together on either side of the main road which takes you first towards Huarte, then to the Esteribar valley, and, eventually, towards the distant Pyrenees.

With little more than 4,000 inhabitants at that time, Villava was basically an agricultural village with two or three medium-sized firms which were taking on those workers who were deserting the increasingly uncertain world of farming. The San Andrés paper mill gave that quiet, rural village the look of pre-industrial tranquillity and, just in front of it, at number two San Andrés Street Miguel was born on 16th July 1964. He was the first child of Miguel Induráin senior and Isabel Larraya.

It is a two-storey house with a small garden, brimming over with roses, set against the main wall. There are, and always have been, geraniums and other plants in the windows, and on the balconies. At the back there is another wide, flower-filled garden which leads into the vegetable patch.

Villava, in the sixties, was a self-contained village in which everyone knew everyone else. To go to Pamplona, so near and yet so far, was something of an adventure, or at least an excursion.

More than thirty years have passed since then and Villava is no longer what it was. The neighbouring village of Burlada is now just a suburb of Pamplona, the capital city of Navarra, and with no geographic or visual boundary to separate the two villages, something of that has touched Villava: it is now almost a dormitory town

1

of more than 8,000 inhabitants, with noise, traffic and workshops. Very few families still live exclusively from agriculture, but one of those which does is the Induráin family.

FAMILY PORTRAIT

There are those who say, with hindsight, that they remember Miguel Induráin senior riding his bicycle out into the country, even that he was pedalling in a particular direction because he was visiting the woman who would later be his wife. Every man has his own genetic interpretation of where a love for cycling comes from. Miguel Induráin, the father, neither confirms nor denies any of this, nor even perhaps remembers it. He prefers to smile, ironically, at anyone who asks him.

Miguel Induráin senior preferred not to listen to the siren calls of industrial development: he was attached to the land, to his vegetable gardens, his fields of wheat, his vineyards and his animals. They provided him with work and with more than enough to support a family which, in time, would grow. After Miguel came Isabel, Nekane (Dolores), Asunción and, finally, Prudencio.

Miguel's father worked hard to give the family a good upbringing and did everything he could to provide for the future of his children, although they all gave a hand in working the fields. Now, when so much has changed in the village and in his own family, we can imagine Miguel Induráin senior surrounded by his children in that corner of the back garden where they all come together for family celebrations. Miguel, the oldest, at the height of his achievements; Pruden, the youngest, in the same career as his brother and taking part with the same enthusiasm while also sharing some of his brother's fame; Isabel, qualified in business management; Nekane, dividing her time between her work as a beautician and the Talde Berri basketball team in the first women's league; Asunción, working as a clerk. The family has certainly done alright.

Chance – and love – brought the Induráin and the Larraya families together in a double marriage: Victor Induráin Eugui, Miguel senior's brother, married Emi Larraya, Isabel's sister. The cousins Daniel, Javier and Luis brought an extra three players to the games, the rushing about, and the general racket between the stone walls that surrounded the vegetable garden and the cornfields of that two-storey house in San Andrés Street. In the big garden the two sets of Induráin–Larraya children ran about, played hide and seek, fought battles, and climbed trees. They rarely went into the street because they had everything they needed in their own little world.

In that same garden the whole clan now gets together to celebrate the success of son Miguel, in the closeness of the family, between bursts of good humour and glasses of that smooth red wine – almost a claret – that comes from the vines lovingly tended by Miguel senior.

SCHOOL-DAYS – A TRIAL

When the time came, Miguel was enroled in the local Lorenzo Goicoa School; in those classrooms he put up with school life from kindergarten to the end of his primary-school days. I say 'put up with' because school books were not exactly his greatest love.

His school friend, Angel María Armendáriz Echeguía, remembers him pretty accurately: 'He was an average student, like all of us, scraping through, although he made more effort than I did. I remember that he usually let me copy the homework the teachers set us. I believe that at home they put a bit of pressure on him and made sure that he finished the homework every evening. Me, I was more careless.'

In the school playground, recalls Armendáriz, they played football together and you could almost be certain that Miguel would play in defence. But, apart from playing sport with the gang, he did little else with them. 'When we got out of school in the afternoon and the rest of us kids used to play around, we usually saw Miguel in his family's fields working with the tractor. Villava was very small in those days, not much more than the one main street; all the rest was cultivated fields.'

That tractor was the Induráin brothers' favourite toy which they had learned to handle seated on their father's knees while he drove it; later, while still youngsters, they would have the nerve to take it from the door of the house to its garage. It was exciting that tractor and they rode it more than their bicycles; it made them feel grown up.

The other pupils in Miguel's school thought of him as 'a bit reserved and timid', one of them recollects, and yet already there

3

were signs of his strength, his power, and astuteness. 'In the autumn we used to play with conkers to see who could throw them the furthest. Miguel used to throw them in a special way, "under-arm" as we say, like the shepherds we saw around here, flinging them from low down upwards.'

Inevitably, of course, Miguel played football. He was also keen on athletics, table-tennis and basketball. But that was after he left Villava: after finishing primary school his parents sent him to the Larraona College in the regional capital, in the Avenue of Pío XII. Miguel was not the only one there since, by family agreement, all the Induráin–Larraya cousins went to that same school. It was a modern building, next door to the university campus and opposite the University Hospital of Navarra. The population growth of Pamplona was bringing the city closer to Villava and the kids of Villava were gravitating towards the capital.

It was then that Miguel got thoroughly involved in sports – any sport. His school friends from Larraona remember him as a 400-metre runner and javelin thrower. He used to beat everybody. 'He was always very strong,' says his mother, 'and in every sport he took part in he stood out because of his physical strength.' His presence was an inspiration when he played sweeper for Villava's local football team, Beti Onak, now in the regional third division. A youngster of great stamina, he liked long-distance running races. 'He even got on to a television programme called *On the Way to a Record*,' says his cousin, Daniel, 'which children from all over Spain used to go to. Miguel did well, but he didn't win.'

Absorbed in sports, and unable to stomach maths and physics, Miguel somehow finished his schooling, and qualified for the Training Institute at Potasas de Navarra, a town artificially created in the seventies around the potash mines. He opted for the tool mechanics course, with the sensible idea that he would be able to help his father maintain and repair the tractors, and agricultural machinery on the farm. 'He had always enjoyed repairing things and manual work,' says his mother, and she proudly shows an enormous steel sliding entrance door for the cars and the tractor. 'He designed and made it.' She is delighted to show it to us. With only one year remaining before completing the four-year mechanics course, he left the Institute. He had decided to devote himself fully to cycling.

4

His father understood and accepted it. There had been bikes in the house ever since the children were babies. 'If it goes badly,' he said, 'he'll always be able to return to working on the farm.'

Villava was beginning to move away from its rural isolation but, even so, when Miguel Induráin decided to make his career out of cycling nobody could have imagined that within a few years the name of that village would be triumphantly spoken about on television and in all the major newspapers.

THE VILLAVA CYCLING CLUB

Miguel Induráin had already made up his mind, even when he was still a student in the Larraona College, that cycling was going to be the centre of his life. A great deal has been written about the origins of that enthusiasm and how Miguel came to see his future so clearly. There is no doubt that at nine years old he was pedalling through the streets of Villava, which were quiet and traffic free in those days; and, according to the story his father tells, his love of cycling was spurred on when, at the age of eleven, he bought him a 'racing machine' after some kid had stolen the old bike on which he had first learned to ride.

AN IRREVOCABLE DECISION

'In our family,' so cousin Daniel tells us, 'the first present they gave us was a bike. So, all of us loved cycling.' Being honest and realistic about his academic limitations, and being mad keen on sport, when, around about fifteen, the moment came to choose, Miguel had no doubts: he opted for cycling, even though the football club Osasuna Promesas* wanted him. 'I told him,' his mother recalls, 'that I would prefer him to be a footballer. That was the better choice, but he'd already made up his mind. "Are you sure, son?" I asked him. "Quite sure," was his reply.'

His father accompanied him when he signed on with the Villava Cycling Club, a local group which all the Induráin boys, five in a row, would end up joining. There were times when they gave the young cycling novices a sandwich and a Fanta for taking part in the races they organised, times when the youngsters who won climbed

---

*The youth team that feeds Pamplona's Osasuna F.C.

up on to the podium with an outsize cup which sometimes had to be given back to the organisers, so it could be used on another occasion.

José (otherwise known as Pepe) Barruso, president of the club and one of its founders in 1975, has a host of personal recollections. It was he who met Miguel Induráin senior when, in the spring of 1976, he came into the headquarters of the club, holding his eldest son – an eleven-year-old lad – by the hand. At that time Pepe Barruso was in charge of the club's 'school' and was recruiting any youngster he could, although this was difficult because something as tough as cycling is not everyone's cup of tea. He remembers that the very first was one Arizcuren, the son of a friend, and after him came a dozen more – among them, all the Induráin boys.

By then they were organising official races, many of them through the streets of Villava itself. 'Today that would be unthinkable,' Pepe says, 'because of the traffic and the inconvenience it would cause. It was a bad circuit then, but it was OK for juvenile races.' He remembers Miguel as a shy lad, who didn't say much, and it was his father who came up to him one day 'so they could enter the lad who wanted to ride in that day's race'. He needed a federation licence and on that first occasion he had to make do just watching. He was annoyed because he had come with his bicycle, convinced that all he had to do was turn up and ride.

JUST GET ON WITH IT

With a licence granted by the Villava Cycling Club, Miguel got his first opportunities to compete, always in nearby villages in Navarra. The boys were taken there by club officials in their own cars and Miguel's father put his at the disposal of the club; between them, the directors and the parents did the chauffeuring, and paid for the petrol. The cycling apprentices were all friends from the village, like Angel María Armendáriz, Miguel's classmate from the primary school, who was envious of him: 'It was the typical kid's jealousy,' he remembers, 'because he and Joaquín Marcos competed in the races run through the streets of the town, and they won them all.'

Years later, when Miguel had got his first stage win in the Tour, Armendáriz met him, driving his car in the main street of Villava. 'He stopped when he saw me and was obviously pleased to talk. His win had really been something in the village and I said to

7

him: "Now they're going to keep their eyes on you and they won't let you win again. They'll keep you well under control" – meaning his opponents. He didn't think so: "You'll see, it's now that I'm going to go better", he told me. And he was right, because that's what happened later on.'

José Ignacio Urdániz, another director and founder of the Villava Cycling Club, shares Pepe Barruso's experiences. He remembers that Miguel came second in his first race away from Villava. That was in the district of Elbetea, in Elizondo in the North of Navarra. Second time out he won, in the little village of Luquin. 'It was there in Luquin,' he recalls, 'that an amusing thing happened to his brother, Pruden, some years later. He had forgotten to bring his cycling shoes, and some other lad lent him his, but he took size 42, and Pruden took 43. With it being tremendously hot the inevitable happened, and we'd already warned him: he had to retire – he couldn't continue with such pain in his feet.' They were heroic times in a sport made for heroes.

His father, and sometimes his mother, too, used to go with him when he was racing. Later, he began to go by himself or with his friend, Alberto Bretón Mendía, who now works in the family saw-mill. Alberto's uncle, Juan Mendía, remembers the time when the two boys went to Barcelona to take part in a championship race: 'They came back so depressed, sadder than anything. Their bikes had been stolen and with what it cost then to buy a new one...'

Pepe Barruso interrupts these recollections: 'We had another boy older than him, Joaquín Marcos, who was a jewel: he used to win everything. When Miguel first arrived on the scene Marcos used to outshine him and it's not true, as I have read, that Induráin was able to win from the first moment. It was only after several races, when they were still in the first year and competing together, that Miguel began to beat him.'

'In the village,' continues Urdániz, 'there was no special love for cycling but there had been some people who were more or less well-known on the amateur circuit, like Pepe Barruso himself, Almárcegui, Lerga, and the López Salas family.'

So, it was then 1976 and the five Induráin—Larraya boys were registered in the Villava Cycling Club: Miguel, Prudencio, Daniel, Javier, and Luis. Urdániz remembers them well: 'They were privileged kids. They never had to go away from the house to enjoy themselves. In all there were ten of them – five brothers and sisters and five cousins, and they spent much of their lives together; they didn't need others to play with. What's more, the boys all went to secondary school together. Of all of them, the one who's seen most around the village, doing his own thing, is Prudencio, the most extrovert.'

'Miguel was strong and powerful: training came as no great effort for him, and that was before they did the kinds of medical checks they do now; then it was more carefree,' says Barruso. He is proud of his role in the club's school and of the outstanding pupil who came out of it. He cannot, however, conceal a certain amount of disapproval: 'In those days all of us connected with cycling knew Induráin; now there are so many fans – everyone is a fan. But the real fans are those who went to watch those youngsters race in the juvenile events. Nowadays it's wonderful to follow the Tour, and I respect those who do, but very few of them are true fans. I realised that during those races when we put up a poster and passed the hat round so that the spectators could contribute to the finances of the club. Many of those who now call themselves fans used to stand back when the hat came round.'

In the school of the Villava Cycling Club they taught the youngsters how to use the gears and not much else. Urdániz reels off the memories: 'Miguel was already using his bike a lot on his own account. He used to take a meal to his family in the fields, to his mother's family's farm at Alzórriz. It's about twenty kilometres from Villava to Alzórriz, and it was usual for him to come and go once or twice a day.'

THE FIRST PODIUMS

Urdániz and Barruso both insist that it was not necessary to repeat things twice to Miguel: 'He got it immediately. Apart from that, he had a magnificent physical fitness which neither of us had yet discovered. In those days the doctor only looked at them rather superficially to see if they were healthy, or whether they had a heart murmur, for example, and nothing more.'

Urdániz swells with pride when he tells how 'Miguel made his mark throughout the period in the different categories, both as a cadet and as a juvenile. He was always the best of his age-group in Navarra. He won all of the cycling school's races; it took him a bit of time to adjust, after changing category to juvenile, but he soon adapted. That boy won some 30 juvenile races, and it never made him conceited. I remember that we used to go in the car behind the race; the boys would be at the finish and we'd never know who had won. With everyone else, when we got there, we could tell how they'd done from their expression – you saw the joy, or the disappointment, on their face. With Miguel we always looked at him and could never guess what had happened at the finish. And the fact is that most of the time it was he who'd won ...'

Urdániz reckons that it was their failure at school which led the Induráin brothers into cycling: 'Miguel didn't like studying, but in his home he wouldn't have been allowed to stop trying.' This was why the academic effort was too much, except in physical education, obviously, and religious studies which, as a practising Catholic, he learned from childhood. 'Pruden,' Urdániz recalls, 'was not allowed to go to the cycling club as a punishment for getting bad marks at school. The fact is they are totally different. Pruden is more open, talkative, more of a joker, better with the girls.'

As a young cyclist Miguel was very obedient, disciplined and determined. That's the view of Pepe Barruso, his trainer for six years: '"But doesn't he have any faults?" the journalists usually ask me. Look, Euskal Telebista, the Basque television channel, were going to make a programme about Miguel – a 'This Is Your Life' kind of programme – and they came to the club and asked us which people they could take to the studio, and who would surprise him. "Well, I'm very sorry," I told them, "but there is no hidden story behind the idol." There was no one at all who occurred to me. The romance magazines would die of hunger with Miguel Induráin. Certainly, on one occasion, the magazine *Diez Minutos* interviewed me and they put words in my mouth. I was supposed to have said that Miguel was a big head, that he said "yes" to everybody and then just did what he wanted. It was all made up. I sent a letter to the editor in protest. It's outrageous that they can just make things up like that.'

It is obvious that the hunger for information created by the Induráin phenomenon has reached everywhere, and anyone who had anything to do with the start of his sporting career has eventually been drawn into this world of assertions and denials.

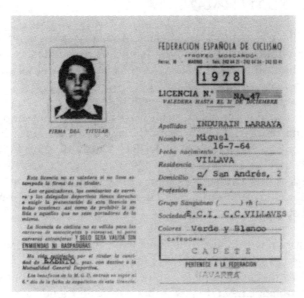

Miguel's licence to ride as a cadet

First kisses on the podium, aged thirteen

RIVAL AND TEAM-MATE

In the Villava Cycling Club, whenever the story of Miguel Induráin is being retold, one person who is always mentioned is Joaquín Marcos, his training partner and the one who, until Miguel's arrival, used to win everything.

Joaquín Marcos is 33, one year older than his former team-mate, and works in a sheet metal workshop in Berrioplano in the Pamplona industrial belt. From the age of eleven until he was twenty-one he was a registered cyclist – with Villava up to the age of eighteen. Then he gave it up. 'To be a keen cyclist was very hard and the year I lost whilst I was doing military service was the turning point. It was an uphill struggle for me to begin again; I tried, but after a year I stopped completely.'

Joaquín disagrees that there was any jealousy between him and Induráin within the same team. 'Nonsense, not at all: we were clubmates. From the time we were little kids, and with the few of us there were, the club was like a family. The parents and the organisers took us in their cars and vans, and we were all friends; we weren't opponents.'

With the passing of the years, Joaquín Marcos doesn't know how to describe what Miguel was like. 'I saw him as very reserved; he didn't say much. He was only assured and felt in his element when he was surrounded by his brother and his cousins, especially Daniel, who was the one he got on best with.' In training he tried to go in the group with them, with his family. Marcos remembers, however, that he and Miguel sometimes arranged to ride together.

They certainly went to the Spanish Championship together. There were four selected from Navarra: those two, Luquin and Miguel's cousin, Daniel. They were together for three days at Ponferrada (in the province of León), but the Navarra group put up a pretty mediocre performance. In the team time trial Miguel retired with sunstroke. In the road race he fell on a descent and fractured his arm; Joaquín Marcos was involved in the same accident but emerged unscathed. He can remember the return to Pamplona in the team manager's car with Miguel's arm in plaster.

'Miguel was a very good bloke: he would always help you if he could. Me, I certainly saw it: he pushed me for a good while so that I could get up the col de Aibar [in Navarra] because I had gone off the back,' Joaquín points out. Clubmate, and rival but nevertheless

12

friend, Joaquín Marcos left the Villava Cycling Club to join a team in the town of Oteiza, and later he went to Kaiku where Héctor Roldán was manager. And then came military service, and it all ended. Even in this Miguel Induráin was lucky: he avoided military service because there was an excess number of recruits.

After leaving cycling, Marcos met Miguel again in Villava where he still lives with his parents. They saw each other after Induráin had turned professional, 'but was not yet so famous' and, of course, they spoke about cycling. Other times since they have bumped into each other in the street 'but we only greet each other and say "Hello"'.

In the Villava Cycling Club there are now more than 100 future cyclists signed on, in training up to the age of eighteen. Naturally they all want to emulate their countryman. 'I warn them,' says Pepe Barruso, 'that if they want to be professionals they will have to sacrifice a lot, because we also make sacrifices for them. The difference is that when they win a race the glory is theirs. They are the ones who appear in the photograph.'

Miguel surrounded by youngsters from the Villava Cycling Club

THE REYNOLDS ADVENTURE

It was 1981 and seventeen-year-old Miguel Induráin was riding the races in Navarra almost like a newborn cyclist. At that time a cycling team called Reynolds was also being born. José Miguel Echávarri, a Navarra man from Abárzuza who had made his professional début with Anquetil's BIC team, had, two years earlier, convinced Juan García, boss of INASA, a firm in Irurzun, to support a crazy project: to sponsor a new cycling team which would be called Reynolds, after the name of the product – aluminium foil – which that firm made.

During 1979, once the idea had been accepted, he set about establishing an amateur team. It was not a bad beginning and in the following season they made the leap into the professional category. Reynolds' second coach, Eusebio Unzué – the brother of a first division goalkeeper – bumped into the young Miguel Induráin in 1982 and decided to bring him into the team. Later he was to say: 'It was our good fortune that we met Miguel when he was seventeen and excelling in juvenile events; we moved him up to the amateur category when he was eighteen and he was only there for two years because he showed so much potential. We agreed that that was sufficient time because, with his physique, we saw he had the potential for a splendid future. And slowly, slowly, but very surely, those expectations we had right at the beginning were confirmed.'

After eight years – as a beginner, infant, cadet and juvenile – in the Villava Cycling Club, Miguel accepted Unzué's offer. It was then 1983 and they came to the following agreement: 150,000 pesetas (£750) per year together with all equipment, including his bicycle. His father signed the authorisation that enabled him to compete, saying to himself: 'If one day he gets tired of riding, he can always return to work on the farm.'

Miguel Induráin's jump to the amateur category coincided with the beginning of the professional careers of Julián Gorospe, Angel Arroyo and Pedro Delgado. It was the year when Arroyo won the Vuelta a España, although afterwards he would be disqualified, and the first time that the organisers of the Tour de France invited Reynolds, which had then been running a professional team for three years, to take part in their great race. It was an invitation which filled everybody with great anticipation, but José Miguel Echávarri decided that it would be better to wait and compete the following year with a young, strong team.

Looking back now over all that Miguel achieved, Eusebio Unzué reckons that one of the keys to that success was the patience of the sponsors, of the managers and of Miguel himself, who was keen to accept the chance of riding beside such charismatic figures. 'I believe that patience is a family legacy,' he says, half joking; 'his manner, his calmness about everything. Also, there's the fact that we, in the team, wanted to bring him on slowly, trying to do things the best way possible. It was lucky, too, that in the early years we found a group of sponsors like Reynolds, who didn't get agitated and start demanding quick results from us, and that Miguel had the opportunity of being able to count on men like Arroyo, Gorospe, Laguía, and above all, Pedro Delgado. They were professionals who, throughout, carried the responsibility of the team, which meant that the personal work with Miguel could be conducted more calmly.'

Unzué's confidence in Miguel's potential was absolute, prophetic almost. 'It sounds like I'm boasting, and it might seem easy to say it now,' says the coach, 'but I definitely said, some years ago, that Induráin might never win a Vuelta a España, but undoubtedly the Tour de France would be his.'

Together with Miguel, in that historic Reynolds team, rode Gastón, González Salvador, Arenas, Navarro Fuster and Pacheco, among others. They won so many races that they beat the record for the number of first places won by a single team.

With regard to his own performances, Miguel Induráin managed six wins in that year, 1983, among them the Amateur Championship of Spain, on 3rd July, in Elda. That triumph, which made him the youngest ever Spanish champion, was decisive: it made him dream about becoming a professional like his idol at the time, Bernard Hinault.

In 1984 he took part in the Los Angeles Olympic Games and ended the season with ten victories. In September of the same year, just in time to compete in the Tour de l'Avenir, he moved up into the professional ranks with a salary touching on a million pesetas (£5,000). He was making progress but he had not managed to overcome that excessively quiet nature of his and the lack of ambition which, although he did not realise it, was prejudicing his chances.

RESULTS

Amateur: 1983

Road Race Champion of Spain
Tour of Salamanca: first overall and one stage win
Champion of Navarra
Tour of Toledo: two stage wins
Star Trophy of Pamplona

First-Year Professional: 1984

Tour de l'Avenir: team time trial and individual time trial
Gran Premio Iberduero
Fuencarral Classic
Aragón Week: first overall, points winner and one stage win
Tour of Navarra: two stage wins and Mountain Prize
Corte Inglés Classic
Tour of Vizcaya: team time trial and leader for three stages
Olympic Games (Los Angeles) road race: did not finish

A VERY PERSONAL PARENTHESIS

We left Miguel Induráin as he was on the point of entering the world of big-time cycling, which is where his own story really unfolds. At the age of 32 he is barely old enough for his biography to be written, at least not in the strict sense of the word. What we can do is write his professional biography, which is what this book is, but we do need to get an idea of the vital ups and downs of his life, and for that we can go little beyond a brief sketch.

Now, when Induráin is at the height of his fame, it is easy to make the same error as many of his fans, or the schoolboys who come up to him and scuffle amongst themselves to greet him, by considering ourselves his lifelong friends. Miguel has an anecdote about that: 'There are those who come up to me and say, "Don't you recognise me? I'm so and so. You remember? We did military service together." The fact is I didn't do military service. I was excused because that year's quota was exceeded!'

So this chapter will be an excursion through the memories and opinions people have of the young Miguel, of Miguel the person, of the Miguel of few words and without the yellow jersey, of Miguel getting off his bicycle – which is a bit like saying descending from heaven.

Miguel is not a man with many enthusiasms other than cycling and sport in general. His team colleague and room-mate, Pedro Delgado, tried to get him into the habit of reading during the evenings when they were away racing, but he didn't have much success. Miguel does have one habit or peculiarity: he always keeps a diary in which he puts down everything he has done during the day, with details about the time, the place, the weather, and other matters of interest. Perhaps one day editors will be itching to get their hands on that voluminous diary.

MARISA, THE COMPANION

Marisa has been Miguel's wife since 14th November 1992. Discrete and reserved, for two years before marrying Miguel she was with the Induráin family party enjoying Miguel's success in the guests-of-honour grandstand on the Champs Elysées in Paris.

Marisa is not one of those who make television appearances as 'the wife of' and she shuns the true-life magazines like the plague. She prefers to remain in the background: since they were married, at the end of the 1992 season, she has rarely been seen at the end of stages or running after her husband at the finish, or even turning up on rest days as many of the riders' wives do, appearing to think that it's their role to give succour to their men after the trials of battle. It's obvious that Marisa López de Goikoetxea is a discrete and sensitive woman.

She is from Lazkao, in the Basque province of Guipúzcoa, and is the same age as Miguel. She completed her business and administration studies in San Sebastián, and worked in the office of the University Clinic of Navarra, which is where they met when, on one occasion, Miguel was at the medical centre for a check-up.

During the three years of their engagement they were rarely seen in public together. They were most often seen, perhaps, in some restaurant or pub in the Iturrama district of Pamplona, but when they wanted to be really alone they went off to a quiet restaurant in Biarritz, or St Jean de Luz on the French Basque coast.

Marisa's first public appearance as Miguel's fiancée was with the Induráin family on the Champs Elysées. It was the prelude to the wedding which took place on 14th November in the chapel of the Colegio de las Madres Oblatas in the Rochapea district of Pamplona.

Miguel spoke of his honeymoon with the eagerness of a little boy: 'We went to Disney World, then to the Bahamas and to Paradise Island,' he would report enthusiastically.

That schoolboyish enthusiasm could be the secret of his success. Miguel has retained, from when he was very young, a certain freshness, a kind of innocence. In the airport at Orly, in Paris, Marisa bought him a surprise present from one of the duty-free shops – a scale model of a 1950s Alfa Romeo. Miguel collects them.

PRUDEN, THE YOUNGER BROTHER

Prudencio, Miguel's younger brother, is also a cyclist. He normally finishes the major races at the back of the field, but generally he does at least finish, which is not something to be sneezed at. He's not particularly worried about where he comes in the overall race classification because his intention at the Tour, or anywhere else, is to help Miguel win, and he puts everything into it, and it's a job he does pretty well. Pruden, as he is known in the family, also has memories of his childhood: 'I was the youngest and, as in all families, even those that get on well together, it's always the youngest who gets a clip round the ear most often. I know I did, and it was Miguel who gave it to me.'

That's probably true, but Pruden was also the one who most often got into scrapes: 'I was the one who was always annoying the others and it was me who ended up crying, too. In all families, as I said before, it's the youngest who ends up in trouble, although Miguel did as well sometimes.'

Pruden and Miguel enjoyed the same things, and used to get the same marks at school – a bit below average: neither of them were too keen on books. They didn't have to put up with any nicknames at school, although Pruden did get to be called Pindu because of the capital P he wore on his green jersey and 'indu' for Induráin. For him, Miguel is always Miguel, while his older brother refers to him as Pruden. Except when he's in a bad mood: 'When he's annoyed with me he calls me Prudencio – my full name. When I hear him calling me Prudencio, I know something's up.'

LIKES AND DISLIKES

Miguel Induráin has been asked about pretty well everything – his likes and dislikes, his past, his present, and his future – and he has patiently answered those questions a thousand times. From all that has been asked of him, and from all he has said, a detailed portrait could be painted of this major figure in world cycling.

'I was born a winner but I was not brought up like one', is what he usually says, perhaps to emphasise a modesty, bordering on humility, within the environment of his family. What he would really like, before each stage, is to eat a couple of eggs with ham because that's what he remembers from when he was a youngster – those late breakfasts in the family kitchen during the morning break from the work in the fields.

He and Marisa have a natural interest in ecology; they like taking long walks through the countryside, or along the Basque beaches where nobody troubles them. Miguel, a modest young man from Villava, the son and the grandson of farm-workers, seems lost standing on the main balcony of the Navarra Government building to receive the cheers of a packed crowd: it's as if the whole thing were a dream. When he returned after his triumph in the '93 Tour he appealed to the the organisers of the reception to forget about the American-style procession they were planning: 'Open-top cars? No, please, I'm not a president,' he had begged.

Miguel is a practising Catholic, but admits 'it has never occurred to me to ask the Virgin for a victory; the important thing is that she gives me good health and protects my family.'.

At the moment Miguel Induráin earns a lot of money, sensibly from a variety of sources. He has an economic interest in a firm that distributes Vélo accessories and he also gets an income from Banesto's sole rights with Francis Lafargue, who is their public-relations manager, and who is also both a friend and a business partner. Lafargue is the one who interprets for him when he appears on French television. He has also invested in a garage with José Miguel Echávarri, in a sports shop and a hotel.

On the day before his visit to Pope John Paul II in the Vatican Miguel could be spotted travelling to the village of Larressore, in the north of the Basque Country, to meet 50 excited youngsters who were waiting impatiently for him. He prefers these kinds of meetings to official ceremonies, and he always has time for youngsters: you just need to watch him at the start and finish of stages, signing his autograph for his cheering young admirers.

Tere Uriz, Miguel's cousin and Marisa's friend, spoke a lot about the time when they were engaged, their aim of having a child 'when the time comes', and of their happiness when the time did arrive. Tere runs the perfume shop Xarel, in the centre of Villava, opposite the town hall, but it was not easy to get her to speak about Miguel: it almost seemed as though there was a family pact 'after the things that have happened'. It is true, she warned, that the Induráins are resentful towards the press: 'At first the family received everybody, even though we're just ordinary, run-of-the-mill people and have never had anything to do with the press. First one journalist arrived, then another, and then photographers, and the television, and all of them were allowed into the house; we'd pour out a glass of wine for them, and give them something to eat, until they began to abuse it. A lot of things have happened which it's better not to talk about.' Tere has had intruders who have even climbed over the garden wall at night; they have stolen photographs from the family album; they have been followed day and night by the *paparazzi*, and they have lost their privacy.

Tere Uriz Induráin is 36, four years older than her cousin, Miguel, and is the daughter of Miguel's aunt on his father's side. She, too, spent her childhood on the farm and in the garden of the family house in San Andrés Street: 'Miguel was very laid back, nothing troubled him. Anecdotes? Well, we're so normal that nothing particularly unusual happened to us. As for me, since I am a little older than Miguel, Daniel, Javier, Luis and Pruden, I didn't really take part in their activities as children but, yes, we usually played ball games together, the boys, and the girls.'

To Tere, Marisa seems 'a really lovely person. She's someone who the more you get to know her, the nicer she seems. I'm sure they get on well as a couple.' Until a few years ago cousin Miguel regularly visited her perfume shop: 'Although he's not a show-off, he likes the minimum – eau-de-Cologne and aftershave lotion.' His favourite types – *Essence* from Loewe or Cacharel. His sisters used to buy it for him, but now it's Marisa's job.

Other than birthdays, the Induráins don't have any set times when they get together but they do so often, almost every day. When Miguel gets back home during the season and takes a rest from cycling in his new house in Olatz, near Villava, his mother calls everybody together, and organises a meal. In the summer this is always in the garden. When the family gets together in the evenings Miguel isn't the one who tells jokes: 'he is the one who laughs', Tere says. She also reckons that when cousin Miguel is in the house, completely relaxed, his favourite distraction is to get himself comfortable on the couch, in front of the television, with a bag of sunflower seeds to chew. She also confirms her cousin's favourite food: 'When he gets back home after a race what he needs is a couple of rashers of bacon and two fried eggs. His mother cooks them, and they are really special to him after the boring diet of pasta and rice when he's away.

21

THE MEDICAL PORTRAIT

As doctor to the Banesto team, Sabino Padilla was one of those who worked the medical miracle for the team and the most obvious person to give a medico-biological picture of Miguel Induráin. The press describes Miguel as a combination of genetic make-up and breeding, strength, and elegance, a man quite different from the average. Sabino Padilla basically agrees: Induráin is a high-performance biological machine and almost the perfect athlete: 'I have been with him for a good many years at Banesto and I confess I still don't know how far he can go physically. With each season that passes he develops further. We certainly have no quantifiable tests which show, accurately, his progression, but we can observe his enormous strength and capacity for recuperation which makes him capable of increasing his volume of work. That's not something all cyclists can cope with.'

He's 6' 1" tall, he weighs 12st. 4lbs and has a normal pulse rate of 36, which can go up to 190 during a time trial. But all that is just the infrastructure; inside there's a complex physical–psychological –biological mechanism which contributes to his superb performance as a cyclist: 'I'm not prepared to give out Miguel's medical and biological data: taken out of context I don't think they would mean anything, and also such intimate data is private. It would be like asking a man married to a film star about the size of his wife's breasts … What I can tell you is that Miguel has a physical potential way above the average, even for other professional cyclists, marathon runners and élite athletes. I have never come across anyone else like him.'

The explanation for Induráin's success is put down to genetics and work, 'and there is no doubt that his genetic inheritance has contributed significantly. For example, it is more than likely – although we have never done a biopsy – that his muscle tissue has a greater percentage of slow fibres than quick ones, and that is a genetic factor. Slow fibres are less susceptible to acidosis – getting saturated with lactic acid – and fatigue, and are better adapted to working medium or long distances.'

According to Padilla, the dual capability, which is very occasionally found in a man who both climbs very well in the mountains and excels in the time trial, is there in Induráin: 'we are talking about an athlete who combines two extremely important qualities in a cyclist: a great capacity for suffering, and an incredible aerobic potential. It makes him capable of sustaining tremendous efforts against the clock and, at the same time, able to use that aerobic potential to get through the mountains without difficulty, even though he is not a born climber. In short, he is an athlete with a high aerobic potential who makes practically 100 per cent use of it. The élite marathon runners achieve between 90 and 94 per cent of their potential; a good cyclist between 80 and 85 per cent; and a normal, sedentary person between 50 and 65 per cent of their potential.'

Sabino Padilla also explains the speed of his pedalling cadence: 'It may not seem so, but, in relation to his weight and size, he doesn't actually use big gears. In Luxembourg, in that memorable time trial in the 1992 Tour, Lemond and he used the same gear ratio, a 54x12, and Miguel took four minutes and four seconds out of him. His advantage had to be attributed to his cadence – he turned the cranks more times per minute. That is another of his main characteristics: a high pedalling rate. He really can ride like a windmill, pushing a gear which others might find too big.'

Miguel Induráin is a dry, fibrous athlete, so Padilla confirms: the proportion of body fat oscillates between eight and nine per cent. This compares with a figure of around about seven per cent for the Olympic marathon runner, Martín Fiz, and six per cent for the Ethiopian distance runners. His morphotype corresponds to the ectomorph – a predominance of vertical lengths over horizontal; he is not what we could call a 'stocky cyclist'.

After Miguel's third consecutive Tour de France triumph Padilla was asked, and was asking himself, how much longer could Induráin go on? 'Well, from the physical point of view, a good few years more because his body is in good shape. However, I don't want to say he's going to carry on winning Giros and Tours because that's a subjective matter: it depends on other variables such as his health, the strength of his rivals, the weather, tactics, and things of that sort.'

This, with all its terminological complications and its technical concepts, is another portrait of Miguel – almost an X-ray vision.

THE INDURAIN SUPPORTERS CLUB

Aitor David has been the president of the Induráin Supporters Club since the day of its foundation, on 27th September 1990 – '*before* he won the Tour and the Giro, I want you to know'. The club was formed with 40 members and its first administrative committee was selected 'from amongst the keenest cycling enthusiasts, and from those who had the most free time because they were shift workers'. In the first meeting after its inauguration the number of members was increased to one hundred. But, as a result of Miguel's victories, the number of applications continued to increase and this created problems: 'It's difficult to say no to the people of the village but we had to set a maximum number because running the club involves a lot of work, if only in the letters which have to be sent to each member.'

One of the established rules is to reject applications from those who are not known or not recommended by an existing member. The problem is those who call from Madrid, from Barcelona, from Portugal or from Mexico. These are, for the most part, men from Villava or Navarra, or the sons of Navarros who work abroad. The Supporters Club is considering, in these cases, permitting some exceptions for membership to the society 'because what they want is to have a membership card to show in Argentina or Germany – nothing more than that. So, if we can arrange for them to have one they'll be happy, although they don't participate as members by right, nor do they pay the fees, for example.'

Aitor David, the president, is a touring cyclist and he's always getting something going. 'The idea of the supporters club,' he explains, 'came from a group of friends and, one way or another, I was the promoter, the one who got most carried away with it. I am ten years older than Miguel but I have been a friend of his for some time.' He admits that he followed Miguel's cycling career from when he was in the juveniles, through the amateur ranks and ended up becoming a real supporter when he joined Reynolds. From the beginning he had a blind faith in him and he followed him in all his races, stage by stage, in Navarra, and the neighbouring provinces. He doesn't disguise the pleasure he gets from being president of the club: 'Although I've also had my share of difficulties,' he admits. 'There's a lot of people and they all have their own opinions, but the majority always give me their support and, up to now, I have been re-elected as president. Why? Do I do it well? I don't know. Perhaps it's through the personal trust I have with Miguel. The unpleasant things come when you plan something and not everybody agrees. But the truth is everything has gone well for us and, in the end, the people have said the governing body is doing it right. We have made hundreds of journeys and we've never had any problems, not even the slightest quarrel in the coach, nothing.' Aitor is satisfied.

An Induráin Supporters Club coach returning from Paris

In the Supporters Club they pay a subscription of 500 pesetas (£2) per month which covers the cost of hiring coaches and other working expenses; they also help the Villava Cycling Club which continues to work with the youngsters and cadets, and the Alas Cycling Club for the amateur-status riders. Encouraging a love of cycling is one of the functions of the club, according to its statutes, and, in pursuit of that, they now invest hundreds of pounds in prizes, a mountain prize, and trophies; but what the kids like most, when they win a race, is a jersey which Miguel Induráin has signed exclusively for them.

As well as being president of the club, Aitor David is a boiler-maker; he is also the joint owner of an engineering firm, together with a neighbour from Villava, Juan Antonio Almárcegui, who is also a cycling fan and president of the Alas Cycling Club. A staunch supporter of Induráin, Aitor David remembers the time when his idol turned professional: 'There were people who said that he

25

couldn't go far, that he was built for one-day races (a 'classics man', as Aitor defines it), that he wouldn't be able to cope with multi-stage races because he was too tall and heavy. It gives me a great deal of satisfaction,' he says emphatically, 'that I forecast great things for him even before he won the Giro. I forecast all that, and those who know me know that I did – although they looked at me as if I was daft.'

The Induráin Supporters Club receives letters from fans all over the world. Curiously, they had a call from Tokyo asking for the 'Song of Induráin', a *jota** composed by a local group: 'I had to play a recording of it over the telephone so they could take down the lyrics,' says Aitor David, with a laugh. The person who had called was a young Japanese girl who spoke Spanish and she said they wanted to translate the song into Japanese. The club also has a more official song, specially composed for the local San Andrés Choir, which is more solemn. They always take tapes of the two songs on the coach journeys 'but the one we put on most is the *jota* because it's more lively for singing in a group'.

The headquarters of the club is in the Jaizki bar and there the yellow jerseys and the pink jerseys, and photographs of their hero are displayed. At some time every year, 'whenever he can, when the man's commitments permit it', Aitor explains, 'the members have a celebration dinner with Miguel at which he hands over the jerseys, signs posters, is photographed with us, and then we have a real ball', says Aitor David.

David hankers for those quieter times when you could still see Induráin walking through the village with friends or at the bull pens during the fiestas. Now that is impossible. 'Sometimes we arrange a meeting in the Jaizki to deal with some aspect of the club and he has to come in through the back, through the restaurant door, and there are usually three or four of us with him. The fact is he cannot go for a walk without people embracing him, asking for his autograph, harassing him.'

The club has not forgotten about Pruden either, the brother 'who has many physical capabilities similar to Miguel'. In all honesty things have not gone so well for Pruden. Unlike Miguel, he wasn't lucky enough to avoid military service because of a surplus of recruits: Pruden had to put up with his year in the military, a year

*A Basque folk tune

26

with no training; he came back and then a crash put him in dry dock for another year. Then it was all uphill, trying to recover what had been lost. 'But he doesn't resent being second best', Aitor argues. 'He knows that, as of now, his brother is the best and that's all there is to it: he accepts it.'

Aitor David confirms this personal description of Miguel: 'He is the most unaffected person you could possibly imagine. He's cool; he doesn't lose his nerve; he's not put off his stroke by anything. His human qualities are almost more striking than his qualities as a cyclist: his patience with people is remarkable. Some complain that he doesn't show his feelings, but that's the way he is, that's his character and he can't change that. We ourselves have felt that he could do a little bit for the club – speak about or mention us when he's on television, but that's the way he is. The truth is he's extremely grateful to us, like when we send him a telegram on his birthday which is always during the Tour, but he's never effusive.'

The Giro and the Tour are experienced intensely in the headquarters of the club, and it is customary for them all to get together in the Jaizki to follow every stage on television. It has reached the point where many of the members have to go off to other bars in the village because of the lack of space.

In Villava, when there is no race going on, they carry on living quietly, in spite of the avalanche of journalists that regularly descends upon the village whenever Miguel wins one of the major tours. Villava is now a place to visit and stay overnight. Many of those who come to Pamplona for the San Fermín Fiesta use their time to get to know the village of Induráin. But it's not just Induráin: Villava is also on the pilgrims' road to Santiago de Compostela, and many of those pilgrims of St James, coming from all over Europe and heading there for their indulgences, stop off at the Jaizki bar, the headquarters of the club, so they can get their pilgrimage book stamped with the seal of Villava.

A KIND OF STARTING LINE

We have taken advantage of the reader's patience to leave Miguel Induráin stranded, at the point where he had just become a professional, while we took this excursion amongst those closest to him, and saw, or interviewed them on their home ground. The important thing, however, and what justifies the attention given to him by his countrymen, and cycling enthusiasts the world over, is his exciting sporting career. The following chapters chart the progress of that career, step by step.

As the reader will see, the difficult years when Induráin was still far from being at the top have been dealt with most carefully. This was done for two reasons: first, we are conscious of the fact that many learned who Induráin was only after he had began to triumph in major races; secondly, we have followed this earlier period in greater depth to try and give a detailed picture of just how arduous a route it is to reach the top and realise the highest ambitions that the professional rider can aim for.

We are going to recount, year by year, the gradual, patient progression of Miguel Induráin: we will accompany him through the hard times of his first years as a member of the peloton in the major tours; we will record what he said and what was said about him. Patient work in the newspaper archives, and a journey of more than a decade through the cycling journals will give us an unrivalled view of the long, laborious, and glorious career of one of the best cyclists in history.

Between signing on as a professional for Reynolds, fourteen years ago, and becoming El Cid of the Tour there is a whole journey of trials and triumphs often unknown to those who have only recently started to follow him. We left the reader on the starting line of this journey when Miguel Induráin, grave and lacking in self-confidence, began to follow his destiny as one of the greats of cycling history.

1985: AN UNKNOWN

Miguel Induráin had joined José Miguel Echávarri's Reynolds team to take part in the Vuelta a España. Still not yet twenty-one, and in his first year as a professional, things were not going badly in this new phase of his career: he had taken two second places – behind Wolf in the Ruta del Sol, and Fignon in the Midi-Pyrenees – to add to his stage win in the Tour de l'Avenir. His eighth place in the Tour de Camp de Morvedre and his twelfth in the Luis Puig Trophy had been rather more modest. That was the full extent of his record as a novice professional.

VUELTA '85: THE FIRST SURPRISE

Those limited successes, however, had passed by almost unnoticed, judging by the surprise with which the media and many fans greeted the prologue stage of the '85 Vuelta. It was won by a prologue specialist, the Dutchman Bert Oosterbosch, riding for Panasonic, but eight seconds behind, finishing as if an engine had been attached to his bike, came Induráin, the youngster with the inelegant style – virtually unknown in the peloton. 'I'd been told about him,' said the nearly displaced Oosterbosch, 'and I'll have to bear him in mind from now on because I only took eight seconds out of him, and I rode flat out, using a 52 x 14.' It was one of the short time-trial stages, of the kind that were typical then: 5.3 kilometres, out and back from Valladolid, and completely flat.

This was almost the first time Miguel found himself facing the press microphones and, with the terseness that was always to characterise him, he simply remarked that the stage had meant a lot to him.

Echávarri, who had placed three Reynolds men in the first ten, was more forthcoming, almost prophetic: 'I believe we are well on the way to the situation where, in the very near future, a Spanish rider can win a prologue time trial at international level. And I think Induráin can serve as an example, and lead the way into that Common Market of great time-trial specialists.'

This was at the time when Spain had only just entered the European Economic Community, when the country was in a hurry to integrate completely with Europe. Miguel Induráin was the advance guard in the transition from the short, gaunt Spanish cyclist – *le petit espagnol* – who stormed up the hills, made a fool of himself in the time trials and just scraped inside the time control on the flat stages; with him it became clear that we had moved on from the time when Spanish cyclists breakfasted on garlic soup: now it was to be cereal and skimmed milk. This was the modern age in which we would go from the happy-go-lucky sportsman to the sporting athlete; from having only the slightest chance of achieving what would have been an astonishing success, to regular, and no longer unexpected, triumphs. From the moment that Induráin started to get on to the podiums what would become important would not be the taking part, but the winning.

But we are getting ahead of ourselves. Let's go back to Miguel Induráin's first turns of the pedal in a major tour. We were in the '85 Vuelta with the novice professional surprising everyone in the prologue.

Problems were forecast for the second stage between Valladolid and Zamora – 177 kilometres of flat plain where any attack would be suicidal; it was perfect for the fast finishers like Panasonic, Peugeot, Safir who weren't going to allow any solo escapes. It was raining on that parched Castilian land and the stage was anything but placid: there were too many riders for so narrow a strip of road and within the peloton there were too many rookies, new professionals, unaccustomed to the wheeling and dealing, the threats, and the posturing. There were dangers on that slippery road and a large group containing Miguel was involved in a mass fall: he was slightly concussed but got up in time to finish in the same group as Panasonic's Eddy Plankaert who won the bunch sprint. In spite of everything he had held his ground and maintained his second place overall.

The third stage was the longest day: 262 kilometres from

Zamora to Orense with three third-category hills which were sufficiently leg-breaking to split the peloton in two, for the first time in that Vuelta. The Villava man will find it difficult to forget that Thursday, 25th April 1985. Those three modest climbs had livened up the stage much more than anyone had expected: the first ascent did the damage and when those left behind – among them the current leader Oosterbosch – realised what had happened, the pace being set was so fast that, by the time they reached the finish in Orense, they had lost more than six minutes to a sizeable leading group. Miguel Induráin finished in that front group which was headed by Skil-Kas's Irishman, Sean Kelly. The result sheet came out and, for the first time in his life, the youngster from Navarra, who had been the sensation of the prologue, climbed the podium of the Spanish tour wearing the yellow jersey.

He was the youngest Spanish rider ever to wear that jersey in the 40 editions of the Vuelta. There was jubilation in Villava and the team celebrated what was, as its director admitted, an unexpected result.

In spite of the euphoria, José Manuel Egido, a columnist sent especially from *Marca*, one of the sports dailies warned: 'A word of caution. There is no way that Induráin can win the race because of his youth and his size. The young man from Navarra will not be able to cope with the high mountains but, for the moment, there he is, wearing the yellow jersey and seeking a place, not yet among the best in the Vuelta, but among the best of the Spanish peloton.'

Induráin himself, visibly proud of his achievement, was modest when the journalists confronted him about his real chances: 'I haven't the qualities or the experience to tackle a Tour of Spain with this particular profile,' he admitted. 'I'm worried about the mountains, but I'll try to keep the yellow jersey as long as possible.'

That unforgettable finish at Orense brought a triple triumph for Miguel: the yellow jersey as leader of the Vuelta; the first Spanish rider on general classification; and the first new-professional. Pretty good going for a novice of scarcely twenty who was aware of the sheer scale of what he was up against.

That humble reply to the journalists was not a matter of false modesty because he woke up from the Orense dream on the very next day, which took the peloton the 197 kilometres to Santiago de Compostela. He very quickly discovered what the responsibility of wearing the leader's jersey meant – the sideways glances, the furtive gestures, the relentless attack on the easy target which the colour of his jersey made him. He managed, although not without some difficulty, to finish just four seconds behind the lone winner, the Italian Gianbattista Baroncelli of the Brianzoli team. For the time being he still had the leader's jersey, but he realised it was not going to be easy to retain it much longer and he acknowledged that, perfectly calmly, when he spoke to the journalists: 'It won't bother me to lose the jersey because I know that it will be very difficult to hang on to it: there are some first-class riders here.'

The fourth stage, still on Galician soil – over 162 kilometres between Santiago and Lugo – was a tragedy. After 58 kilometres a dog crossed between the riders and brought the peloton down. There were shouts, groans, curses, sirens, blood; there was Doctor Astorqui, the Vuelta's medical officer, saving the life of the Mallorcan rider, Jaume Salvà, with mouth-to-mouth resuscitation as he lay suffocating on the road; the Belgian, Ludo Loos, was taken urgently to the intensive-care unit with head injuries. While the peloton continued the race in the most sombre mood, Noel Dejonckeere (Teka) and René Martens (Fagor) were exchanging punches every time they happened to come near each other. This sordid affair, which they both perpetuated, culminated at the finish with a blow from Noel which left René unconscious and needing attention in the ambulance. As if that wasn't enough, during the final circuit around the walls of Lugo, the sprinters' dirty war began way out, with elbow jabs, zigzagging and violent switches of direction.

Eddy Plankaert won it, having blatantly blocked Sean Kelly, and, in the middle of the bunch, deeply affected by it all, was Induráin. It had all been too much for a novice, but he had come to see the value of team work when all his Reynolds colleagues pulled out the stops to chase down the Zor rider, Juan Fernández, who had escaped in the confusion after the crash and, for a few kilometres, had been the leader on the road. For the time being, then, Miguel Induráin remained race leader, but it had been very hard, and enlightening. The Vuelta a España, like all the major professional races, had a vicious side and there was no room for standing on ceremony. He took note.

The following stage, between Lugo and Oviedo, brought them very close to the mountains. Two hundred and thirty-eight kilometres, with three moderate climbs in the final part when they were already leg-weary, it was the last step before passing into the high mountains. Fede Etxabe prevented the fifth consecutive win by a foreign rider by coming in one second ahead of the top sprinters. Again they all finished together, and it had not been difficult for Miguel Induráin to stay with the train which had kept a jealous vigil and prevented any rider 'with possibilities' from going clear. So those first stages ended like a dream; now even the most optimistic fans were surely thinking that he wouldn't last out, and that his yellow jersey would be gone by the time he crossed the finishing line the following day, at the lakes of Covadonga – which is exactly what happened.

The team directors had all indicated that they thought the race would break wide open on the top of the Fito, the first category-one col of the 1985 Vuelta. The Colombians went over first, with Parra in the lead, but on the descent Sean Kelly came past like a streak of lightning and only the strongest managed to follow him, all the way to the slopes of Covadonga itself. It was Kelly who made the selection but, in the finish, his strength failed him. Pedro Delgado, then riding for MG Orbea, won and the overall classification was, as expected, turned upside-down. Induráin, who knew that he was not going to be able to retain the leader's jersey, saw it pass to the Segovian who would later be his team-mate and would share his triumphs. The man from Navarra came in thirteen minutes down on Delgado, exhausted but in one piece. It had been wonderful while it lasted, wearing that yellow jersey for the first time, in his first Vuelta. Now he had to carry on, and it was all uphill, both on the road and in the struggle to lift his morale. But it had been worth the pain.

José Miguel Echávarri, who saw how his team collapsed on those very hard climbs, remarked wisely: 'There's a long way to go still and now we'll have to try other tacks. We will carry on fighting: we lost the jersey, but not our spirit.' It was a lesson to learn.

After the set-back at Covadonga, and with the race now in the high mountains, the young Induráin simply returned to the peloton. At that moment in time it was, perhaps, the best place for him. From there on he was completely at the disposal of Gorospe and Gastón, the Reynolds team leaders, so long as he had enough strength left to support them. And to finish – to get to the finish was like a passing-out parade into the professional ranks that he had recently joined, and was the toughest task imaginable.

After his bad time in the Asturian heights the young man from Villava had dropped to the middle of the classification table.

Five days later, after they had passed through the Calvary of the Pyrenees, he was still there, now in 79th position out of the 129 survivors, but an eternity, 1-28-59, separated him from the leader, Robert Millar. The severity of the route had brought about a major split and a large section of the peloton had moved above him. For several days, now, the reporters had stopped speaking about Miguel Induráin: there was nothing to report.

The peloton returned to the flat. Four stages in which the battle-hardened veteran rouleurs fought for seniority based on cutting others up, sticking in their elbow and generally not giving a damn. Four days which went from damp cold to sultry heat, in which Miguel did enough to maintain his position and to reflect, from the back of the peloton, that this was a serious business. He'd assumed the role of domestique particularly well and, after the Covadonga stage had brought him down to earth, he'd been working to get Julián Gorospe into the best possible position before the final time trial. This, they said, was going to be decisive. Obviously Induráin, too, felt he had some chances on that stage and said as much to the journalists: 'The route tomorrow suits me well and I shall try my best. But now all that remains for me is to finish the Vuelta and to fight, with the whole team, to put Gorospe at the front.' The Navarra man assumed his domestique role and recognised his limitations.

The stage that awaited them was one of those time trials which nowadays would be a beauty for Miguel – 42 kilometres out and back from Alcalá, not completely flat, but undulating some 1,000 feet. This stage, it was reckoned, would determine the final outcome of the Vuelta, but that was not what happened – at least, not in the way that had been expected. It was won by Pello Ruiz Cabestany, who had been the best-placed Spaniard at 1-55 behind Millar. He reduced his deficit by 40 seconds; Gorospe also improved but Peugeot's Scotsman held on to the yellow jersey. Induráin, after the anonymous mediocrity into which he had sunk during the previous thirteen stages, rode an excellent time trial finishing in eleventh spot, only 1-59 slower than Pello. In spite of this fine performance he remained 84th overall, 2-01-57 down on Millar.

The penultimate stage now lay in wait for the exhausted peloton and again it was uphill. Between Alcalá de Henares and the Dyc Distillery were 200 kilometres containing three first-category cols. There were only 107 survivors left and, just when nobody was expecting it, the race was turned upside-down. It was the Kelme rider, José Recio, who made the moves, continuously threatening to break up the peloton on the three climbs. On the last one he joined forces with Pedro Delgado and, between them, they ended up destroying every forecast for the outcome of the race. Delgado allowed Recio, who had made so much of the running, to cross the line first. At 3-29 Kelly lead in a group of eight; at 6-50 Millar and Cabestany arrived, while Julián Gorospe was lost from sight, 9-34 down. So, Perico* Delgado, who had been in sixth place at the start of the day, 6-13 behind the Scotsman, now flaunted his virtually unassailable yellow jersey.

Thus they reached Madrid. On the last stage Miguel Induráin failed to get into a break and finished back among the stragglers – such are the hazards of being a novice. Pedro Delgado would be the winner after the courtesies of that unremarkable final day. It was a great finale for him, an unexpected winner of the 1985 Vuelta a España. It was also the baptism of Miguel Induráin, the gawky domestique from Reynolds, who was riding for the first time in the professional ranks and who had had Villava holding its breath during those four stages when he wore the yellow jersey. Not bad going for anyone in their first confrontation with one of the three big tours.

TOUR '85: A BRIEF ENCOUNTER

José Miguel Echávarri again counted on Miguel Induráin when it came to the Tour. To be honest, Reynolds was a pretty modest outfit in such a select peloton, which numbered 180 of the best riders. Eduardo Chozas and Iñaki Gastón were the only members of the team with any remote chance of not making themselves look too ridiculous, at least.

Miguel Induráin, already worn down by a particularly hard Vuelta, set off in good spirits, on 28th June, in the prologue – a 6.5-kilometre circuit at Plumelec. The memory of that prologue stage at Valladolid had raised the fans' expectations of his ability to ride against the clock, but it proved harder than anticipated and the power of the specialists took the novice Induráin by surprise: he

*Perico is a nickname for Pedro.

35

finished one minute slower than the best time put up by Bernard Hinault. He was in a very ordinary 100th position.

Worse was to befall him by the finish of the 256-kilometres of the first road stage at Lanester. He was caught out by the break, and finished in a small group of back-markers, 2-01 behind the winner, Matthys. In the general classification he was 3-04 off the leader, Vanderaerden, and 173rd out of the 178 still surviving. And the hell had scarcely begun.

The following day was a repetition of the events of the previous stage. Two hundred and forty-two kilometres of flat and frenetic riding, between L'Orient and Vitre, again brought Matthys to the line first. Miguel Induráin once more paid for his inexperience, finishing 9-01 behind Matthys and practically the whole of the peloton. After no more than three days riding, he was in last position, 17-35 down on the leader, Vanderaerden.

The third stage was a team time trial of 73.8 kilometres from Vitre to Fougères – too long for the limited strength of the Spanish teams by contrast with the experience and authority of outfits such as Panasonic, or La Vie Claire who were the joint favourites. Yet Reynolds was always in the hunt and proved to be the best of the Spanish teams, losing only 2-10 overall to the lightning fast La Vie Claire. Despite not being able to count on Julián Gorospe, Echávarri's specialist over that type of course, this was not a bad result. The young Induráin, however, who it was hoped would shine in the battle against the ticking hands of the clock, had remained on the back of the string of Reynolds men and did well just to get to the finish. Afterwards the youngster explained: 'It's a real shame that I'm not in my best form. I was a key man for this stage, but I was the one who contributed the least. I've had a heavy cold for several days. As for whether I continue in the race, it all depends on the doctor. I believe I am the only Spanish rider, in recent years, who has taken part in two of the big stage-races in his first year as a professional.'

For Miguel Induráin all the alarm bells were ringing. He was doing badly, in 177th position in the race which Vanderaerden continued to lead, while a summer bronchitis was bringing him to the point where he would have to abandon the Tour.

The fourth stage – 239 kilometres between Fougères and Point-Audemer – took the race along a winding route with three third-category and several other fourth-category hills. The peloton had to sweat buckets and suffer stretches of pavé, and Induráin couldn't do it, not even on the first of the climbs, the Mortain. Forty kilometres into the stage the Reynolds doctors decided that it would be pointless to prolong the agony: Miguel Induráin abandoned the race and returned home. So ended his first Tour as a professional on 2nd July 1985, on the brink of the San Fermín fiesta in Pamplona.

Bernard Hinault was the winner in Paris; Eduardo Chozas, in eighteenth position, was Reynolds highest finisher and the team ended seventh in the team classification.

As befitted his age, Miguel Induráin was moving into the hardest stage of his apprenticeship. For some impatient people he was finished but, in fact, this is the time when the character and steel of a champion is forged.

TOUR DE L'AVENIR: A RAY OF LIGHT

José Miguel Echávarri was not about to let his young novice, who had demonstrated his professionalism in his début year, rest from his labours. So, he included him among those taking part in the Tour de l'Avenir. This was a kind of thirteen-stage 'mini-tour' for professional and amateur riders whose common denominator was their youth. In the 1985 Tour Reynolds and Seat-Orbea were the only Spanish representatives, and Echávarri had delegated the management of the team to Eusebio Unzué; their chances revolved around Rubén Gorospe and Miguel Induráin.

It was a mixture of good and not so good for the Navarra man in the first five stages: after an acceptable eighth-best time in the prologue he went back into the mediocrity of the peloton in a race which was being fiercely disputed at a rattling pace. Perhaps, in this brief account, it may be difficult to understand the significance of the time differentials (in comparison with other major stage-races). In a race of fairly short stages in which the total distance is not that long, the gaps between the riders do not become as big as in, say, the Tour. To give an example: on the fifth stage Miguel Induráin was lying 64th in the general classification, but the advantage that the leader, the Swiss rider, Benno Wiss, had over him was only 4-41.

But let's return to the reality of the race itself, on that sixth stage which covered the 91 kilometres between Albi and Revel. In spite of the intense heat, a strong pace had been imposed from the very first kilometres. Continuous threats and frustrated attacks came and went until, at kilometre 55, at the top of Miquellou, Levainne attacked, drawing Miguel Induráin on to his back wheel. A perfect example of relay work between the two of them prevented the pursuing peloton from getting close to them and they came into the final straight with an eleven-second advantage. Miguel Induráin was the quicker of the two and won the sprint. Going up on to the podium at Revel was the happiest moment for him: since that fourth stage in the Vuelta he had not known the joys of winning.

Now in much better spirits the Villava man put up with the three following stages in the high mountains, holding on and not missing too many chances. He was keeping out of trouble in 54th position, 1-9-47 behind the Colombian, Martín Ramírez, who headed the classification.

Another day worthy of mention was 14th September, with a 30-kilometre time trial between Lourdes and Tarbes – a distance that ought to tell the reader something. Miguel Induráin 'demolished' his opponents, said the journalists. He 'crushed' them – just like now. Half a minute was a huge advantage over such a short distance and it was exactly 30 seconds that he took out of second-place man, Jean-François Bernard.

The race ended in Plaisance, two stages later, with Martín Ramírez winning and Induráin 50th overall, at 1-8-49.

So Miguel Induráin's first year as a professional came to an end. He had made his first ventures into two of the major stage-races – the Vuelta and the Tour – and discovered that they were not so fierce as they had been made out to be. Those unexpected four days in the yellow jersey in the Vuelta were like a dream. But Miguel was a realist and, realistically, 1985 had definitely not been a fruitless year: his overall results could reasonably be said to have been more than acceptable.

José Miguel Echávarri and Eusebio Unzué, who had first noticed the kid from Villava pedalling furiously in juvenile races, didn't disguise their satisfaction with Induráin's season. The moment was coming when he would assimilate all that he had learned in that first, harsh experience. The rough diamond needed patient, unhurried polishing, but he had all the time in the world on his side.

RESULTS

Tour de l'Avenir: two stage wins
Tour of Burgos: prologue stage win
Ruta del Sol: prologue stage win
Midi-Pyrenees: prologue stage win
Tour of Spain: leader for four stages
Tour de France: abandoned on stage four

1986: APPRENTICESHIP

Miguel Induráin's first professional season had had its ups and its downs, and he knew that what he had to look forward to was a long and arduous apprenticeship; it would be worth it in the end but he had come to realise that it was definitely not going to be easy. And so, in that spirit, on 22nd April 1986 he began his second Vuelta a España, in the Reynolds squad, once again directed by his mentors, José Miguel Echávarri and Eusebio Unzué, and led by the forever-promising Julián Gorospe and the inconsistent Angel Arroyo.

VUELTA '86: SURVIVING

It was a sophisticated Vuelta in 1986, beginning in Palma de Mallorca and ending in Jerez, and would climb some of the biggest cols, with mountain-top finishes in the Sierra Nevada, the lakes of Covadonga, Naranco, and San Isidro. These magnificent mountain stages contrasted with a total of some 70 kilometres against the clock in which the favourites could recoup their losses – if they had made any on the peaks.

Joint favourites of the 170 participants were Sean Kelly and Laurent Fignon among the foreigners; among the home riders the choice fell between Pedro Delgado, Angel Arroyo, Julián Gorospe, Pello Ruiz Cabestany, and Marino Lejarreta. So the die was cast and each man to his own task: the favourites to do their job, and the domestiques to support them.

The prologue stage, five kilometres along the Palma sea front, saw Thierry Marie in flying form. The Frenchman in the Pegaso-System U team flashed past the finish, averaging more than 50 kilometres an hour, to make the best time. Miguel Induráin, as was now almost customary in the prologue, was the quickest of the Spanish riders; six seconds down on the winner, he was satisfied when he spoke to the journalists: 'I was hoping to be among the leaders; I've done a good time trial and I'm pleased.'

It was put to him, however, that, taking all his races into account, he hadn't exactly been brilliant, as if only immediate success would do from someone who had merely shown a certain amount of promise. Miguel replied quietly, and auspiciously: 'I am making progress, little by little, and I recognise that I am still too young to be among the top riders. But I'm in no hurry because things are going reasonably well for me.' As he indicated to them, he was there as a domestique; that was his responsibility and he knew it: 'I have come to work for whoever is going best. I will try to ensure that someone in the team can secure the best position in the classification. The important thing is that we work together so that everybody is satisfied.'

Grave, serious-minded in his declarations – just like now, just like always – Miguel Induráin knew that he enjoyed the confidence of his director. Echávarri analysed the performance of his best-placed man on that stage: 'I think he has put in a great race and he's matched the best international specialists, like Marie and Peiper. I believe that each one was placed where they deserved to be and Miguel was among the best, and inside the time we predicted.'

The first stage, beginning and ending in Palma, would take them through almost the whole of the island, some 190 kilometres. Reynolds' French rider, Marc Gómez, went clear at the 38-kilometre point and stayed away, in what was to be the winning break, for the remaining 152 kilometres. The peloton of more than 100 riders which had woken up too late to the situation arrived 2-33 behind. In that group, in 90th position, was Miguel Induráin, and in the general classification, now headed by his team-mate, Gómez, he was fourth overall, 2-20 down.

The second stage, after the peloton had been transported by land, sea and air, was a 182-kilometre circuit, starting and finishing in Barcelona, with the climb of Montjuïc in the middle. The Asturian, Jorge Domínguez (Seat-Orbea), was first over the line in a race broken up by a thousand skirmishes.

Miguel Induráin was not feeling well after the return to the mainland and he lost his chance of getting into any of the breaks. He finished in 150th position, 1-52 down on Domínguez, which relegated him from his fourth place of the day before to 103rd overall, 4-12 behind his colleague, Marc Gómez, who was still wearing the yellow jersey.

Lost in the peloton, and way down in the general classification, Miguel Induráin pedalled steadily through the next few stages until the first serious selection took place on stage five, between Haro and Santander. They were now in the mountains with Miguel surviving in the guards-van: first the lakes of Covadonga, the Calvary where he had lost his short-lived, but well-deserved yellow jersey the previous year, with a string of riders coming in laboriously at the finish; then, the hill climb of the Naranco in which he put up the 125th 'best time' – and this, remember, a time trial, albeit an uphill one. Induráin was still not the real Induráin, quite obviously.

He survived that first mountain test as best he could and, by the end of stage nine, he was 111th overall, 1-9-47 behind the yellow jersey which, by now, Robert Millar was wearing.

They returned to the flat and to another opportunity on stage eleven – a 29.6-kilometre time trial around Valladolid. Induráin rode comfortably and recorded the eighth-best time after overtaking the three riders who had set off in front of him, and almost catching the fourth. For a long time he was on the top of the provisional leader board. 'He has been simply sensational, impeccable,' said José Miguel Echávarri. 'He went off full of motivation and determination, and he dominated the situation throughout.' Looking back now on that performance, it was a foretaste of the time trials the Navarra man would be giving us a few years later.

The race went relentlessly back into the mountains on the twelfth stage and returned to the level roads again on the fourteenth. Miguel lost time on the climbs and didn't get into very many of the breaks on the flat. He was arriving unhurriedly at the stage finishes – what difference did it make? – conscious that he had to toil through the race with aspirations no greater than his own limitations would allow him.

Stage seventeen was the 191-kilometre trek from Jaén to Sierra Nevada and Induráin finished among the back-markers. He was now 102nd overall, 1-53-36 down on the current leader, Alvaro Pino. Felipe Yáñez, who won the stage for Zahor, was no real threat to the favourites. The following day brought a distressing picture – the string of some 116 riders as they reached the top and crossed the finishing line on the hardest finish in the Sierra Nevada. Some could kiss a final goodbye to any hopes they might have had and there were teams that were totally crippled. Things were that bad for Reynolds: of the two team leaders Arroyo abandoned and Gorospe arrived outside the time limit. Set against that, the 23-02 that Miguel Induráin lost was not so disastrous and, as sometimes happens, he went up to 96th overall because of the retirement of other, even more exhausted riders. Alvaro Pino, who managed to survive it all and hold on to the leader's jersey, was now 2-14-02 ahead of him.

The riders might have expected a little rest in the following days, with gentle riding over totally flat roads, but there was always somebody who kept taking the peloton by surprise in the middle of its siesta. It didn't turn out to be too serious, however, as attacks in the final stages are usually carefully watched over and whoever is wearing the yellow jersey by that time seems to sprout wings. This appeared to be what was happening to Alvaro Pino, now securely established in the lead.

The 1986 Vuelta ended with a 20-kilometre time trial at Jerez which wasn't expected to affect the Gallego man's likely victory. In fact, Pino left nothing to chance and won the stage himself. We should note, however, that, being a time trial, it brought out the very best in Miguel Induráin: he finished 35 seconds down on the leader and was listed as sixth, although he recorded the same time as the fifth man, Pello Ruiz Cabestany.

Thus, Induráin survived the Vuelta in 92nd position overall and 2-17-17 behind Alvaro Pino's yellow jersey. In his first attempt, the previous year, he had ended up 84th, a bit higher but, at 2-24-47 down on Delgado, the gap had been a few minutes wider.

His apprenticeship was tough – it had to be if the youngster was ever going to become hardened – and there were times when he hardly realised that he was making progress. But Echávarri and Unzué knew it: they were polishing their rough diamond.

TOUR '86: BEATEN BY THE MOUNTAINS

In his second year as a professional Miguel Induráin was following the same programme as in his first season. Toughened up in a hard, frantic Vuelta he again signed on for the biggest of the major tours.

In the '86 Tour de France, beginning on 4th July, Induráin was a domestique in a Reynolds team that was seriously weakened by the absence of Arroyo. With Julián Gorospe known to be in poor form, Laguía and Celestino Prieto were selected as team leaders.

The route for that Tour was expected to favour the climbers, giving the Colombians and the Spaniards, therefore, real chances. The peloton, 210 strong, was the largest in the history of the race, and, logically enough, the French press made Hinault and Fignon joint favourites.

For the prologue – 4.6 kilometres along the Parisian Periferique from Boulogne to Billancourt – the French press also spoke of Induráin as one of the experts at short distances against the clock and therefore among those hoping to be the first to wear the yellow jersey. Julián Gorospe who was taking part, somewhat out of form and without any major ambitions, was also optimistic about the young man's chances: 'It's a pity that Arroyo is not here this year,' he told the reporters, 'but we have some strong men who can really do something, like Miguel Induráin.'

These pre-race auguries were not bad, and nor were they groundless: in the one year he had been a professional cyclist, Miguel Induráin had certainly shown what he was capable of. However, he didn't have the greatest luck in the first trial, coming in seventeenth, ten seconds down on the time set by the first race leader, young Thierry Marie. Echávarri was none too pleased with Miguel's performance, although he did try to make excuses for him to the journalists: 'Maybe Miguel Induráin has not done as well as was hoped; it seems that he had some trouble finding the right gear. These mistakes in such short distances cost too many seconds, but what's for certain is that they don't usually turn out to be all that important.'

La Grande Boucle began at hectic speed: those first days were tough and Induráin was soon catapulted towards the back. He was learning to ride in that position in the peloton, sometimes as a rearguard, sometimes in service of whoever in the team needed him, until he decided to show himself.

The fifth stage – 124 kilometres of flat roads between Evreux and Villiers-sur-Mer – was very suitable terrain for chancing one's luck. After various escape attempts, Plankaert and Miguel Induráin jumped out of the peloton, at kilometre 107, to chase down Van der Velde and Pelier who had been away since kilometre 16, without a reaction from the main group. Towing the Belgian, the Navarra man got away from the peloton and gained ground on the two who had

44

escaped earlier. They partially succeeded in bridging the gap, reducing the deficit from six minutes to one minute. At the finish Van der Velde came in first, two seconds ahead of Pelier; Plankaert came in at 39 seconds and, in fourth place, one second further back, came Miguel Induráin after a tremendous effort. The main group arrived at 1-15. Van der Velde now wore the yellow jersey while Miguel Induráin, at 5-20, had lifted himself to 86th overall.

As usually happens – unfair though it is – the journalists crowded round Induráin, who had been the principal animator that day, and asked him what had been the point in making the escape. The point was he had wanted to win the stage: 'That's what I was trying to do,' he told them, 'but it wasn't to be. I don't know if it was the ideal moment or not, but the truth is that it's very difficult to break away from the peloton when it's on the look-out. What's more, Plankaert got on to my wheel and I had to work that much harder. In the final stretch I realised there was nothing doing and I threw in the towel.'

It was a good day's work for Induráin, although his team had been somewhat uninspired, but they were still in completely flat country and he was going to try again.

Stage seven – 201 kilometres from Cherbourg to St Hilaire – and anything could happen. There were certainly a number of small escape attempts but, up to the 182-kilometre mark, the peloton was still all together. It was at this moment that Miguel Induráin decided to make a decisive move and, after a steep slope, he attacked strongly, pulling away a small group of riders. This group got to the finish with more than two minutes on the main peloton. Ludo Peeters won the final sprint with Miguel third. There was a new overall leader – Pedersen – and Induráin was the top Reynolds rider, 3-26 down, and 53rd overall.

It was clear that in this, his second encounter with the Tour de France, Miguel Induráin wanted to make his presence felt. His powerful attack had broken the field in two, and only the greater experience of Peeters and Kieffel when it came to a sprint finish, deprived him of the stage win. This is how Tito Irazusta, a reporter for one of the major Spanish radio networks, described the great performance of the almost unknown Miguel Induráin: 'He doesn't put on any airs. He'll appear in all the papers as the hero of the day, but he won't let that go to his head. He is a serious young man who, in spite of his youth, knows how to keep his feet on the ground and

45

that there's no way of knowing what today's joys will become tomorrow.'

Induráin himself commented on his superb performance in the stage: 'At the moment I'm feeling fine. It's very difficult to get a good position in the Tour, and I believe a fourth and a third is something to be pleased with. There were a number of attacks being made and seven others joined on the back of one of mine, and we got away. I was doing well in the sprint, but it was a pity I couldn't get up to Peeters.'

Miguel had had few opportunities to speak at such length with the journalists. They asked him to forecast the next time-trial stage, but he passed that over with a laconic 'anything can happen'. Thinking then of his own limitations, he added: 'The mountains are where I don't go so well and I don't know how I will be able to respond, although I'm confident that I'll cope with them. Everybody here is talking about how hard some of the cols are; they are even saying that there is so much snow it's possible the route will be cancelled.' This, perhaps, was wishful thinking. But reality is stubborn and he had to come down to earth again. As always in the Tour the euphoria was on one side and the efforts of the Navarra rider on the other.

The following day – stage eight – the 204 kilometres between St Hilaire and Nantes were covered at a frantic pace. The finish was a mass sprint which Plankaert won ahead of 185 others. Induráin finished with the same time in 180th place. Pedersen remained in yellow after what was an uneventful day; Miguel, only 3-28 back, was 54th. He was not doing badly.

Awaiting the 191 survivors, on the ninth stage, was a 61.5-kilometre individual time trial which started and finished in Nantes. As Induráin had remarked, two days earlier, 'anything could happen'. What did happen, in fact, was that Hinault destroyed all his immediate rivals. 'From another galaxy', reported the Gallic journalists. That was in reference to Hinault's feat, but it reminds us of what would be said, a few years later, in reference to a different rider. On that day Miguel Induráin finished 2-11 down, in thirteenth place. It was not by any means a bad performance and his time brought him up to nineteenth in the overall classification, 3-56 behind Pedersen who was still in the yellow jersey. Of the Spanish riders, only Gorospe had recorded a better time than Miguel who admitted at the finish: 'It was too long for me; the only time I've ridden such a distance against the clock was in a team time trial and so you can't compare the two. I had a very bad stretch over the last few kilometres, but I am pleased with my showing and with the time I made.'

Then came the Pyrenees and the race became hell.

The 217-kilometre twelfth stage from Bayonne to Pau would bring about the first significant selection in the race – at least, that's what was anticipated. Two first-category climbs – Burdincurutcheta and the Col de Marie Blanque – strategically placed at the beginning and end of the route, together with four fourth-category hills, two second-category, and a third-category turned the stage into a closed shop for the pure climbers. As was now becoming customary, everybody was looking towards the Colombians, but it was Pedro Delgado who came in first, with Hinault on his wheel. Bernard Hinault took over the yellow jersey and the extreme difficulty of those first steep slopes had cruelly scythed away a good number of riders, among them Induráin. So his second Tour ended, again prematurely. The race would be won by the American Greg Lemond and Alvaro Pino would be the leading Spaniard, in eighth place, 33 minutes down.

The Tour had ended for Miguel Induráin but, in contrast to the first time, his retirement attracted far greater attention: he was now being talked about in the press. After he had returned to Villava, he said: 'I left the Tour with a certain sadness because it hurts to have been living it and now following it from so far off. The first stages were positive for me but I recognise that, in general, I didn't go well.'

The Pyrenees had hardly begun when they became an impassable barrier for Miguel Induráin. In those days he was seen as a good rider but a weak climber. He, himself, didn't altogether agree with that picture: 'I can manage reasonably well on the hills but the mountains in the Tour are something else again and the stages are so long, too. The truth is I couldn't take it and I quit.'

He had just turned 22 and already he was rubbing shoulders with the best riders in the world. This is how he saw those impressive first experiences as a professional: 'At first you are a bit scared. People are nervous; there are a lot of falls which frighten you, but then you get a bit of confidence and you start to ride more calmly.'

The kid from Villava was gaining all he possibly could from the experience, throwing himself into his riding with more self-confidence and a total dedication to making it, just as his mentors, directors, and teachers were asking of him. Having studied the raw material in some depth, Echávarri and Unzué were shaping each of his capabilities to the utmost; preparing him for flying high.

TOUR OF THE EEC: THE SENSATION

In 1986 the classic Tour de l'Avenir was renamed the Tour of the EEC. Perhaps this was because of the apparent approach of full European integration (although, after Maastricht, this has not been so clear). With a less difficult profile than on other occasions, the Tour brought other novelties like the route itself and stage finishes outside France – in Portugal, Spain, and Italy.

Again Reynolds put in an appearance, with virtually the same selection as the previous year: Rubén Gorospe, Miguel Induráin and Marc Gómez were their strongest men.

The brand-new Tour of the EEC started in Oporto with a 4.8-kilometre prologue stage and the best time was put up by Miguel Induráin in an astonishing 48.7 kph average speed. The Navarra man, as the reports said, 'was flying' on his bicycle; full of strength, he took off with the very first thrust of the pedal and his pace didn't drop for an instant through to the finish. To get an idea of Miguel's power in that stage you simply have to bear in mind that the eleven seconds gap between him and the second-place man was greater than the gap between second and twentieth!

So Induráin set off in the yellow jersey for the first road stage, 162 kilometres from Oporto to Viseu, but lost it on the third stage when he arrived at the finish in Salamanca 8-38 down on Roy Knickman. Through an opportunistic escape, the sprinter from La Vie Claire was now the overall leader.

The 134-kilometre sixth stage from Vitoria-Gasteiz to the Navarra capital of Pamplona was made hard by a strong cross-wind. Reynolds, regarded as the Navarra team, tried throughout to control the race. Then, twenty kilometres from the finish, there was a break provoked by Knickman himself which required more effort to neutralise. The escape group was absorbed back into the peloton but then Juan Martín Zapatero (Zor-BH) managed to get away to finish alone, 33 seconds ahead of the leading group containing the top riders, among them Induráin. Knickman stayed in yellow and Miguel, at 7-20, was sixth overall: he was no prophet in his own land.

The journalists were keen to listen to what he had to say – he was now recognised as having some sharp insights – but, whether out of shyness or whether on the instructions of his director, Eusebio Unzué, the Villava man went straight back to his hotel after the finish. Unzué spoke to the press for him and made the appropriate remarks about the chances of his pupil: 'I continue to have every confidence in Miguel and in him making further progress in this race. All my riders are responding very well and I hope they will continue doing so in the remaining stages, in spite of the fact that we have now reached the most difficult terrain. If things don't go well for Miguel Induráin in the mountains I will be more relaxed about it than anybody else because that will ensure he's in the right condition to win another time-trial stage.'

The following day was going to be hard, above all because of the psychological weight of being on the brink of the toughest stage of the race. The 196 kilometres between Pamplona and Pau were full of attacks, threatened escapes, and sudden changes of pace. A group containing the top riders arrived at the finish together. The sprint was won by Jokin Mijika – once more by centimetres – from Miguel Induráin. Knickman held on to the yellow jersey and Miguel was now fifth at 7-10.

In the eighth stage, which took them the 133.5 kilometres from Pau to Luz Ardiden, Miguel Induráin showed that if, up to now, he was known as a time triallist and a sprinter, he was no longer falling back in the high mountains. Laudelino Cubino was first to reach the summit finish, but with a tremendous show of strength Miguel came in fourth, 3-04 behind. The race was now wide open although Knickman, with great difficulty, was still holding on to his lead. Induráin was up to second place, 5-25 down, wearing the green jersey of points leader and looking forward to the next time trial where, at the very least, he would be aiming for another stage win.

On the tenth stage – 27.5 kilometres against the clock at Carpentras – Miguel Induráin was again devastating. Able to keep his machine moving perfectly throughout the whole of the pedal stroke he returned an invincible average of 45 kph. If we had to hand a video of that stage it could sit well with any of his more recent time-trial victories. He cut three minutes and seven seconds from Knickman's lead; now he was just 2-18 behind with four stages left.

It was on the following day, the eleventh stage, that the Navarra man recovered the lead which he had lost after winning the prologue. In the 186 kilometres between Carpentras and Gap the race was broken open again. The leader, more than twenty minutes behind on the day, was worn down and had to abandon the Tour. A small group broke clear and worked with such determination that only the strength of Induráin at the head of the peloton prevented a complete overturn of the general classification. Denis Roux won the stage and Induráin, finishing in with a small group, 4-50 behind, took over the yellow jersey from the retired Knickman. He now had a lead of 1-10 over the Frenchman, Patrice Esnault, in second place.

The 109-kilometre twelfth stage from Gap to Briançon was very tough, ending on the slopes of the Col de Izoard. Induráin weathered the most difficult moments steadfastly, almost with something in reserve, and his team did the rest. The boy from Villava came in fifth at the finish, 26 seconds behind the stage winner, Alexis Grewal. He stayed in yellow and now it was Grewal who was second, 54 seconds down.

The thirteenth and final stage, covering the 91 kilometres between Sestrières and Turin – in Italy now – was a carbon copy of the day before: strong attacks from Esnault and Grewal, and that continuous sitting on their wheel by Induráin which, nowadays, from witnessing his most glorious triumphs, has become so familiar to us. The finish was a desperate sprint with Christian Chaubet hitting the line first. And, for Miguel Induráin, his first big international victory: overall winner of the Tour of the EEC.

To judge the real worth of that victory by the 22-year-old Miguel, in his second year as a professional, it's helpful to realise that the Tour of the EEC, or Tour de l'Avenir, was the most important race open to amateurs and professionals. Induráin was now able to put his name alongside cyclists of world renown. Two years before the race had been won by the then world championship runner-up, Charlie Mottet. In 1982 Greg Lemond had been first, just a short time before he won the world professional title. Other previous winners like Pascal Simon (1981), the Russian, Souko (1978 and 1979), Baronccelli (1973), Martínez Heredia (1974), Zoetemelk (1969), Gimondi (1964), Mariano Díaz (1965), De Rosso (1961) had also reached the highest levels in world cycling.

This brief excursion is perhaps worth making, if only to understand just what that victory, which now seems so trivial, must have meant to the young cyclist from Navarra who at first seemed cut out only for riding against the clock. He had learned to live with the high climbers and to perform in the sprints, thereby giving consistency to his classification. After his lap of honour Miguel showed just how over-joyed he was: 'This win has been the greatest happiness of my sporting life since, in a way, I was not expecting it because I lost the lead even before the most difficult part – the mountains. In the beginning my aim was to win some stages and get to Pamplona as leader. That didn't happen but, in the final stages, I found myself in good health and tremendous form and I was able to overcome that terrain well, and I can even say comfortably. I admit that the mountains scare me a little but so long as I'm feeling strong they are less difficult; you suffer when you're not at your best, although in the Vuelta and the Tour I've now learned what it is to suffer on a bicycle.'

His team-mate, the Frenchman Marc Gómez, had this to say about Miguel's bearing: 'Rarely have I seen a youngster of his age, faced with that responsibility, react so calmly. He's very observant and his racing brain makes up the rest.'

After his final yellow jersey in Turin the French newspaper, *L'Equipe*, was reporting: 'He is a champion who is discovering himself and who will grow with this victory. If tradition is anything to go by, in the not very distant future Miguel Induráin must figure among cycling's élite.'

The value that the French put on Induráin's win brought him an invitation to compete in the Grand Prix des Nations which took place a few days later in Cannes. It was an 89-kilometre individual time trial and the 21 riders invited to take part included the best of the international peloton.

The Grand Prix was run on 28th September in the most dreadful weather: Spain's representatives, on a circuit that was made perilous by rain and dense fog, were Gorospe and Induráin. A spectacular fall brought Induráin down when he was not going badly. This ordeal was eventually won by Sean Kelly; Induráin, who was fourteenth at 4-27, and Gorospe, fifteenth at 4-38, played quieter roles.

After this fleeting competition appearance, Miguel went back to his winter quarters. In other words, he went back to the most intense, detailed and patient preparation for the future. José Miguel Echávarri, Eusebio Unzué and all the technical staff at Reynolds were bringing him on sensibly. That might well have been the foundation of his victory.

But we cannot forget, in a brief biography of one of cycling's major figures, that other feature of the sport – the warm affection of the fans, of friends and family – without which those who dedicate themselves to this hard discipline would be nothing more than sadly postured knights riding their aluminium machines. Villava was waiting for Miguel Induráin once he had fulfilled his obligation to the Grand Prix des Nations. The whole of Navarra was waiting for him and his colleagues, friends, and teachers at the Villava Cycling Club had prepared a huge reception for him. It's worth describing it in some detail to get an impression of the significance of, and the affection behind, that first, almost improvised tribute.

Miguel got into Villava at seven in the evening, accompanied by Echávarri and Unzué. Scores of youngsters and members of the Villava Cycling Club were waiting on the outskirts of the village to accompany him, pedalling towards the town hall. There, hundreds of people, who had been waiting more than an hour, greeted him with a tremendous ovation and with popular songs played by the local brass band. Induráin got out of the Reynolds team car, nervous and emotional, and, after the first hugs and handshakes, he was practically carried towards the activity room together with the municipal councillors. At that moment the Mayor of Villava expressed his gratitude to everybody who had assembled there 'to join in the tribute to such an unpretentious man as Induráin'. He congratulated him on his victory in the Tour of the EEC and took advantage of the situation by calling on the regional government to give more help to the sport.

The declaration whereby Miguel Induráin was granted the first Gold Medal of the municipality was then read out, and then he was handed a parchment, a Villava celebratory neckerchief, a neckerchief of the Beti Onak handball team – these neckerchiefs have a profound symbolic significance in Navarra festivals – and given the best wishes of the school children of the district. The Navarra regional government also sent him its congratulations together with news that he would be awarded the Gold Medal for Sporting Achievement.

After receiving all these awards and messages of congratulation, Miguel Induráin, for the first time in his life, went triumphantly out on to the main balcony of the town hall, in his home town, and gave his thanks for the tributes that had been paid to him with the brevity and naturalness which he still displays today: 'I was not expecting it, still less so many people.' With a show of oratory that began to resemble a speech he ended, emotionally: 'For me, this day has been as important as the day I won the Tour of the EEC. This reception and the Tour of the EEC gives me strength and encouragement to continue racing and fighting to achieve more victories.'

RESULTS

Tour of Murcia: points winner
Tour of Burgos: stage win
Tour of Spain: 92nd overall
Tour de France: abandoned on twelfth stage
Tour of the EEC: overall winner and two stage wins
Grand Prix des Nations: fourteenth

Miguel Induráin greeting the villagers of Villava after the Tour of the EEC, his first major international triumph

1987: LITTLE MORE THAN A HOTHOUSE

After his excellent victory in the Tour of the EEC, at the end of the 1986 season, Miguel Induráin was scrutinised by various experts. There were medical examinations, massage and sessions on the fixed rollers designed to improve the efficiency of his every muscle. Then there were psychological sessions, too, looking to give a youngster who scarcely believed in himself the mentality of a champion. Echávarri was confident in placing his raw protégé in the hands of Francesco Conconi, the Italian doctor who had helped Moser to beat the hour record; he worked skilfully and patiently.

Conconi's initial diagnosis was that Miguel's muscle power was impressive and he had a rapid rate of recovery, but that his weight – 13st 5lbs – was a definite handicap. That was in December; in February the consultant returned, and his weight was down to 12st 6lbs without any reduction in his physical condition.

Echávarri decided that Induráin would ride the 1987 season without any major demands being made on him: he had no intention of wearing him out. It would be sufficient to grab some stage wins and victories in minor, but still reasonably tough, races: in fact, he was to take a stage in the Tour of Murcia, two in the Catalan Week, and secure victory, together with three stage wins, in the Tour of the Mining Valleys, and first overall in the Tour of Navarra. Those competitive appearances were to become Induráin's way of tuning himself up for the major tours – a practice which he continued throughout his career.

VUELTA '87: AS FAR AS HE COULD

The 1987 edition of the Vuelta a España began on 23rd April with the outcome full of uncertainty. One hundred and seventy-nine riders from eighteen teams set out from Benidorm with the last-minute announcement that Alvaro Pino, the Galician in the Zor-BH squad who had won the previous year, was suffering from tendinitis, and would not be starting. Among the foreigners there was plenty of speculation on Moreno Argentin (Bianchi), Sean Kelly (Kas), Laurent Fignon (Systeme U) and Luis Herrera (Cafe de Colombia). Among the home riders, the usual names were again being trumpeted: Pedro Delgado, Marino Lejarreta, Pello Ruiz Cabestany, Vicente Belda, Iñaki Gastón and Julián Gorospe. Together with Arroyo, Gorospe was joint leader of Reynolds who had been joined by Seur as sponsors of the team. No doubt some were betting on Miguel Induráin as a candidate for the podium. To be realistic, however, Miguel came to the Benidorm prologue labouring under a heavy bronchitis which he was hoping to get rid of as the race progressed.

Benidorm was like an oven, with the kind of temperatures normally expected only in summer. This didn't stop the riders giving it everything. The Belgian, Jean Luc Vandenbroucke (Kas), flew round the 6.6 kilometres in 8-09, an average of 48.5 kph, to record the best time. Induráin was 25 seconds slower, in seventeenth position, thereby confounding those who considered him a prologue specialist and were predicting a better time. But what those enthusiasts didn't know was that Miguel was seeing the doctors that very morning, even before his training ride, because of his bronchitis. However, he was not too dispirited at the finish of the stage: 'I knew it would be very difficult to win here because the circuit suits Vandenbroucke very well, but I was hoping to be among the top ten and that wasn't to be. The important thing, though, is that I am getting over the bronchitis and I was able to ride flat out.'

In the next two stages he settled for riding in the middle of the peloton, but the third stage was awkward: 35.4 kilometres against the clock in a circuit around Valencia. Before the start, Induráin, who in other circumstances would have been regarded as a potential winner, spoke to the journalists: 'Today is a big day and I want to be among the leading riders. Little by little I am going better; on the other hand, it's not advisable to press too hard in these stages unless you're feeling in good physical shape.'

Sean Kelly was super quick in that time trial, averaging almost 50 kph, and was in the yellow jersey at the end of the day. Induráin, finishing with the fourteenth-best time, remained twelfth overall, 1-57 down on the Irishman. However, he was satisfied with his performance: 'It needed a great effort to cover those final metres because the cross-wind and the bronchitis didn't let me pedal as strongly as normal, and on occasions I lost my rhythm. In spite of everything, and given my present poor physical state, I'm pleased with my time because I beat men who were putting more store by this stage than I was.'

He was not just making excuses. The medical attention he'd been getting had alleviated the bronchitis but hadn't cured it. He struggled on through the next few stages which lifted the race towards the tops of the Pyrenees, trying not to miss too many chances and staying among the top fifteen overall. That is, until the race entered Andorra and the climbs became a real ordeal. He came through the three mountain stages pretty well wrecked and down at 57th overall, 16-26 behind the German, Raymond Dietzen, who was then in yellow.

On stage nine, from Zaragoza to Pamplona, there were 180 undulating kilometres where Reynolds, the Navarra team, were hoping some opportunities would come their way because of their better knowledge of the area – this was their home territory. But it was the modest Dyc-Lucas rider, Felipe Yáñez, who won. He had escaped from the pack with 112 kilometres still to go and held on to reach Pamplona, exhausted, but still with 2-20 over the whole peloton. Esparza led in the charge, with Induráin in 38th place. There was no change overall: Dietzen stayed in yellow; the Villava man stayed 57th, at 16-26. The prediction that one of Echávarri's boys would win came to nothing, but the Reynolds squad had been very active throughout the stage. At the finish Induráin explained: 'We had to try something simply because the race was on our own ground, but it was not an opportune moment to spend energy when we are getting close to two very hard mountain stages. Our intention is to work for Gorospe who is our best-placed rider on general classification and has a chance of winning.'

The race became severe again as the route took the riders into the Cantabrian mountains. On the Alto Campo, at the end of stage ten, Induráin finished last but one: he was wrecked. It was a terrible day in which all the fury of the elements was let loose: snow, the freezing cold and getting soaked to the skin was not exactly the ideal medical treatment for his bronchitis.

If that wasn't enough, what lay in wait for the peloton on the following day's stage were the 179 kilometres from Santander to the

56

lakes of Covadonga. The battle-hardened veteran, Marino Lejarreta, told of the dread that had spread among the riders in the face of what they were having to put up with. In the event, it was the Colombian Luis Herrera who proved his mettle and, by the same stroke, took over the leader's jersey. Miguel Induráin finished fourteen minutes down in 103rd place; overall he was now limping 42-40 behind Herrera.

There were no major complications on the next stage, the 142 kilometres to Oviedo, but even on such an uneventful stage Miguel Induráin found he could go no further. The pace was fast and he found himself twelve minutes down, and, worse still, showing no signs of recovery. He had managed to get through twelve stages in a poor physical condition that had been aggravated by the awful weather on the Cantabrian and Asturian climbs. Aware that he had no chance himself, he had put all his effort into supporting his colleague, Gorospe, and, although he regretted depriving the team leader of his help, he decided to take the advice of his team director, and dismounted. This was his third encounter with the Vuelta and the first time he had abandoned the race.

The 1987 Vuelta a España was won by Luis Herrera who became a true national hero in Columbia. He won it, perhaps – or perhaps not – thanks to the fact that Sean Kelly had to quit, three stages from the end, because of an enormous boil which prevented him from sitting on the saddle. Reynolds had a more than reasonable tour, finishing ninth in the team classification, with Arroyo, their top rider, eleventh, at 8-15. Once more, Julián Gorospe faded and ended 39-18 down in 31st place. Miguel Induráin went through a real ordeal before abandoning the Vuelta a España, a race which still has not seen him on the top of the podium.

TOUR '87: THE HARD APPRENTICESHIP

On 1st July 1987 the 74th edition of the Tour de France started in Berlin. A total of 207 riders, from 23 teams, were taking part in a race which, on paper, was going to be tough: a prologue and 22 stages to cover 4,100 kilometres with more than enough in the Alps, and a total of 90 kilometres against the clock. The press, as usual, was putting forward its favourites for the annual *Grande Boucle* which, this year, had the added interest of unpredictability.

On the day the race began the French specialist journal, *Vélo Magazine*, published a kind of order of merit, according to which those with the best chances were: Stephen Roche (Carrera); Laurent Fignon (Systeme U); Robert Millar (Panasonic); Sean Kelly (Kas); Claude Criquelion (Hitachi); Andy Hampsten (7 Eleven); Jean-François Bernard (Toshiba-Look); Urs Zimmermann (Carrera); Luis Herrera (Cafe de Colombia); and Charlie Mottet (Systeme U). The Spanish press, for its part, favoured Fignon, Roche, Kelly, Millar and Herrera among the foreigners. As for the home riders there was the hope, without much conviction, of a surprise by Pedro Delgado (riding for the Dutch PDM squad) and some stage wins for Induráin, and Blanco Villar.

After his retirement from the Vuelta Miguel Induráin came to this, his second 'big one' of the season, with rather low morale. In their conservative way Reynolds-Seur again had the unpredictable Angel Arroyo to beat their drum. Julián Gorospe was no longer joint leader – he had been substituted by the Frenchman, Dominique Arnaud – although he could always be kept in reserve if necessary. Miguel Induráin was once more listed as a domestique but, if the opportunities presented themselves, he would be given the chance to go for stage victories. In short, Reynolds, as a modest team in such aristocratic company, were really setting forth just to see what they were capable of.

To see what all 207 riders were capable of there was the 6.6-kilometre prologue in Berlin – an unusual setting for the Tour of '87. The time trial proved unpropitious for the favourites and it was the Dutchman, Jelle Nijdam, riding for Superconfex, who recorded the best time, flying through at 51.45 kph. Of the rest, one who didn't fail was Miguel Induráin, who, in spite of the strong head wind and problems with his disc wheel, achieved a very acceptable eighth place, ten seconds down on the winner. He was once more in his element as a prologue specialist. Surrounded by journalists after the race – he had, after all, been the highest-placed Spaniard – he explained: 'I am satisfied with my time. I believe that on a normal, conventional bike I would have gained another second or so. The prologue was tough and I think I attacked too soon, and I felt the effects of that in the final stretch. Right from the start I was on a 52x12.'

During the first five stages Miguel Induráin survived with more pain than glory. He kept himself in the least-exposed, most anonymous part of the peloton which, from the pace it was setting, seemed to have gone wild. At the end of those five days he was laying 75th overall, 7-29 down on the current leader, the Swiss, Eric Maechler, but he was not happy: 'I'm not at my best,' he told the journalists. 'Up to now I have restricted myself to riding in the bunch and avoiding the crashes, which is quite normal at the beginning of this type of race. I would like to do something special in the Futurescope time trial but I have looked at the route book and the course is very difficult, although the distance [87.5 kilometres] doesn't worry me.'

The start, then, had been at a crazy pace. The seventh stage was on the feast day of Saint Fermín and, as was now traditional, the whole of the Reynolds team were sporting red neckerchiefs. 'Today was a very special day for us,' said Miguel to the journalists. 'We wanted to dedicate a win to Saint Fermín, but it wasn't to be. Aiming for a win is easy; achieving it is the difficult bit. But I'm confident and I hope that one of these days I'll be able to escape, before the Pyrenees. There, it'll be a different story.'

The following two days on the flat were heavy and extremely hot. Likewise, the peloton was languid and slow-moving with scarcely any surprises, or overall changes. What was awaiting the riders was the major test of stage ten – 87.5 kilometres against the clock from Saumur to Futurescope. Induráin was not going 'entirely at his best' as he, himself, recognised and, bearing in mind that he was a specialist in this type of event, the press didn't give him any peace the day before this vital stage. He was hedging his bets: 'It is a long time trial, too long for what suits me. I don't know if I'll have enough in reserve to keep going well through to the finish. Last year, in the Nantes time trial, which was 71 kilometres, I was very tired in the last ten.'

The long time trial was won by Stephen Roche at an average of 44.2 kph. Charlie Mottet took over the yellow jersey and Induráin managed a quiet fourteenth place, 3-12 slower than Roche. In the general classification, however, he went up to 26th place and 8-44 separated him from Mottet. Miguel had not lived up to expectations. 'I was wrong to press so hard at the beginning,' he reasoned. 'I realised this at the feeding station [kilometre 36] and although I was getting reports by that point, the urge to do well and the information about the seconds I had lost on Blanco Villar and Steven-Haagen, who were setting the best times, didn't do me any good. It has been a very hard day and I've only ever competed in something like this in the Copa Baracchi. In spite of it all, I'm satisfied with the time I put up.'

Two more interminable stages brought the smell of the Pyrenees to the nostrils of the peloton. Induráin was the highest-placed rider in his team but Angel Arroyo, 66th overall and 13-55 down on the leader, remained Reynolds first choice. Everybody would have to work for him.

Miguel came out of those two cruel days in the Pyrenees unsteady, but in one piece. The slopes of Marie Blanque, Saudet and Luz Ardiden had wreaked havoc on the roll-call of participants. To get a general idea of how things were going for Reynolds after the transition stage between the Pyrenees and the Alps, it is enough to say that Induráin was the best placed in his team and he was 89th overall, and 55-19 down on race leader, Mottet. In the overall team classification they were 21st and Echávarri was not able to hide his disappointment: 'Some of my riders still haven't justified their presence here. Nevertheless, I believe we will not go back empty handed this year. We need to get stuck in and carry on the progress of previous years.'

Angel Arroyo, the would-be team leader, was demoralised and announced his intention of quitting. In reality, the team now had no real chance and it was pretty much a case of every man for himself.

It took seven stages, seven stations of the cross, for that particularly tough Tour to get clear of the Alps. Like almost all of those who had no significant aspirations, Miguel Induráin was just concerned about getting through them, somehow. He was almost detached from that fight to the death between Pedro Delgado, who had taken over the yellow jersey on the legendary Alpe d'Huez, and Ireland's Stephen Roche. Miguel emerged from the wicked Alpine stages in 104th position, 2-52-41 behind Perico.

For those like Miguel it was a relief to realise this race, which had turned into a torture, was nearing its end. He would be a mere witness (although he would learn from it) to the electrifying duel which would be decided, for sure, on the following day, because the 38-kilometre individual time trial around the town of Dijon was to be decisive. It was all about whether Roche, riding against the clock, would overcome Perico's feeble advantage. The press reporters had completely forgotten that a time trial of that length was ideal for a certain young man from Navarra. Hidden now at the tail of the field, and with legs tired from such an exhausting race, he was still able to shine over that distance. François Bernard, riding for Toshiba, made the best time and Stephen Roche confirmed the forecasts, and snatched the *maillot jaune* from Perico Delgado, in spite of the Segovian defending it with every bit of strength in his body.

This thrilling fight so monopolised the reporters' attention that there was scarcely a mention of Miguel Induráin's magnificent performance – head of the leader board for two and a half hours, and finally overtaken by only the top five riders, he was even quicker over the 38 kilometres than Perico Delgado who set off in the yellow jersey. Induráin made the sixth-best time of the day, 2-35 behind Bernard, the winner, and he moved up to 97th in the general classification, 2-52-45 down on Roche, the new leader. Among his countrymen, only Marino Lejarreta recorded a better time than Miguel who was again surrounded by journalists. He regretted that he had not done even better: 'It was a power circuit which was perfectly suited to my strengths and it was a real pity that I didn't manage to win. I went off really hard, looking for victory. The most difficult section was half-way round, that small hill, since there was a certain amount of wind. To finish a Tour de France as lively as this is a real triumph. It's not a bit like the "little event" that I won last year.'

In spite of everything Induráin was content. That monstrous Tour of '87 was about to end and he had gone conspicuously well on the penultimate stage. All that remained was the farewell ritual, 192 kilometres between Créteil and the Champs Elysées in Paris where the survivors would put on a reasonable show for the fans, while at the same time respecting the yellow jersey.

And so it was that the American, Jeff Pierce from 7 Eleven, came home a few seconds in front of the general group in a routine race which confirmed the Irishman, Stephen Roche, as overall winner, and allowed him, in his best-ever season, to complete the Giro–Tour double. Within smelling distance of victory – 40 seconds back – was Pedro Delgado. On that ceremonial final day Induráin made no great effort: he came in 127th, with the back-markers. Overall he ended up 2-53-11 down in an unremarkable 97th place.

So this chapter of Miguel Induráin's 1987 season closed. The Tour had been a crazy 26 days and the young man from Villava, for the first time in his professional life, had made it to the finish. A nervous glance back at the previous two attempts reminded him that in the first, in 1985, he got no further than the fourth stage, because of bronchitis and, maybe, a touch of stage fright; the second ended through exhaustion on the twelfth stage. On this, the third occasion he finished, perhaps not well, but he got there. And he remained convinced that he could, with difficulty, cope with even more overwhelming tiredness than he had already endured. It could be that getting through this race was the beginning of a deep determination that some day he, Miguel Induráin, would give people something to talk about in the biggest bicycle race in the world.

RESULTS

Tour of the Mining Valleys: first overall and three stage wins
Tour of Navarra: first overall
Tour of Murcia: one stage win
Tour of Spain: abandoned on stage twelve
Tour de France: 97th overall
Catalan Week: two stage wins

1988: A TIME FOR PATIENCE

The following season saw Miguel Induráin hardened from the bitter-sweet experience of victory and defeat, and still with the whole of his sporting life ahead of him. He had learned to share the peloton, escape groups and the back of the bunch with great figures, with charismatic riders from whom he made the effort to learn. It was a time to take things calmly, to be patient. That patience was perhaps a family trait, but it meant that, at 23, he was in no hurry to monopolise the podium.

José Miguel Echávarri and Eusebio Unzué had agreed that they would take as much time as they needed to continue developing their raw protégé. Although Miguel Induráin was now becoming a recognised cyclist, it was not wise to cash in on that; they would go slowly and try to do things properly. The Reynolds company which was forking out the money to sponsor the team – even to the extent of signing up Pedro Delgado for the season – was not losing its nerve, nor demanding immediate results. So they decided to keep Miguel Induráin as a definite for two of the 'big ones' – the Vuelta and the Tour – and to try their luck in the Tour of Catalunya and some of the minor races, but without wearing him out, or putting too much pressure on him. He could continue to make his slow but inexorable progress.

VUELTA '88: AT THE EXTREMITY

The 43rd edition of the Vuelta a España, following the custom of earlier years, was going to begin in the Canary Islands. There would be 3,431 kilometres to cover, in 21 stages, with 180 riders taking the start. The peloton was definitely lacking a number of stars and the

63

absence of Perico Delgado provoked some controversy. Riding now for Reynolds, he preferred to keep himself back for the Giro and the Tour. The forecasts favoured Sean Kelly and Alvaro Pino in what was to be an unpredictable Vuelta beginning on 25th April.

Miguel Induráin was the third string in the Reynolds team, led again by the eternal Arroyo–Gorospe tandem. As for the rest, it was a pretty handy squad with José Luis Laguía and the Colombian William Palacio forceful in the mountains, Pedro Díaz Zabala as their sprinter, and strong domestiques in Rubén Gorospe, Jesús Hernández Ubeda, José Enrique Carrera and Javier Luquin. Miguel remained an option if one of the team leaders failed.

The eighteen-kilometre prologue was a new kind of time trial, for both pairs and teams, and, because of its novelty, nobody dared bet on the outcome. Ettore Pastorelli, Carrera's first-year professional, was the cleverest in all this and, when the final computation was made, he found himself in the yellow jersey. Miguel Induráin finished first in his group in the series and for a long time was scenting victory, but he ended up marked down as 56 seconds behind the Italian.

The journalists, who just didn't understand that new and complicated system, congratulated Miguel for his good prologue performance, but the Navarra man didn't hide his disappointment: 'It would have been a dream to win such a difficult and bizarre stage as this. My morale was the same as when I made my Vuelta début and was leader for four stages after the Valladolid stage. The circuit suited me very well: it was flat and although I was worried about the wind, it was never blowing hard. What's more, we worked out the relays very well and there weren't any problems. At the end it was a matter of who was the quickest and, in spite of the sprinters in my group, that was me.'

With that first hurdle over – and it was a bit of a nightmare, not because the race was difficult but because of the extraordinary system of calculating the result – the riders faced the mountains in the first stage, and a team time trial in the second. Induráin left the islands 22nd on general classification, 3-19 down on the leader, Laudelino Cubino.

Now on the mainland, the peloton had to put up with the dangers, the crashes, and the ups and downs of four interminable stages that took them from Alcalá del Río to León. Miguel Induráin avoided as many obstacles as he could and fought as well as he knew how on the flat plain. At the finish in León he was 32nd overall and 10-38 separated him from the yellow jersey which Cubino was still wearing.

Now the first significant selection had been made, the peloton was facing the seventh stage from León to the ski station of Brañalín. The high mountains were beginning with two painful stages. All in all, Miguel's ordeal to the top of Brañalín did not go too badly – he finished 51st. The 6.8-kilometre hill climb, the following day, up the Naranco, was not the ideal distance, nor gradient, for the Villava man: he took 1-57 longer than the winner, Alvaro Pino. From these two stages Induráin emerged in pretty good shape – in 30th place overall, 23-59 down on Cubino.

One day on the flat and then they were back in the mountains at Valdezcaray but Miguel continued to keep his spirits up: he knew he was pedalling soundly enough, with no major worries nor, unfortunately, with any great ambitions. Now he had to face up to the Pyrenees from where the wind was already blowing, on the twelfth stage between Jaca and Cerler.

He emerged from the three days in the Pyrenees in poor shape; it had been a mediocre performance. Stage fourteen, from Seo de Urgel, and he was down to 69th overall with the gap between him and the leader, Laudelino Cubino, now more than an hour. Even more discouraging was the fact that Angel Arroyo, Reynolds' team leader and best placed overall, had abandoned because of a strange fever. Disappointment and loss of heart had spread through the ranks.

Nor was there any respite during the three flat stages which brought the peloton back on to the plain. They were ridden very fast and the continuous attacks were alarming for anyone with serious ambitions. Induráin did make one unsuccessful attempt to get away on the long flat stretch between Albacete and Toledo, but he hardly managed to get out of the general ruck.

The boy from Villava was off the back at the finish at the Dyc Distilleries, now in the Madrid hills, while, at the front, things were hotting up for the final show down. Sean Kelly was getting threateningly close to the then leader, Anselmo Fuerte, and the following day's time trial would give the Irishman certain victory in the Vuelta. Induráin was not riding well, as was obvious to anyone who was following his painful performance. He explained: 'I began the Vuelta able to ride at a very reasonable pace and then, instead of improving, I found myself getting worse, day by day. The flu ruined my plans and on the Col de Los Leones my legs gave out: I didn't seem to have any strength left. At the speed at which it has been ridden, it's very difficult to recuperate. I came into this Vuelta wanting to be among the first five but the flu has prevented me from making the most of my chances.'

It was like a premonition. The following day the penultimate stage was fought out: the 29-kilometre race against the clock from Las Rozas to Villalba was likely to determine the final outcome. Kelly was favourite and he lived up to it, winning the time trial with enormous authority. He would wear the yellow jersey of the undisputed winner through the streets of Madrid. Anselmo Fuerte couldn't match Kelly's pace, nor even finish inside the top ten. And Miguel Induráin? In other circumstances he would have been regarded as the logical person to put up the best time, since the distance and the terrain were ideal, but he didn't even count among the forecasts. In fact, he didn't do badly, finishing eighteenth in a time 2-31 slower than the winner. Overall he was now in 56th position, 1-19-48 down on Sean Kelly.

And so to the formality of the final stage, the 202 kilometres between Villalba and the finish in Madrid, which was supposed to be a promenade. Kelly reached the finish wearing the yellow jersey, while Dietzen stole a few seconds from Fuerte – enough to snatch second spot – in a battle which ended with a crash involving riders from both of their teams.

Miguel Induráin did not get to experience the supporters' enthusiasm as the race arrived in Madrid. At kilometre 52 of that final stage of the 1988 Vuelta a España he abandoned; on top of the flu dragging him down, he now had a touch of tendinitis which was impeding his pedalling. It was, he would later say, one of his biggest disappointments.

It doesn't require much insight to realise that Miguel Induráin quit the race for the simple reason that he couldn't go on any more. Anyone who knew Miguel, anyone who lived near that small world of professional cycling would understand that, after going through stage after stage of a very tough tour of Spain, you don't just pack up and go home a few kilometres from the end. Quite simply, Miguel could go no further. Both Echávarri and Unzué realised that it was not worth prolonging the agony, even though it was such an extraordinary retirement. They withdrew Miguel from the race.

After the crisis of mind and body had been overcome, they sent him back to work once more. Another trial by fire was awaiting.

TOUR 1988: THE GLORY OF THE DOMESTIQUE

The 75th edition of the Tour de France was going to start on 4th July without a clear favourite. The absence of Greg Lemond and Stephen Roche, winners in the two previous years, had left the top step of the podium in Paris vacant; *la Grande Boucle* would begin without an heir apparent. Those in the know were speculating on Pedro Delgado, although his chances had been somewhat reduced after his failure in the Giro; Andy Hampsten, winner of the Italian race; and Lucho Herrera, the recent winner of the Dauphiné. As ever, of course, all-rounders like Jean-François Bernard, Urs Zimmermann, Sean Kelly, Erik Breukink or Charlie Mottet were thought to be in with a chance. The most chauvinistic faithfully continued to put their money on the now somewhat faded Laurent Fignon. For the Spanish supporters and commentators, Pedro Delgado was the only possibility. At least nobody was putting forward any other name and, it should be said, the man from Segovia had been signed up by Reynolds, so he would not be riding in a foreign team this year.

In this squad which, in this edition of the Tour would be going for everything, Miguel Induráin figured, once more working in support of his leader, and out to make an impression himself in the time trials. Since his retirement in the Vuelta, Miguel had been absent from practically all competition, getting fully prepared for a Tour which was thought to be vital to Echávarri's Navarra team. However, not everything was completely peaceful in the Navarrese garden since neither Arroyo nor Gorospe were used to working for somebody else, and Delgado was Reynolds one and only team leader.

The prologue stage of the '88 Tour was totally unusual: a six-kilometre team time trial between Pornichet and La Baule in which each rider's time would not be used to effect the general classification but only to determine who would have the honour of wearing the yellow jersey the following day. An even greater innovation was that the complete team would ride the first five kilometres then, with a kilometre to go, only one rider from each team would carry on to the end.

67

For Reynolds this final warrior could be either Gorospe or Induráin, according to what people were saying the day before. In fact it was the Navarra man and he didn't do too badly. Quickest through the first five kilometres was the Weimann–La Suisse squad; Reynolds were not so sharp, taking 23 seconds longer and ending up fifteenth of the 22 teams. Over the final kilometre, from the point where one rider left the remainder of his team, Carrera's Bontempi was the fastest. Miguel Induráin was six seconds slower in eleventh place. So he did improve his team's overall performance, but it was the Italian, Guido Bontempi, who would start the next day's first stage in the yellow jersey.

Four dead-flat and diabolically fast days were a delight for the rouleurs, and the flat-out wizards. The last of these stages coincided with the start of San Fermín and the Reynolds riders wore their red neckerchiefs. Not that it did them any good: the team leader, Pedro Delgado, had fallen one kilometre from the finish and none of his team had been able to arrive in the leading group. 'It was a pity Pedro fell,' commented a saddened Miguel who had been continually dragging along the peloton. 'I don't know how it happened because I didn't see it, but after the break it was a real blow. We were not paying enough attention to the break that Kelly, Bernard and the others made; then we were held up in the peloton. When he saw who'd got away Echávarri told us to get up to them and we really pressed hard, but we couldn't catch them. We did reduce the gap, though.' Lubberding was now in yellow and, 2-02 down, in 62nd position, was Induráin.

The sixth stage, 52 kilometres against the clock between Lievin and Wasquehal, was where the first serious selection was expected. Here, Sean Yates went like the wind and beat the most reputed time-trial specialists. Miguel Induráin was also thought to have a good chance, but it was not his day. He finished 2-12 slower than the winner, in 38th place. He went out too strongly: at fifteen kilometres he was equalling Yates' time but, little by little, he was running out of steam and he finished in a time that was no better than moderate. Even so, it did bring him up to twentieth in the general classification, which Nijdam was now heading.

Up to this moment Induráin had been more than doing his job of pacing Delgado. José Miguel Echávarri, having got over his displeasure at what had happened on San Fermín's Day, was insisting that everybody had to work for the Segovian, and that

'Gorospe, Induráin and Luquin formed the backbone of support for Perico.' With regard to the Villava man, he added: 'Everybody knows the nature of Induráin and if he pulls through, as he has done up to now, we will be satisfied. I was hoping that he would do a good time trial, but while at the beginning he was very good, later on he dragged. He is a man who is growing in cycling and he is not yet tuned to the level needed for the Tour.'

The four progressively more hilly stages which brought the peloton close to the Alps showed that Induráin had already learned his lesson and was trying not to miss his chances in the main group: he needed to be vigilant, and, where necessary, to accelerate. He was maintaining his composure, eighteenth overall, 2-55 down on the then leader, Bauer.

Reynolds went into the Alps in good spirit. The first day they were concerned with sheltering Perico, taking stock of their own strength and that of the others. The second day was very tough and dramatic, with the team devoting itself entirely to defending Pedro Delgado's escape. He had attacked on the lower slopes of Alpe d'Huez, drawing Steven Rooks, to whom he conceded the victory, on to his wheel. The failure of the other favourites began on that day's starting line with the retirement of Fignon, and continued with the general decline of Kelly, Breukink and Zimmermann. Delgado was in the yellow jersey and Reynolds' hopes began to be realised. The whole team had worked to protect Perico's escape and it didn't matter that Induráin, for example, reached the finish 20-25 behind in 63rd place. The overall classification was now led by Pedro Delgado and Miguel was 42nd at 23-21.

Stage thirteen was an individual time trial of 46 kilometres in the area of Santenay over a somewhat lumpy route. It was an absolute rout by Delgado who took almost a minute out of his nearest rival. Given that this was his speciality, Miguel Induráin made an unusually modest time – 8-06 slower than Perico. Overall he went down to 44th but, as he explained to the journalists: 'I didn't set out to ride the stage flat out because I have to preserve strength for the Pyrenees. Now everyone in the team has a duty to Delgado and so we did what was expedient.'

José Miguel Echávarri, who was cautiously not counting his chickens, in spite of the evident superiority of Delgado, reinforced what Induráin had said: 'It is very important that men like Julián Gorospe, Miguel Induráin and Angel Arroyo remain in good form

69

since their support will be very necessary for the battle of the Pyrenees.'

That final Pyrenean test arrived with stage fourteen where Delgado widened the gap between himself and his nearest rivals, and Miguel Induráin came in a worthy 41st at 10-03. It was a day when all the Reynolds men had ridden themselves into the ground in order to get the leader away. Miguel, up to 39th overall at 32-47, was shattered at the finish. As he explained: 'It's been an extremely hard day and we have worked overtime to control every attack. I think I have accomplished my mission throughout all these stages although I admit that today I finished pretty well worn out. All the same, I hope to get to Paris to celebrate Perico's victory.'

They were not going to have any respite, however, neither Induráin nor any of the other 176 survivors. What lay in wait for them on the fifteenth stage – 187.5 kilometres from Saint Girons to Luz Ardiden – were a second-category, three first-category and two special-category cols. The day's hero was Laudelino Cubino, of the BH team, who finished alone on the summit of Luz Ardiden, almost six minutes ahead of the second man. But Pedro Delgado increased his lead still further and it mattered little that Induráin finished 42nd, 20-16 down, and that overall he was lying 37th, 47-01 behind his team leader.

Two quiet, relaxed, relatively unimportant stages with, much to the delight of the sprinters, bunch finishes, ended in speculation and rumour: French television was insisting that Pedro Delgado had tested positive at one of the drug controls. This misery went on for the next two stages: the short but leg-breaking eighteenth and the tough, pure mountain stage nineteen. The violent controversy that surrounded the analysis and counter-analysis of his presumed doping had descended on Perico; it preoccupied the commentators far more than stages which were of little consequence other than to show that Delgado still had enough spirit to increase his overall lead. It all ended in the International Jury issuing an official statement that the Segovian would not be sanctioned.

For Miguel the three remaining days were continuously exhausting, sparing nothing in support of Pedro Delgado, driving the peloton, pacing his team leader, finishing at the back of the bunch if necessary so long as it served the purposes of the person he was there to support. This was the hard, thankless task of the domestique which only those with the right qualities can effectively fulfil. And

Pedro Delgado arrived victorious in Paris: mission accomplished. Of the four Tours in which Miguel had competed this was his best result – 47th overall, and 1-02-54 behind his team-mate and race winner. The press commented on his remarkable performance, not so much for his stage placings but for the reliability and devotion he brought to the defence of his team leader's yellow jersey. He was always there when Delgado needed him, offering his help even to the point of exhaustion. Perico himself recognised this, especially regarding the stage that had brought him the yellow jersey when Miguel paced him so quickly on the descent: 'I asked Induráin to keep going as long as he could. I think that's where I did the most damage to everybody because Miguel made a sensational descent; he was even dropping me at times', said Delgado after his triumph.

Miguel Induráin, judging his own performance in that memorable Tour of '88, was as laconic as always: 'It's made me very happy, just as when I won the Tour de l'Avenir some years ago. Apart from my satisfaction at contributing to Delgado's victory, I have definitely responded better than I was expecting. Every time the mountains are less hard for me and on this occasion I've found it much less difficult to face up to them.' He really was developing.

THE SURPRISE OF THE VOLTA

After finishing the Tour Miguel Induráin and Julián Gorospe asked José Miguel Echávarri for a rest. It had been an arduous few months and they were down on the rivets after ensuring Pedro Delgado's triumph in Paris. Miguel's break lasted until 2nd September, the starting date of the 68th edition of the Volta a Catalunya.

Theoretically, that edition of the prestigious Catalan tour was particularly wide open: among the Spaniards the favourites were reckoned to be Pedro Delgado, winner of the Tour; Juan Fernández, bronze medallist in the recent World Championships; and the previous year's winner, Alvaro Pino; of the foreigners Giuseppe Saronni, Sean Kelly and Eric Breukink all had a real chance.

It was a tough, six-stage race with 136 riders, from seventeen teams, covering a total of 998.4 kilometres. Miguel Induráin was one of those included by Eusebio Unzué in the Reynolds squad; he was there, as can easily be imagined, to give his support to Perico Delgado, the undisputed team leader.

71

The first stage, 156.8 kilometres around an urban circuit in Salou, was won by Mathieu Hermans, at the head of a fast-moving group that had taken 1-56 out of the second group which contained all the main figures, Miguel Induráin included.

The second day's stage of 191.8 kilometres, between Salou and Sant Joan Despí, went to the Teka rider, Alfonso Guriérrez, who led in a twenty-strong group in which Miguel Induráin was twelfth. The rest of the field finished in bits and pieces; the stage had been hard, with attacks coming non-stop.

The third stage was a double: a 16.8-kilometre team time trial between Hospitalet and Barcelona, followed by a 111.6-kilometre road race from Barcelona to Platja d'Aro. The Italian team, Del Tongo, put up the best time with Reynolds ten seconds back in fifth place. In the second part of the stage the Pole, Czeslav Lang, got the better of his two companions in an escape group which took a scant nine seconds out of the main group. Del Tongo's Franco Ballerini was now wearing the leader's yellow jersey and Miguel Induráin, who was riding a reasonably comfortable race, was tenth, twelve seconds down on the Italian.

The fourth stage included a first-category and a second-category col in its 175 kilometres from Platja d'Aro to Manresa. These were jittery climbs with a succession of escape attempts which, as soon as they were countered, provoked new attempts. Shortly before the finishing line Miguel Angel Iglesias accelerated, taking Miguel Induráin on to his back wheel. Iglesias finished in front but the eleven seconds which the Navarra man snatched from the peloton took him up to second overall, just one second behind Ballerini.

The fifth stage was reckoned to be the *etapa reina* – the queen of stages: 187.8 kilometres between Bagà and Super Espot with four major climbs. Whoever won this stage, they said, would win the Volta. How wrong they were. The winner, after a hair-raising escape, was the Basque, Arsenio González, riding for Teka; out of the pursuit group – which included Induráin – jumped Laudelino Cubino to finish second, 7-27 down. At 7-46 came Marino Lejarreta, Pino and Induráin, and then the string of survivors continued to arrive at the finish with large time gaps between them. Cubino had leap-frogged into the overall lead while the Villava man held on to his second place, a threatening seventeen seconds adrift – threatening because the sixth and final stage – again a double – included an individual time trial of 29.7 kilometres – the perfect distance for Miguel Induráin. The second section, 128.4 kilometres from Tremp to Lérida, was likely to be routine, or, at most, a case of control and vigilance.

This time there was no denying the forecasts: Induráin was devastating against the clock and it earned him overall victory in the Volta. Miguel's domination of the time trial was secured in brilliant style, pedalling firmly and setting a strong pace from the outset which enabled him to beat even the mark set down by the organisers as the probable best time. He came in with a 25-second advantage over Laudelino Cubino who had also had a great ride and fully deserved his second place on the stage.

The evening section was, as can be imagined, purely routine: the Reynolds team carefully controlled the race until the stretched-out peloton came to the finishing sprint which was taken by Toshiba's Dutchman, Jacques Hanegraff. For the first time Miguel Induráin had won the Volta a Catalunya.

So finished Miguel's 1988 season. Very few believed in him when he began his professional career; there were even some who maliciously dismissed his win in the Tour of the EEC as 'luck'. Two waiters celebrated the Fiesta of San Fermín with the bet that he was incapable of climbing the 'Cuesta de Beloso' – a popular hill on the main road from Zaragoza towards the Navarra capital. With that enormous frame of his, with that hunched body, the kid would never amount to anything, so it was said. Those dismissive judgements, the scepticism of so many prophets of doom, had been destroyed by the end of the 1988 season.

On his return to Villava, still in the warm glow of his success in the Catalan tour, Miguel Induráin opened up to a local journalist, Pedro Lanas: 'This season I've had a bit of everything. At the start I was going well, as you could see in the Costa del Sol and the Tour of Galicia. Then I really prepared myself for the Vuelta and hoped to get among the top placings, but the flu and tendinitis forced me to abandon. In the Tour I again began to go well and got back in tune, and so I've had a good end to the season.'

The podium of the Volta was not a bad end to the season but, in spite of having won it with authority, Miguel still didn't really believe it: 'I was hopeful at the start of the Volta despite the fact that the race was far from being easy because of the particular men who were competing in it and the toughness of the route. Nevertheless, the win has taken me completely by surprise. I was hoping to do a good race but I had no illusions about winning up until the time trial on the last day. I didn't see myself as an overall winner until after the time trial.'

Nothing was easy, to judge from Induráin's description of that '88 Volta: 'It was fought out during every stage, in spite of the heat, the mountains and the difficult terrain. It had been a real battle right to the end and there was no way of knowing who would end up the winner. There were rivals like Marino, Pino, Millar, Cabestany, who failed in the time trial, and Cubino – he's a difficult man to beat ... In the end, the triumph was mine.'

He said it almost as if he was apologising, as if that victory was too much from someone whose job was as a domestique, and who was paid for being a domestique, as if being the winner was purely coincidental. However, there was something of the rebel in that young man who was beginning to know the smell of success: 'I've been winning races for two years,' he said, 'or at least making a mark in them, but without any recognition. That is why winning the Volta, with the prestige that it implies, has meant a great deal to me. At least it will get rid of that thorn I've had in my side for the last couple of years.'

The fact is that the boy from Villava now knew himself to be more experienced, hardened, more his own man: 'I found I was very much at ease in the Volta; it was like when I won the Tour of the EEC, only now I feel more mature and then you don't suffer so much, and you know how to go better in the race.'

Nobody would guess that throughout that time Induráin thought he was never going to be a 'Tour-man': 'The truth is that it's very difficult to get to be one. There are very few because the Tour requires a specific preparation and very particular qualities. You have to be a great climber and that's where I fall down a bit. Perhaps I do better in shorter races, of four or six days; and, also, I can play my best hand if there's a time trial.'

These were the worries of a man who considered himself a mediocre climber and who perhaps lacked the ambition – or the opportunity – to race as a team leader: 'I still have a lot to do,' he said. 'I'm not a complete rider. In one Vuelta I do well, in another I do badly. I still don't have a very clear idea about how well I ride. Perhaps in a couple of years I will do a bit better and I might be a little more consistent in my performances. I don't see myself as a team leader; I'd be rather afraid of that because the team leader has so much responsibility. At the moment I enjoy a certain amount of freedom because Perico is there for the major races. If you are the leader they are always going to be pressurising you in all the Vueltas and I'd be afraid of that, or at least it would be something to be concerned about.'

He described his progress and his deficiencies: 'This year I've maintained my form in the time trials. Where I have certainly improved has been in the mountains and over long distances, but in the mountains I still need to improve further because they take too much out of me and as the days go by I find I'm paying for it. I need to make myself a bit tougher, for my body to be a bit more ready to accept punishment and put up with it better.'

It was clear that his mediocre performances in the Vuelta a España had left a deep mark on Miguel Induráin, as he spoke of his coming season: 'I still haven't worked out what I'll be doing next year. However I would like to ride well and compete, above all, in the Vuelta, which has been a failure for me in these last two years. Perhaps that is the thing for me, winning a Vuelta a España. The Tour is still too far off for me. The Vuelta is more accessible, closer to how I see myself as a cyclist.'

Doubtless Miguel didn't know the hidden intentions of José Miguel Echávarri and Eusebio Unzué, both obsessed with their team carrying off the individual victory in the Tour. They had done it with Perico and they had the same ambition with Induráin. What's more, for those who believe in premonitions, there was the omen of Unzué's remark all those years ago: 'It could be that Induráin will never win a Vuelta a España, but it's certain that he's going to win a Tour de France some day.'

A few days later the Reynolds team, its technical staff and its riders, received a tribute in Pamplona for the brilliant season it had achieved.

RESULTS

Tour of Galicia: one stage win
Tour of Spain: abandoned on last stage
Tour de France: 47th overall
Tour of Catalunya: first overall and one stage win

1989: READY

For Miguel Induráin the 1989 season began very differently from the previous year. He had shown obvious progress, both physically and in terms of his self-confidence. He was now a de-luxe team member of the Reynolds outfit and only restricted to that because Perico Delgado was its indisputable leader; however, Echávarri and Unzué were agreed that he should do more than merely help his team leader. So they entered him for one of the early season classics, the Paris–Nice, confident that, in a short stage-race like this, Miguel would perform well on his own behalf, without having to direct all his efforts towards someone else's triumph.

PARIS–NICE: DEBUT

Miguel Induráin was Reynold's main protagonist for the 1989 Paris–Nice; Pedro Delgado and Julián Gorospe were also taking part, but they were there more to get some kilometres in their legs than anything else.

The race began on 5th March with a 5.3-kilometre prologue time trial through the French capital in which Thierry Marie made the best time. Induráin was one second back – in second spot, but ahead of Fignon, Roche, Breukink and other renowned top riders.

The first stage, 170 kilometres between Gien and Moulins, went to the Belgian, Etienne de Wilde, who won the sprint from the whole bunch. The overall classification remained the same as the day before.

In a mass sprint at the end of the second stage, from Moulins to Saint-Etienne, it was de Wilde again and, thanks to the ten-second bonus, he also took over the leader's jersey. Induráin was now third, eight seconds down on the Belgian.

The third stage was a team time trial over 58 kilometres at Berguezes and Reynolds completely lost out: they finished 1-51 slower than the winning Toshiba squad who, with that victory, were able to put their new professional, Frenchman Laurent Bezault, into the leader's jersey. Induráin slipped to sixteenth overall, 1-19 down on Bezault.

Some changes in the overall table were expected to take place on the fourth stage, 207 very tough kilometres between Vergèze and Toulon Mont-Faron. On the bottom slopes of Mont-Faron, Bruno Cornillet and Miguel Induráin jumped clear, and there was a truly thrilling battle between them. The Frenchman won in a tight sprint, but the seconds that Miguel gained brought him up to fifth overall; he was now just 45 seconds behind Marc Madiot, the new race leader.

The 181-kilometre fifth stage took them on from Toulon to Saint Tropez. On the only climb of the day, the Vignon, Frenchman Gérard Rué and Miguel Induráin escaped. Here we were seeing the Villava man climbing easily, almost fearlessly. On the descent they increased their advantage; Miguel allowed his fellow escapee to take the stage, while the minute they took out of the peloton was enough to eliminate the advantage of the four riders ahead of him on general classification. With only two stages to go Miguel Induráin took over the white jersey of race leader, with a gap of 22 seconds over second man, Marc Madiot.

The sixth stage, between St Tropez and Mandelieu, was a route of 190 kilometres with a climb fourteen kilometres from the finish. With the whole of the Reynolds team working for him Miguel Induráin didn't have too much trouble defending his lead. The stage went to the Dutchman, Adri van der Poel, in a 30-man sprint, leaving the overall classification unchanged from the day before.

All that was left was the final day which was going to be a double. The first part, a 100-kilometre road race from Mandelieu to Nice, ended in a mass finish, won by the Italian, Adriano Baffi, and made no important difference to the classification. The second part was a ten-kilometre mountain time trial, from Nice up the Col d'Eze, and it lived up to expectations: the best time was made by the Irishman, Stephen Roche, who was the only man capable of snatching the white jersey from Induráin. But the 32 seconds he took out of the Navarra man were not enough: Miguel made a great climb and came in with the second-best time, and overall victory.

There could not have been a better start to the 1989 season. He couldn't get so emotional about winning the Paris–Nice as he did about his win in the Tour of the EEC – his first international success. On the other hand, reaching the podium of the Paris–Nice was obviously not a matter of outstripping a group of amateur cyclists, however brave and full of promise they might be, but of overcoming rivals of the class of Stephen Roche, Marc Madiot, Peter Winen, Eric Caritoux and others who figured among the *crème de la crème* of the international peloton.

On his return to Villava the Induráin telephone didn't stop ringing, and there were not only congratulations or demands from journalists, but also tempting offers for his future professional career. His market value had risen enormously, confirming his development as a rider but, to all the proposals he received, some more honest than others, Miguel replied that his contract with Reynolds had another two years to run, and then he would see. His reputation was growing, but his increasing popularity was also a burden: it was the price to be paid, something that did not really fit with his quiet personality but he had no choice but to pay it.

In his comments to the journalists he explained his triumph in the Paris–Nice: 'Perhaps I took them by surprise. In a race containing so many mountains they were not thinking about me, so I took advantage of that to catch them unawares. It's no secret that I'm not too fond of the mountains, but I am learning how to deal with them and get through them as well as I can.'

He also talked about his complete understanding with the staff and fellow riders in the Reynolds team: 'Here, at Reynolds, they have always helped me and known how to support me, explaining what might happen at any time, how far I could go and motivating me to carry on further. In bad times their advice has always been invaluable.'

The Miguel Induráin of that first outing of the 1989 season was a different man: he had brought forward his preparation by a month and trained hard. In Navarra there had been scarcely any rain, nor had it been cold, and, notably, there had been no sign of the catarrh and flu from which he often suffered. Things could not have begun better.

They continued to get even better when, some days after his win in the Paris–Nice, Echávarri decided to enter him in the International Criterium. In the first of its three stages Bezault provoked an escape which contained the best of the field: Marc Madiot, Lemond, Mottet, Fignon, Roche ... and Induráin. A handkerchief could have covered the lot of them at the finish and it was clear that the race was going to be between those seven. The second stage, in the mountains, was so placid that it was won by the track-rider, Lino. The third stage, a decisive time trial at Avignon, was won by Induráin and, with it, the International Criterium. He overtook his minute man, Fignon, and beat those 'superstars' – Visentini, Breukink, Mottet, Roche, Bernard and Lemond, in that order. And that was that.

From the offers which rained down on him after his victories in the Paris–Nice and in the International Criterium, Echávarri decided that Miguel should ride the Milan–San Remo. In this classic of classics he put in a modest performance, finishing half-way down the field, 1-50 behind the winner, Laurent Fignon. He also took part in the Liège–Bastogne–Liège and finished tenth in a race won by Sean Kelly. What Induráin was really doing in these events was getting his legs tuned up for the Vuelta a España, a race he was entering for the fifth consecutive time and which continued to be one of his professional frustrations.

VUELTA '89: TEAM LEADER

The 1989 Vuelta was preceded by almost a year of controversy surrounding the Reynolds team. The absence of Pedro Delgado from the previous year's race because he was reserving himself for the Giro gave rise to some slanderous remarks, virtually accusing Echávarri of treason against his country. Not even the Segovian rider's triumph in the Tour enabled the Reynolds Director to escape the charge of defeatism and denying the Spanish public the chance to see their best professional cyclist in their most important race. The row almost ended in Echávarri's resignation, before the storm eventually calmed down. Even so there was great anticipation about the announcement of Reynolds' plans for the '89 Vuelta a España.

On 20th April José Miguel Echávarri gave the official list of the cyclists who would be participating in the race to the press, announcing that Reynolds would be running 'at 80 per-cent'. In response to their pressing questions, he told them that the team would consist of Miguel Induráin, Julián Gorospe, Pedro Delgado, William Palacio, José Luis Laguía, Jesús Rodríguez Magro,

Dominique Arnaud, Javier Luquin and Melchor Mauri. In the event of them being needed, they were counting on Juan González Salvador and Abelardo Rondón as reserves.

Having resolved the first mystery – Pedro Delgado would be riding the Vuelta – Echávarri went on to announce the surprise: there would be three team leaders: Delgado, Gorospe and Induráin. However, to all intents and purposes, it would be Induráin who would carry the weight of the race, and would have the other two as de luxe team members in support. 'In principle,' he said, 'Induráin will be the chief card we are going to play. He has shown that at the moment he is the best in one-week races and he is becoming a fine, mature professional. For that reason we are going to give him this opportunity, even though we know full well that it might not work. We will give him as much support as is necessary and it won't matter if he fails. In that event we will count on Delgado or Gorospe. In short, we are going there with three strong arrows to our bow.'

The Vuelta a España began on 24th April with a very poor foreign representation which meant that, theoretically, the race was between half a dozen favourites. The forecasters were speaking of Delgado, Pino, Parra, Lejarreta, Induráin and Dietzen. Perhaps a shiver ran down Miguel's spine, knowing that he was among the candidates for victory.

A total of 209 riders, from 21 teams, took the start at La Coruña, in a 20-kilometre prologue, very like that of the previous year. It was really a case of three stages in one, but to explain its complications would take too long and probably leave the reader none the wiser. The first winner and wearer of the yellow jersey was the veteran, Mannix Lameire, in a race full of incidents, skids and falls. The rain made things difficult for Miguel Induráin and he finished the ride 30 seconds adrift of the leader, and, due to the eccentric system of classification, after such a bizarre stage, he found himself in 158th place.

The first ten stages were a nerve-wracking affair, over dreadful winding roads, buffeted by wind, but mainly flat or, at most, slightly undulating with a few small hills. The Colombian, Omar Hernández, wore the yellow jersey and Miguel Induráin, fifteenth overall at 3-20, kept himself continuously at the front of the peloton, watching, and being watched: he was not Reynolds' key man for nothing. The race was becoming exasperatingly monotonous, with none of the start-line favourites making any kind of attack.

The journalists, for want of anything else to write about, were reduced to speculating, and Echávarri had to refute certain rumours about the relationship between Induráin and Delgado, both leaders in his team: 'Both Delgado and Induráin will fight in the interest of whichever of them is best placed,' he said.

Some journalists were also stirring up rumours about the state of Miguel's health and morale because he was refraining from taking the initiative in the race. The Villava man gave them their answer: 'I'm feeling fine. I have climbed well on some stages and that has given me confidence in myself. I hope that everything continues like this and that I perform well in the hard mountain stages that are coming up. The Vuelta is a very long race and there's no need to get worked up too soon. The final week will be the decisive one.'

The hour of truth came on stage twelve: its 186.5 kilometres between Lérida and Cerler could clear up the uncertainties. The summit finish at the ski station of Cerler could decide the race or, at least, bring about the decisive selection. It was an epic stage: a long escape by the Frenchman, Esnault, who was brought back on the first slopes of Cerler; then a do-or-die attack by Pedro Delgado, and while four Colombians managed to hold on to him, they couldn't deprive him of the stage win; and an extraordinary effort from Miguel Induráin, offering his wheel to Delgado and doing the work so that the Segovian man could make the definitive break. Induráin himself finished in seventh place, 46 seconds down on Perico. In spite of everything, Delgado's winning margin was not enough to take the lead away from Hernández in the overall classification in which Miguel was now ninth, at 2-59. To outside appearances at least, this was a moment of indecision for Reynolds. Gorospe, who was suffering from complete exhaustion which had relegated him way down the field, was definitely out of it, while Delgado, the best placed, could now be regarded as the one and only team leader. However, Echávarri declared that he had certainly not ruled out Induráin and both men were saying that they were at the service of the other, if it were necessary – their times would decide it. They seemed calm and showed no signs of tension.

The peloton left the Pyrenees decimated, having passed through the sieve of the first, and for some, the final selection. Again it was downhill and then, almost immediately, the road was heading steeply upwards again. Miguel was optimistic when he talked to the press before stage fifteen, the 23.4-kilometre hill climb up to the ski

81

station of Valdezcaray, which was likely to prove decisive: 'I feel fine and I'm going to compete for the stage win. There are several men all with possibilities, but I believe I can be amongst the best and I'm certainly going to try. It's going to be tough but I'm confident of a good result.'

In the event it was Pedro Delgado who showed the best form, in a demonstration of hard hill climbing against the clock. Induráin, who at least rose to the occasion, finished in tenth place, 1-51 slower than the Segovian.

Overall, the Colombian, Hernández, lost the yellow jersey to another of his fellow countrymen, Martín Farfán. Miguel, at 2-37, was tenth and Delgado, two seconds behind Farfán, was in second spot. Yet still Echávarri had not decided – at least not publicly – if Perico was the sole team leader. Prolonging his indecision, perhaps, was the long time trial in Medina del Campo, still to come.

There was no relaxation during the sixteenth stage with two first-category climbs towards the end of the 193 kilometres that took them from Haro to Santoña. It proved to be a lively race in which the Colombians lost out. It was won by the German, Peter Hilse, two seconds ahead of a group containing Induráin. Pedro Delgado took the yellow jersey from Farfán and Miguel, 2-35 down, went up to ninth overall.

Then came stage seventeen, the terrible stage to the Lakes of Covadonga. At that moment everything pointed to Perico, now in yellow, being Reynolds' single, undisputed team leader. Further-more, in the previous stage Induráin had worked hard on the front of Delgado's group to open up a gap between him and the Colom-bians. However, before the ride to Covadonga Miguel was still talking somewhat ambiguously: 'Today's stage is very dangerous, but it is also a beauty for whoever is in form, and that's Perico. I'm also hoping not to lose too much time because I don't want to say goodbye to the race with so far still to go. I have great hopes for the long time trial at Medina del Campo and we'll have to see what happens before then.'

Perico and Miguel, being room-mates, used to study the profile of the stage every day, and what was lying in wait for them – 228 kilometres between Santoña and the Lakes of Covadonga – was, on paper, the hardest stage of the race. And so it proved to be, not only because it was so relentless, but also because there were a lot of serious falls on the descent from the Col de Fito due to the bad state of the road. One of those to come down was Miguel Induráin who suffered shock and severe bruising to his left wrist. Alvaro Pino won the stage and over-confidence nearly cost Pedro Delgado the yellow jersey. Induráin, despite his misfortune, was well placed, finishing seventeenth at 2-17. Delgado remained at the head of the overall classification with Miguel ninth at 3-05.

According to the emergency medical team Miguel Induráin's injury required an X-ray to ascertain how bad it was. A shiver ran through the Reynolds headquarters at Cangas de Onís when Miguel was led, in great pain, to the radiologists. Echávarri seemed not to want to face facts when he declared to the press: 'Induráin is fundamental to our team right now and he is not ruled out, though the pain he is suffering suggests it could be something serious. If that were the case it would considerably affect the way the team is performing and maybe break the run of luck we've had till now.'

Once more the Lakes of Covadonga had cast their spell on Miguel Induráin. It was there that he'd lost that longed-for yellow jersey in his first Vuelta of 1985, and there where he abandoned the race in 1987. On this occasion, in 1989, his Vuelta was once again coming to an end at that spot. The medical team indicated that he had a 'Colles' fracture in his left wrist and a bone in the lower arm also broken.' The Vuelta doctors explained that 'there has been no displacement of the bones; he should only need a plaster cast for the next few days, but he cannot continue in the race. The injury will be cared for in Navarra and ten days should be enough for him to get back into training on the bicycle.'

At the summit of Brañalín, where stage eighteen finished, Miguel sported his left hand in plaster and spoke philosophically to the journalists: 'I shall rest for a few days, and I hope to be back on the bike soon. There's a lot of the season still left for me.'

With a serious fracture fortunately ruled out, the doctors took the view that he could be ready for the Tour. From now on he would have to follow the Vuelta from home, in the hope that he would see Perico going on to win. It was a hope that was realised: Delgado finished victorious in Madrid and from the splendour of the podium he sent an emotional message of gratitude to his team-mate who had paced him when he most needed help, and to whom a large part of his victory was due. Perhaps that was the major satisfaction for Miguel after his fifth participation in the Vuelta a España which had been superb while it lasted.

TOUR '89: FIRST WARNING

The 76th edition of the world's most important cycling race began in Luxembourg on 1st July with 189 riders from 22 teams. Pedro Delgado, Laurent Fignon and Stephen Roche were rated favourites, with Breukink, Hampsten, Mottet, Parra, and Herrera given an outside possibility.

The two months since the unfortunate break in his left wrist had been more than enough for Miguel Induráin not only to mend his bones but also to return to good racing form. Again Echávarri was counting on him for the Tour with the clear aim that he should devote himself to supporting Pedro Delgado, the top favourite, in his bid to repeat his triumph. Joining the sponsorship of the Reynolds team, both in promotion and with their cheque book, was Banesto, who would, the following year, become their sole sponsor.

A 7.8-kilometre individual time trial set the '89 Tour on its way. The press made Induráin favourite to win the prologue and he didn't deny that he'd be delighted to be 'wearing the yellow jersey on the first day'. It wasn't to be, however: his was the seventh-best time, ten seconds off that recorded by Eric Breukink. But this was not the only, nor the most serious, disappointment. Incomprehensibly, Pedro Delgado arrived on the starting ramp two minutes and forty seconds late which left him in last place overall, 2-54 down on the Belgian. The press, especially the popular Spanish journalist José María García, who, ever since Delgado had failed to take part in the 1988 Vuelta, had frequently attacked the Segovian and, by implication, Reynolds team directors, did so again after Perico's extraordinary mistake: he recommended that the team should appoint a more responsible leader. Miguel Induráin, to avoid any misunderstanding, declared: 'Personally I'm in very good form, but nevertheless, I don't think I should be the one to lead the team. As soon as I got here I made it clear that I had come to give my closest possible support to our team leader, for as long as my strength holds out and I've had no change of mind. We've got to make up the ground we've lost and pick up Perico's morale.'

The first stage, still in Luxembourg, would be a double: a 135.5-kilometre road race in the morning and a team time trial over 46 kilometres in the afternoon. The morning section saw an escape by Carrera's Portuguese rider, Acacio Da Silva, who took 4-40 out of the main field in which Induráin was riding a bit too comfortably in

125th position. In the afternoon Reynolds lost four minutes to the winning team, Super U, for which they blamed Perico Delgado's inexplicable lack of form. Echávarri's team had begun extremely badly and spirits were at rock bottom. Miguel Induráin was 161st overall, 7-13 down on Da Silva – too big a time gap to reorganise team strategy and for him to take over responsibility from Delgado who was now last but one overall, 9-57 off the lead. And there had only been two stages.

Criticism of the Segovian intensified, as did the Siren songs that were being played in Induráin's ears. Some journalists were magnifying the amount of time which Perico had cost him in the team time trial, the stage which had ruined any chances that the Navarra man might have had. Miguel didn't enter into any of this: 'No,' he insisted, 'I haven't lost my chances, quite simply because I didn't come into this Tour for the sake of my position overall. Losing four minutes doesn't matter to me; our choice was, and is, Pedro, and we've just got to recover the time we've lost. At the moment,' he said, referring to the Segovian's loss of form in the team time trial, 'if we just leave him alone his morale may drop even further. We want to show him, right now, that the team is supporting him, to see if he picks himself up. I'll try to get a stage win, perhaps in one of the time trials. That's all that I'm interested in – that and fighting as hard as I can because things are going pretty badly for us in the overall classification.'

Delgado did revive in the long, 73-kilometre stage five time trial and the race rediscovered its excitement. Greg Lemond made the best time and Perico was second, 24 seconds slower, which brought him up more than a hundred places. Miguel Induráin was a useful twelfth, 3-12 behind the American who was now in the yellow jersey. Overall the Navarra man was 7-35 down in 37th position.

The pace was frenetic and the bumpy roads shattering in the interminable days which took the peloton down to the Pyrenean cols. The ninth stage, 147 kilometres between Pau and Cauterets, had two first-category and one special-category climbs, and the press was now beginning to speak of a three-way battle between Lemond, Delgado, and Fignon. This was their conjecture, but, in reality, what happened was that Miguel Induráin exploded and proved that he finally had the measure of the mountains. He came in first after a stage in which Echávarri's team strategy had been masterful, riding with an authority which, as *Diario Vasco* reported, 'aimed to show what he's really made of'. Miguel combined a series of accelerations and decelerations with Pedro Delgado, who finally urged him to attack on the Col d'Aubisque. The Segovian also finished high up, in third place, 1-29 down on the Navarra man; sandwiched between them was Anselmo Fuerte. Greg Lemond held on to the yellow jersey and Induráin, now eighth overall at 5-37, was getting close to the top riders, while Delgado was threatening from eleventh place, 6-24 down. The day could not have gone better for Echávarri's men.

Miguel was happy after his achievement at Cauterets and once again made his position clear to those detractors who were suggesting a change in team responsibilities: 'Our aim in the team is to continue getting Delgado well placed. He is the team leader and it is he who can win the Tour, and with that aim I shall carry on helping him in every way I can.'

Delgado redeemed his earlier mistakes in the Pyrenees while the media were remarking on the magnificent strategy Echávarri's team had brought off. Among the riders, Miguel Induráin's style, strength and intelligence had not passed unnoticed. As the Galician leader of the BH team, Alvaro Pino, remarked: 'If Induráin continues to make the progress he's made this season he could become the Eddy Merckx of Spanish cycling.'

Little changed in the three flat stages which transferred the peloton to the Alps. Here, stage fifteen awaited the 152 survivors – a 39-kilometre mountain time trial from Gap to Orcieres-Merlette, with two first-category climbs, one at the finish. It was the Dutch PDM rider, Steven Rooks, who made the best ascent, while Miguel Induráin was a surprising third at 49 seconds, with Marino Lejarreta finishing between them. Overall, Lemond had snatched the lead back from Fignon, Delgado remained fourth at 2-48 and Induráin was down to 11th, 7-27 back. After his good result in the stage he was again hounded by journalists for his analysis of the race: 'It's always important to be among the leaders and I believe that third place is in line with that. Perhaps we had thought that Delgado would be our leading rider but he wasn't able to be, although the fact that he has remained in front of his chief rivals is a good sign for the remaining stages.' It was his 25th birthday and he had begun trying to speak in public in that distant, impersonal style, somewhere between the shy and the solemn, which today we recognise as his trademark.

After three days in the Alps in which Miguel shouldered the responsibility of supporting Perico, helping him both defend and attack to enable the Segovian to hang on to his aspirations of repeating his Tour victory, many foreign journalists were asking about Induráin: they wanted to know more about the youngster who was riding the perfect Tour on Pedro Delgado's behalf. 'Delgado's heir apparent', Spanish television was calling him; others were courting him as 'the cyclist of the moment' and predicting a splendid future for him. Famous champions were talking about him: Raymond Poulidor: 'He has innate abilities which get better day by day. He is still a little green and he should not be in a hurry, but this man will go to the very top'; Eddy Merckx: 'I love his style, his way of riding and, above all, descending'; Luis Ocaña: 'He has a great build and muscle power. If he knows how to take advantage of it all he's soon going to make us very happy. If he were not Perico's second, Perico would have found it difficult to do the things he has done.'

This was no mean thing for somebody just turned 25. As for the remainder of the Tour, any hope of making Fignon crack seemed lost and it was almost impossible to hope for a miracle on Delgado's part. The Tour arrived at the gates of Paris with Miguel Induráin sixteenth overall, 30-32 down on the yellow jersey, but there was no let up in the amount of interest the press was showing in the youngster from Villava who had been almost invisible in previous editions of the race. He had improved ostensibly and he had lost the reverence he once had for the major tours. 'I believe my prospects are pretty good', he said of himself. 'I regard myself as a rider who has made a lot of progress and I have ambitions now not only for the small tours but also for the big ones. In the Vuelta a España I went well; now I'm doing reasonably well in the Tour, although I recognise that the length is a bit of a strain for me. But if I'm well prepared, with the years I've got left and the physical strength that I must develop, I can aim high.'

Those 24.5 kilometres of the final stage between Versailles and the Champs Elysées were against the clock. They represented the last opportunity for Lemond, 50 seconds down, to take back the yellow jersey from the French cycling hero. The whole of France was rooting for Fignon. In the very last stretch, however, Paris witnessed the American's reversal of fortunes; mortified, they could only wonder how their idol took 58 seconds longer than his fierce rival.

Greg Lemond won a Tour which had been exciting right to the very end and Fignon wept for the loss of what was, perhaps, his last chance. Delgado, who had such a disastrous start, finished on the podium, third overall. Miguel Induráin's performance in the final stage was rather modest – 1-39 down on Lemond, the seventeenth best time. 'I faded a little at the end', he admitted. He also finished seventeenth overall, at 31-21. The previous year he had ended up 47th, 1-03-15 behind the winner, Perico Delgado.

So, for Miguel, the 1989 season had finished on a much more promising note than the previous year. With the '89 Tour at an end, *L'Equipe* published a review of the event and its protagonists. Speaking of Induráin, it read: 'That lanky young man called Miguel Induráin, with an easy smile and elegant pedalling, has, at 25 years old (his birthday was in the middle of the Tour), amazed friends and strangers alike. Induráin won the stage at Cauterets at an incredible gallop, with the entire peloton after him. He showed that he is now mature enough to aspire to victory in a big stage race.'

The Spanish commentators were forecasting that Miguel's next success would be in the Vuelta a España, remembering that almost certainly Perico would give the race a miss to prepare for the Giro and the Tour. The team would be known as Banesto the following season and they were predicting that Induráin would be a prominent member of it.

RESULTS

Paris–Nice: first overall
Avignon International Criterium: first overall and one stage win
Milan–San Remo Classic: fourteenth
Liège–Bastogne–Liège Classic: tenth
Pamplona Criterium: first
Alquerías Criterium: first
Subida al Naranco: second
Tour of Switzerland: seventh overall
Tour of Spain: abandoned on stage seventeen after a fall
Tour de France: seventeenth overall and one stage win

Miguel Induráin, on the podium in Paris,
with the Italian, Claudio Chiappucci

Miguel Induráin, wearing the yellow jersey through the streets of Paris, on the
last stage of the Tour de France

Three moments during the Grand Canary Islands Criterium of 1994
(*Micael Lögfren*)

Induráin on the climb to the Lakes of Covadonga in the 1995 Tour of Asturias, where he suffered a major setback. *(Jesús Farpón)*

Two moments on the ascent of the Col de Somiedo in the 1996 Tour of Asturias, which Miguel won.
(Jesús Farpón)

Winner of the 1996 Tour of
Asturias *(Jesús Farpón)*

Miguel handling different means of
communication *(Jesús Farpón)*

Reading the Spanish press reports in
Pamplona before the start of stage eighteen of
the '96 Tour

Miguel Induráin and his brother, Pruden, with their parents before the start of the eighteenth stage of the 1996 Tour de France

Miguel Induráin kissed goodbye by his wife, Marisa, and his son, Miguel, before the start of the Pamplona–Hendaye stage of the '96 Tour

Members of the Banesto team, with Miguel's son, just before their lap of honour on the Champs Elysées

Miguel Induráin at maximum effort in the Bordeaux–Saint-Emilion time trial, where he would record the second best time

1990: FINE TUNED

Miguel Induráin was now a considerable asset to Banesto. What he required, and what both Echávarri and Unzué were thoroughly committed to, was serious work on his mental preparation. In addition to his physical capabilities, the competitive sportsman needs to develop the mental qualities of a winner; it was no more than a matter of fine-polishing the rough diamond which, in the 1989 season, had already begun to shine. The work of shaping those athletic qualities also meant that his trainers and doctors arranged an operation to correct Miguel's nasal defect, thus preventing the sinusitis he frequently suffered from.

Also in 1990 Banesto took over responsibility for what had been the Reynolds team. They renewed the contracts of almost the entire outfit, including the technical staff, and Miguel Induráin signed for two years with the option of an extension.

PARIS–NICE: IN CASE ANY DOUBT REMAINED

The 1990 season got going for Banesto with the Paris–Nice classic which, for Miguel, brought back pleasant memories of his previous year's victory. Echávarri took his most powerful team, with Delgado and Gorospe accompanying Miguel. A repeat victory for the Navarra man was thought likely now that he had proved his growing ability in the Tour, although here he would have to thwart Fignon, Lemond, Roche, Bugno, Moreno Argentin, Ekimov, Mottet and Rominger – names which were being bandied about in the French press, along with Delgado, and Induráin, as possible winners.

The race consisted of eight stages and began on 4th March with a nine-kilometre individual time trial in Paris where the French

89

sprinter, Francis Moreau, made the best time. Induráin, was second, three seconds slower.

The next stage unfolded over a distance of 178 kilometres between Orleans and Nevers. The Belgian rider, Etienne de Wilde, won the bunch sprint. Overall, things remained the same.

On the third stage, the longest, from Nevers to Lyon, another Belgian, Carlo Bomans, came in first at the head of a reduced group which included Miguel Induráin. Thanks to those precious few seconds gained over the main group the Navarra man was able to put on the white jersey of race leader.

The fourth stage was a team time trial at Saint-Etienne where the Histor squad beat Banesto's time by 58 seconds. The leader's jersey now passed to Roche and Induráin went back to seventh overall, 47 seconds down on the Irishman.

The 179 kilometres of the fifth stage took the riders down to Marseilles and, although Baffi won the sprint, that resolved nothing as far as the overall classification was concerned: Roche remained in white; Induráin remained seventh, still 47 seconds down.

On the queen of stages – 164 kilometres between Marseilles and Mont-Faron – Miguel Induráin produced a demonstration of pure power and physical strength. When he accelerated on the lower slopes of Mont-Faron nobody could stay with him and he came home first with a gap of 1-02 over his closest rival, Stephen Roche. Miguel had recovered the leader's white jersey and now, in the two remaining stages, he would need to defend it from Roche and his other major opponent, Fignon.

The 178-kilometre seventh stage went from Toulon to Mandelieu and was a triumph for Chiappucci: he led home an escape group that finished 25 seconds up on the main bunch, which contained all the principal figures. Induráin maintained his overall lead with Roche still at fifteen seconds and Fignon at nineteen seconds.

The final stage, stage eight, was a double: a 102-kilometre road race between Mandelieu and Nice, followed by a hill climb of 12.5 kilometres up the Col d'Eze. The first part of the stage proved uneventful; now all Miguel had to do to complete the double was cope with the hill climb. Bernard made the best time followed by Leblanc at 30 seconds, Roche at 34 seconds and Induráin, fourth, at 41 seconds. It was enough and, for the second year running, Miguel Induráin ended up winner of the Paris–Nice.

'It was a hard fight,' he would say back in Villava with the telephone ringing non-stop with messages of congratulations. 'It was all worth while because we had to be there anyway for training purposes, so nothing could really have gone wrong.'

The French press, although it didn't appear surprised by the result, was full of admiration for Miguel:

> Induráin continues to be the master. A man of great class, capable of standing on the very summit of world cycling. (*France Soir*)

> Induráin, the rough diamond. A champion of champions has been born. (*L'Equipe*)

> The strong man from Pamplona has shown us, on the mountain climbs of the Faron and d'Eze, that he is the best and, faced with such form and such class, nobody is in a position to deny the exorbitant possibilities that are hidden in his legs and lungs. (Philippe Bouvet, French TV)

> Induráin fully deserved his victory. The winner in 1989, his triumph in the 40th edition has crowned the Navarra man as the best early season cyclist in the international peloton. (*Le Figaro*)

VUELTA '90: MORE GRIEF THAN GLORY

Miguel Induráin came to the 45th edition of the Vuelta a España all set to break the bad spell this race had cast over him. Again, there was a scarcity of strong foreign riders and, among them, only Rominger, Bernard, Dietzen, Ampler, Parra, and Herrera were thought by the commentators to have any remote chance of winning; by and large, though, they were again going for a home victory tossing up between Delgado, Etxabe, Gastón, Lejarreta, Induráin, Fuerte, Pino, and Blanco Villar.

A total of 219 riders, from 22 teams, were taking part. At the outset Banesto was the strongest, and Echávarri's double act of Delgado and Induráin, with Julián Gorospe always waiting in the wings, was charged with upholding that reputation. It was a sign of the times that everyone now knew Miguel Induráin: the journalists were begging him for interviews and kids for his autograph. He, 'Big Mig' as some people were calling him, had to comply, trying to be amiable with everybody, conscious that he was now a public figure.

The Vuelta began on 24th April in Benicassim with a three-up 11.5 kilometre time trial. Banesto were powerfully represented by Delgado, Induráin and Gorospe, but it was ONCE who won with their trio of Cabestany, Mauri, and Fuerte, taking 45 seconds out of the Banesto men who ended the day in third spot. Echávarri was not very happy with that result, in spite of Induráin saying, 'We did everything we could.' Perhaps that defeat would be the tonic the star team needed.

Echávarri's strategy had not yet been clearly defined although on the fifth stage, with its Sierra Nevada summit finish, everybody was working for Induráin. In the painful procession of ones and twos which usually marks the arrival of the peloton at a mountain-top finish, Induráin came in fifteenth. Klimov was wearing the leader's jersey and the Villava man was sixth overall at 3-01.

In that 1990 Vuelta of fluctuating fortunes it was Gorospe who took over the yellow jersey on the sixth stage. From then on Echávarri would have to defend the lead held by his 'third man'.

Nothing altered in the dangerous, nerve-wracked transition stages towards the next set of mountains, which again turned out to be the destroyer of hopes and strategies. Stage eleven, from León to the ski station at San Isidro, was a tough 203 kilometres containing two second-category and one first-category cols, and a special-category mountain finish. First to the top was the Lotus rider, Carlos Hernández, and a great ride by Induráin gave him fourth place, 46 seconds back. But Gorospe crumpled and it was the Italian, Marco Giovanetti, riding for Seur, who now put on the yellow jersey. Miguel, at 3-04, lay seventh.

The fifteenth stage, a 24-kilometre hill climb at Valdezcaray, was eagerly awaited and Miguel Induráin, who was considered favourite to win the stage, was clearly optimistic: 'I've given the best possible account of myself in the mountains, where I didn't have to attack. What I had to do was defend myself against other people's attacks because there are better climbers than me. I went well in the Sierra Nevada and then in the mountain stages of Asturias, and now it's my turn to do my utmost to put in a good ride in the Valdezcaray time trial.'

Then, as can happen, everything went totally wrong. Toshiba's Jean-François Bernard made the best time, while Induráin struggled home 34th, 5-16 slower than the Frenchman. Overall, Giovanetti increased his lead and Miguel slipped to eighth. What he was saying now was in complete contrast to what he had said on the eve of the race: 'I am disappointed with the time I did. The head wind in the final kilometres took too much out of me and at certain times I was just shattered. Now, although I'm still not going to throw in the towel, the overall classification is going to be very difficult for me.'

The race passed over the Pyrenees of Aragón without pain or glory, and without Echávarri's tactical variations between Perico and Miguel (or both at the same time) giving the unexpected, but solid leader, Marco Giovanetti, any trouble.

Nor was anything resolved by stage twenty, a 40-kilometre time trial at Zaragoza, ideal for those capable of pushing a big gear. The best time was put up by Ruiz Cabestany, with Induráin 51 seconds slower in fourth spot. With Giovanetti now looking an almost certain overall winner, Miguel was lying sixth, 3-26 down.

It was stage 21, 188 kilometres through the Madrid mountain range from Collado Villalba to the Dyc Distilleries, that finally settled it. There was a series of do-or-die attacks from Banesto but Giovanetti didn't buckle. The pace was entrusted to Pedro Delgado who pulled a group of twelve determined men clear of the main bunch. None of them was willing to be dropped and the Frenchman, Denis Roux, won the sprint. After them came the group containing the top riders, but Induráin had been unable to hang on to them. The Navarra man finished 35th, in a group which arrived three minutes behind. Giovanetti was now practically assured of victory in the Vuelta, with Miguel in seventh place, 6-22 adrift. Pedro Delgado had got closer to the Italian: he was in second spot, 1-28 down, but by now it was too late.

So to the ritual of the final promenade, the victory parade, the podium and the yellow jersey for Marco Giovanetti, the Italian who achieved his win, almost by chance, on the first col of stage eleven. Miguel Induráin finished seventh, Pedro Delgado second and Banesto, who had been unable to cope with the power of the ONCE squad, had to console themselves with second place in the team competition. When asked about the performance of his two team leaders, José Miguel Echávarri replied enigmatically: 'Pedro began the race in very strange form and ended like Pedro; Miguel began very strongly and then stopped being Miguel. I think that's the only explanation.'

This was not a Vuelta with a prodigious number of renowned international figures yet it was won by a foreigner, furthermore an unexpected one of modest talent. On this occasion, the team leaders, among them Miguel Induráin, were simply not on top of things.

TOUR '90: THE GREAT SACRIFICE

It looked as if *La Grande Boucle* of 1990 would be as spectacular as ever, with a prologue and 21 stages needed to complete the tough 3,415 kilometres of the world's greatest race. Taking the start would be 22 teams and a total of 198 riders. The betting odds were showing a marked preference for safety: as if nothing had changed in a decade, they were still putting forward Lemond, Fignon, Delgado, Roche and Bugno as favourites, while the French press, perhaps in spite of itself, came down in favour of Pedro Delgado as the most likely winner. Echávarri had made it absolutely clear before the start that the Segovian was Banesto's indisputable number one: 'We are going out with our mind fixed on Perico's chances; he is our man for the podium in Paris. And for that he can count not only on his own talents but on two exceptional supports – Miguel Induráin, and a balanced team thoroughly committed to its team leader.'

Those were Banesto's strengths. Miguel, according to Echávarri, 'is currently in fine form and will be a fundamental prop in the team'. Thus there were no doubts about the Villava man's role in this Tour.

The prologue, 6.3 kilometres against the clock in a circuit around Futurescope, went to Thierry Marie. Miguel Induráin made the eighth-best time in a race where the wind was the main influence.

The first stage didn't set out from Futurescope; it was, in fact, a double: a 138.5-kilometre road race in the morning coupled with a 44.5-kilometre team time trial in the afternoon. The morning was stirred up by a four-man escape which took more than eight minutes out of the peloton. Thus, the Canadian, Steve Bauer, found himself the unexpected race leader. The afternoon went to Panasonic and Banesto finished with a two-minute deficit in sixteenth place. With Bauer, then, in the yellow jersey, Induráin lay 109th, 11-51 back. It was a bad start.

94

Those early stages turned out to be harder than anyone had envisaged, even before the riders had seen the sun. It was a frenetic race through the wind, the cold and the rain. On the fifth stage Fignon, Giovanetti and Hermans dropped out, and abandoned the race.

Then came the longest of the time trials, the 61.5-kilometre stage seven. The evening before, Miguel Induráin, who was counted among the favourites, was saying: 'I don't know if it will go well or not, but of course this weather definitely doesn't suit me: I'm very susceptible to getting colds.'

But San Fermín must have been looking after him because just as Miguel came down the starting ramp it stopped raining and the man from Navarra had a sensational ride. He was beaten only by the Mexican, Raúl Alcalá, and for a long time, until Alcalá's arrival, he was top of the leader board. Finishing in second spot, 1-24 slower than the Mexican, Miguel jumped to fourteenth place overall, 11-01 down on Bauer who remained in the yellow jersey.

Stage ten saw the beginning of the Alpine climbs and the temperature fell even further. Claveyrolat won, Induráin didn't do badly, finishing twelfth at 2-29 on an extremely hard stage in which, at last, Delgado began to show his true mettle. Overall, Ronan Pensec robbed Bauer of the yellow jersey and Induráin climbed to twelfth place, 10-44 down on the new leader.

Stage eleven was the toughest of the Alpine stages: a total of 182.5 kilometres from St Gervais with one first-category and two special-category cols, the second of which was the summit finish on Alpe d'Huez. Gianni Bugno won with none other than Greg Lemond on his wheel and they both took 40 seconds out of Perico Delgado. Miguel Induráin, who had drained his strength pacing Delgado to the foot of Alpe d'Huez, understandably finished 40th, 11-55 back. Pensec seemed to have established a solid lead overall and Miguel was lying 31st at 21-51. Delgado was lying sixth at 11-05. He was Banesto's best option and, for his cause, Miguel Induráin had sacrificed himself, riding himself into the ground. As Gianni Bugno, winner of that year's Giro, commented: 'There are few cyclists riding in this Tour who would devote themselves to their team leader in the way that Induráin has. His effort is admirable. I take my hat off to him because he has shown what he's made of. He did an excellent job and, although it did me a big favour, he did it totally in support of Delgado. I really admire him.'

Miguel had already learned to suffer unselfishly and without complaint. As Miguel Arrieta, one of the team trainers, commented to one of the cycling journalists: 'I am still waiting for the day when he blames me for something that's gone wrong; I usually tell him that some day he will complain, but it doesn't happen. He is a most impressive guy and there's no one else quite like him.'

The twelfth stage was a mountain time trial of 33.5 kilometres in which Eric Breukink made the best time with Delgado second, 30 seconds slower. A poor start ruined Miguel's chances of winning, but he finished with the third-best time, 43 seconds behind the Belgian. Overall, he was now lying 24th, 20-01 down on Claudio Chiappucci who had taken over the leadership from Pensec.

After the rest day came stage thirteen, from Villard-de-Lans to Saint Etienne, 149 kilometres with a tough profile. It turned out to be a turbulent day, won by Eduardo Chozas. He arrived together with four others who had escaped, including Delgado's most immediate rivals, Lemond and Breukink. Again it was Miguel who saved Perico, leading the chase that brought the gap down to 30 seconds. Induráin, himself, came in ninth, 36 seconds down, and overall he went up to nineteenth, 15-44 behind Chiappucci who continued to wear the yellow jersey.

Stage fourteen, 205 kilometres between Le-Puy-en-Velay and Millau, was another hard slog, ending in a first-category climb. It was Miguel's twenty-sixth birthday and once more he found himself frantically pacing his team leader until Perico, with his strength gone, dropped back on the final slopes of the Millau. Lejarreta won the day by 24 seconds from Induráin.

All the press continued to extol the sacrifices being made by the man from Navarra. This was his sixth Tour; he had been treated indulgently, initially pampered by Echávarri and Unzué, but, in the previous Tour, he had been put to work, harshly, almost cruelly, in the service of his team leader. Now he was doing it all again, surrendering himself for the benefit of Pedro Delgado who, after this stage, admitted as much: 'I think that by staying with me Miguel was prevented from winning this stage. I recognise what it has cost him. He is my right arm, my left arm and even my legs. I owe him a great deal and alongside him I feel completely secure.'

Stage sixteen, with its finish at Luz Ardiden, was expected to be decisive. As in the '89 Tour everybody anticipated that the demands of this majestic stage would reveal the definitive outcome of the Tour, and the know-alls with little faith were talking of Lemond, of Chiappucci, of Delgado, of Lejarreta, and of the Colombians; but it was won by Induráin. He did it again, just as he did in 1989, and by then we ought to have become familiar with the triumphs of that youngster in the Pyrenees. He finished alone at the top, ahead of Lemond and all the rest. Again Perico faltered and even Davide Boifava, Director of the Carrera team, for whom Chiappucci had held on to his yellow jersey by a slim five seconds from Lemond, offered the view that 'Delgado is not in good form and, personally, I think that if anyone in Banesto has any aspirations towards victory, it must be Induráin.'

Miguel, once he realised that Delgado was finished, kept going at his own pace without stopping to think about what was happening behind him. His victory was, however, accompanied by controversy over the tactical wisdom, or miscalculation, of Echávarri. Induráin, who was overjoyed and applauding himself as he reached the summit of Luz Ardiden, was absolutely sincere when he replied to the journalists: 'For me it's always important to win one stage, although I must insist that my effort in this Tour has consistently been to support the team effort on behalf of my team leader. But from time to time it's great to win a stage and I must say that I am very happy to have done it, especially this stage, ahead of those who seem to be in the best position to win the race.'

Echávarri recognised that it had become a real uphill struggle for Delgado to win the Tour, but he didn't want to give up completely. After that stage the Segovian rider was third overall, 3-42 down on Chiappucci. Sometimes strategists pay dearly when they stick to their guns and, faced with the insistence of the journalists, he ended up explaining 'operation Induráin': 'Miguel is a rider who is going far. In this Tour he has reached a level that he can still improve upon, and become the rider who, from the outset, we always thought he would become.'

The peloton's survivors left the Pyrenees behind and the fans remained with bitter-sweet memories of Induráin's explosive effort and the demise of Delgado who, they said, had suffered an attack of colitis. With Paris not far off now there were no other major changes in the race, except for Banesto: on stage seventeen Delgado lost third place and was now in danger of not stepping on to the podium.

The journalists were blaming Echávarri who, more than anything, wanted to prevent any confrontation between his two top men. The criticisms mounted: he was the person judged responsible for having lost the race. Angered by some of the journalists, Banesto's Director declared: 'There's a lot of cheap stuff being written, but it all stems from the fact that this has been Miguel's best Tour and Perico's worst. If, before the start of the race, I'd presented Induráin as the leader of the team, they would have said that I was crazy.'

The penultimate stage of that Tour was a tough individual time trial: 45.5 kilometres at Auphelle in which everyone would have to prove their own worth without team leaders or domestiques. Breukink won, Lemond grabbed the yellow jersey from Chiappucci and Miguel Induráin finished fourth, 40 seconds down. Delgado was eighth at 2-21. The die was now cast and the Tour of 1990 decided. Lemond won, Perico did not reach the podium, and Miguel made what was, up to that point, his best ever Tour, tenth overall and 12-47 down on the yellow jersey.

However much humility Induráin wanted to show, however much disciplined team loyalty, it was evident that Spanish cycling had taken one step further towards international prestige. 'Perico is dead. Long live Miguel' said one banner on the Champs Elysées. At 26, Induráin's aspirations seemed unlimited. He was beginning now to welcome his family and friends who travelled far to see him triumph, and that was a good sign: it gave him heart as he, himself, recognised: 'When I was first across the finishing line at Luz Ardiden and saw my brother and sisters, my cousins, and friends from the village in the front row, cheering me on, that gave me more strength than all the training I'd ever done. I remembered others from the village, people from the Villava Cycling Club who helped me when I was an amateur.'

Those first days at home, after returning from the Tour, were, on this occasion, dominated by a round of non-stop questioning by journalists, but he was longing to enjoy himself among his own people, before he became engaged in other races following his magnificent performance in the French tour.

On 12th August he was unstoppable in the San Sebastián classic. He climbed as well as anyone until the moment when he made his escape on the Jaizkibel, doubled his lead on the steep descent and finished on the San Sebastián Bulevar 2-24 ahead of his immediate pursuer, the Frenchman, Jalabert.

RESULTS

Tour of Spain: seventh overall; Banesto second in team competition
Paris–Nice: first overall
Tour de France: tenth overall and one stage win (Luz Ardiden)
Tour of Burgos: third
San Sebastián Classic: first
Pamplona Criterium: first
IFPC: fourth place, 1000.5 points
Nominated Best Sportsman from Navarra (Department of Culture
& Sport, Government of Navarra)
Nominated Best Spanish Sportsman of the Year (Association of
European National Olympic Committees)

1991: A YEAR TO REMEMBER

By 1991 Induráin was unquestionably a star, with his name now ranked among the highest in the cycling world. Along with his colleague, friend and rival, Pedro Delgado, he renewed his contract with Banesto for a further two years, during the first of which he would earn about half a million pounds. Meanwhile, the work of the masseurs, doctors and psychologists intensified in order to ensure that Miguel would be on top form for the new season which was expected to be crucial to his future.

VUELTA '91: BY A HAIR'S BREADTH

As in previous years there was a paucity of major foreign riders in this, the 46th edition of the Vuelta a España. Parra, Alcalá and Giovanetti seemed the only ones capable of creating problems for the domestic riders, among whom Miguel Induráin was, by almost unanimous consent, the clear favourite and the press was endorsing him over these prestigious rivals, as well as Lejarreta and Cubino.

On this occasion Banesto put forward just one, incontestable team leader, Miguel Induráin, who would be strongly supported by Jokin Mujika, Uriarte, and the two Gorospe brothers. Once again, Perico Delgado was being held back to concentrate on the Giro and the Tour.

The '91 Vuelta had a considerable preponderance of time trialling, with the mountains concentrated in the final stages, and it opened on 28th April with a three-up time trial over a nine-kilometre circuit at Mérida. It was won by ONCE, which put Melchor Mauri into the yellow jersey; the Banesto trio was third, twelve seconds back.

The time gaps produced by the second day's team time trial stayed virtually unchanged until the sixth stage from Albacete to Valencia – despite the dangers through which the peloton had passed in the intervening days, with strong winds, breaks, threatened breaks and crashes. Mauri remained in the yellow jersey and Miguel lay 21st, 1-58 down. Then came the first contact with the mountains; up until then it had been more like a peloton of crazy tourists, falling off their bikes with unusual frequency.

The peloton seemed to wake up on the Mallorcan stages. The yellow jersey inspired a devastating performance from Melchor Mauri in the 47-kilometre time trial. He gained 56 seconds on Induráin, the favourite on paper, who made the fifth-best time. After that eighth stage Miguel was laying seventh overall, 2-54 down on the Catalan, Mauri.

Returning to the mainland, the shape of that year's Vuelta continued to delight the sprinters. There were some mad, elbow-barging bunch sprints which made scarcely any difference to the gaps between the top riders. It was all very twitchy, but otherwise there was not much to report.

With stage ten, from Lloret de Mar into Andorra, came the high mountains and the cold, and even snow. The Italian, Guido Bontempi, won on a day when the riders really had to prove what they were made of. Everybody knew, Miguel Induráin especially, that in the following days there would be the cruellest selection of the peloton. Stiff with cold, the riders came face to face with the hardest part of the Vuelta: the eleventh stage between Andorra and Pla de Beret even had to be suspended because of the snow.

Stage twelve finished in Cerler and 34 riders arrived outside the time control. It was won by the Russian, Ivanov, while Miguel Induráin rode what Echávarri, himself, called the 'perfect race'. He kept a close watch on his nearest rivals, controlled them and gained time by attacking where the terrain suited him best. He finished on the summit of Cerler in fifth place, 45 seconds back from Ivanov. Overall, Mauri clung stubbornly to the yellow jersey, but Miguel had now climbed to fourth, 1-51 down.

The peloton was decimated by this epic in the Pyrenees. Induráin lost his two principal supports, Gorospe and Mujika, who were eliminated by the time control at Cerler; henceforth he would have to depend on himself, and the help that his second-string domestiques could offer him. Almost without pause for breath the race was once more full of drama, on stage fourteen, at Valdezcaray: the mountain time trial had to be cut short by eight kilometres because of the snow. The Colombian, Fabio Parra, put up the best time with Induráin 2-17 slower. Mauri, who was sixth on the stage, was heroically hanging on to his overall lead; Miguel stayed in fourth place, now at 2-33.

There was no let up in the stages that followed. The fearful Lakes of Covadonga didn't turn out to be disastrous for Miguel Induráin on this occasion, but neither his effort nor his good ascent were sufficient to get him close enough to endanger Melchor Mauri. Herrera won the stage and Miguel, coming in fifth, one minute back, only reduced the gap on the leader to 2-05.

They still had to climb the Naranco on the seventeenth stage of this interminable Vuelta. Cubino was quickest and Miguel, fifth at 13 seconds, carried on nibbling away desperately at the lead which the phlegmatic Mauri had over him. Still 1-46 behind, Miguel remained fourth overall, with Lejarreta ahead of him in second place and Fede Etxabe third.

Stage nineteen, a 55-kilometre out-and-back time trial at Valladolid, brought the last opportunity to oust the unexpected leader, Melchor Mauri, who had worn the yellow jersey non-stop since stage one. Miguel Induráin, himself, said he felt in fine form. Once again, however, wearing the leader's jersey gave the Catalan wings: he simply took off and resolved everything. He was more than a minute faster than second-placed Induráin, who, although he went up to second overall, remained 2-52 down on the leader. Miguel confessed to not enjoying the ride and was clearly surprised at the amount Mauri had taken out of him: 'Yes, he surprised me. He took a minute from me which is a lot, but at the same time it's not a lot because in 50 kilometres you've only got to get a little bit careless and you lose seconds, and, here, it's difficult to get them back. All the same, we won't be throwing in the towel until we arrive in Madrid.'

Two days later they did arrive in Madrid, with Melchor Mauri exhausted but victorious. Miguel tried – and how he tried – on the penultimate stage when Mauri was going through his worst moments, but the Colombians didn't help any, and nothing came of it. Melchor Mauri, the Catalan in the ONCE team, finished in glory on 19th May. A makeshift leader, he rode triumphantly through the Spanish capital in a race that had been marked by the absence of real climbers and by the suspension of the first mountain stage.

For Miguel, it was his first Vuelta as absolute team leader. He started as one of the firmest favourites and finished second, 2-52 behind the Catalan. He laconically summed up his own performance: 'I was there on every stage.'

TOUR '91: ENTERING INTO HISTORY

As usual the Tour had no problems in assembling the finest peloton of sprinters, climbers and all-round riders. With 198 riders making up 22 teams, the 78th edition set off in scorching temperatures and at fearful speed throughout the first few days. Favourites, according to the forecasters, were Lemond, Breukink, Bugno, Fignon and Delgado, while some die-hard supporters were still giving Lejarreta a chance.

Echávarri, once again following his wait-and-see policy, put forward a trio as Banesto's team leaders: Delgado, Induráin, and Jean-François Bernard. The race itself would decide, but this time he had made one variation: he was placing equal confidence in Miguel and Perico, and they would start with identical chances. It was a new challenge for the Villava boy.

The prologue stage at Lyon went to the specialist Thierry Marie, with Miguel Induráin seventh, nine seconds behind the Frenchman. The following days, supposedly exploratory, were fought out at a diabolical speed. The peloton was restless and full of enthusiasm. In those first stages, it has to be said, Banesto was off the pace, lacking initiative – and San Fermín's cloak had hardly yet fluttered. There was constant adverse criticism in the Spanish press aimed at the Banesto team and its Director. Things stayed like this until the end of the seventh stage, the eve of the long, 73-kilometre time trial between Argentan and Alençon. Thierry Marie was in yellow; Miguel Induráin was 48th at 3-32 and Pedro Delgado 55th at 3-40. But, worse than that, the main rivals of the Banesto squad (which in the team competition was twelfth out of the 22) were ahead of them: Kelly, Lemond, Breukink and Alcalá were all in the top ten overall.

The day before that time trial Miguel was worried. He was not one to show his feelings, but the confusion of the first week had created a tense atmosphere. Echávarri, however, was confident about his chances against the clock and that was no bad sign. 'It's a very long way and I don't know how I will respond,' said Miguel before the start. Then he went out, gave it everything and made the best time. Only Lemond, eight seconds slower, was anywhere near him while the rest were more than a minute further back. Lemond now headed the overall classification while Miguel had jumped to fourth place, 2-17 down on the American. The feast of Saint Fermín was still on and in Pamplona they were celebrating their country-man's fully deserved triumph.

With that over and done with, Echávarri continued to rely on the joint leadership of Miguel and Perico (twelfth overall at 4-30), and Banesto now figured second in the team classification. It would depend on how things went, but, for the moment, there was little else to do but wait for the mountains. Meanwhile, Miguel had his twenty-seventh birthday.

With the Pyrenees came the French revival: Mottet won at Jaca, on stage twelve, and Leblanc took over the yellow jersey. Miguel, who had seen Herrera and Fignon jump away, set out after them, and finished sixth, 6-49 back. It was a very difficult stage which paved the way for the hardest of the entire race.

It was on that very stage, the next day, that Miguel covered himself with glory. Between Jaca and Val Louron, over the cols of Pourtalet, Aubisque, Tourmalet, and Aspin, before the finish at the top of Val Louron, Induráin won the Tour. In a spine-chilling descent of the Tourmalet, only Claudio Chiappucci could stay with him; with the two of them taking turns on the front, they stayed away until the final summit where Big Mig allowed the Italian to cross the finishing line first. He put on the yellow jersey and his gap over the second man, Charlie Mottet, was more than three minutes.

In the Banesto team there was euphoria, Echávarri ceaseless in his praise for the intelligence with which Induráin had carried the stage: 'once again Miguel has shown his brains'. The man from Navarra, pursued by the press, replied simply: 'Of course I am the favourite because I've got three minutes on the second man. But from now on you'll see all the attacks coming our way.' Pedro Delgado, who had finished almost a quarter of an hour behind Miguel, now had a very clear function in the Tour – simply returning the service which Miguel had given him the previous year. It was a job for which he had the necessary dignity and wisdom.

Villava went wild: 'Yesterday,' said his mother, 'we couldn't go out because of the number of people who came to congratulate us,

104

but from the fireworks we heard and from what our friends told us I think the whole village had taken to the streets, celebrating the news.' Isabel Larraya added: 'When Miguel telephoned yesterday, I tell you, he was more interested in how we were getting on with collecting in the barley, and other family news, than in the business of the yellow jersey.' The Miguel Induráin Supporters Club threw an improvised party which went on till dawn; it was a prelude to the final victory celebrations.

He still had plenty more to do, knowing full well that there would be some determined assaults on his lead. On stage sixteen, at the foot of the Alps, Induráin received all the help his team could give to neutralise an escape by Bugno, Fignon and Chiappucci. On the stage to Alpe d'Huez, Bugno made a further attempt and it required another combined team effort on the mountain to draw the sting from the Italian who won the stage and moved up to second overall; he was now the major threat. Miguel, who was second on Alpe d'Huez, continued to hold on to his three-minute overall advantage. Claveyrolat won the last of the mountainous stages, one which Miguel was able to control without too much difficulty.

During those days a headline in *L'Equipe* read: 'I couldn't care less about being Spanish', claiming to quote Miguel – but the press love to misrepresent things. According to the text what he had actually said, which was not mentioned in the headline, was: 'I don't consider myself to be Spanish, in the traditional sense. For example, I am afraid of bulls and when I was young I never ran with the bulls. I laugh at the thought of being Spanish because I don't have any patriotic fervour.' The journalist, perhaps trying to trap him, narrowed things even further and asked him if he was a Basque: 'I am from Navarra, which is practically the same thing – we live in a very small area. At first, the Basques started calling me "Mikel"; Madrid people called me "Big Mig", which is more friendly; in France I am called "Migüel", but I call myself "Miguel".' Later, faced with such dirty tricks, he would learn to measure his words carefully.

All that remained was stage 21, the final opportunity to take the yellow jersey away from Induráin, but there was no let up by the Navarra man: he made the best time, and then had the wit or ingenuity to comment afterwards: 'I didn't set out to win, but when I was half-way through I realised that I was going well.' That was no overstatement. He finished splendidly with a 27-second gap over second-place Bugno, whom he now lead by 3-36.

105

That was the final margin, the next day, when he finished triumphantly on the Champs Elysées, where thousands of people from Navarra provided a colourful note. He was the fourth Spanish cyclist to win the French tour since it was inaugurated in 1903. Only Federico Martín Bahamontes (1958), Luis Ocaña (1973) and Pedro Delgado (1988) had preceded him.

Induráin had won a race which is the preserve of great champions and he had won it comprehensively. Newspapers throughout Europe were having to improvise quick biographies; this was the moment for eulogies, currying favour and general euphoria. Miguel, perhaps because of his own character, preferred to put it all in perspective: 'It is a big day in my sporting life,' he told the journalists, 'but I have also had other very happy days which were important to me. OK, they were not very major races, but they meant a lot to me, although this is perhaps the most important in my professional life.'

With Echávarri after the conclusion of his first Tour de France victory

There were also moments of hypocrisy, of warm regards to those who, a short time before, had borne the brunt of insults. Miguel, in his moment of glory remembered those who had made it possible: 'I owe a great debt to José Miguel Echávarri because he has been my Director ever since I became a professional. He has known how to support me, pushing me at the right moments, not letting me have too much responsibility when things were not going too well … In other words, he has known how to bring me on, without rushing me, taking years over it. That work, I believe, has been fundamental.' And he remembered Eusebio Unzué, from whose hands he passed when he became a professional and whose advice encouraged him to make the jump from amateur status. He also remembered his team-mates, who worked unstintingly to help him get on to the top step of the podium, just as on other occasions he had worked for them.

He remembered that Villava had also won the Tour because, in spite of the fact that there, in Paris, were his parents, brothers, closest friends and most resolute fans – two busloads of them – back at home almost seven and a half thousand people, and hundreds of journalists were following every turn of his pedals during his lap of honour. Then, on his return, they would tell him about it. In the Jaizki bar, headquarters of the Induráin Fan Club, famous ever since Miguel put on the yellow jersey at Val Louron, there were the comings and goings of microphones, and taperecorders throughout the morning and half the afternoon of Sunday, 28th July. National, European and American broadcast channels were waiting for the comments of members of the club, of those who had spent some days on the Tour following Miguel, of those who just knew him. The moment when their champion pushed his pedals for the last time in that Tour of '91, the official in charge of the fireworks set off a tremendous racket; there was champagne, the singing of 'Paris is burning, Paris is burning' mingling with the new classic 'Induráin–Induráin–Induráin' popularised as an anthem on the sunny side of the bullring during the San Fermín fiesta.

Miguel did not see the madness from the excitement of the podium, but he knew his countrymen and he had a sense of it. It was the fairy-tale which they couldn't really believe was true: 'It's incredible to see him there, among such famous people.' Then there was the weight of fame that was descending on him: would he be able to put up with it? 'Certainly, you can be sure of it. He's not going to get embarrassed, nor is he going to become conceited or anything like that.' On the television he came across as calm, smiling almost indifferently: 'He has just won the Tour de France and it seems like he's just got up from a siesta.' That was the tempo of Villava, deeply moved and proud of its son.

The rest were there, making their presence felt on the Champs Elysées and turning Paris into a carnival of red neckerchiefs. Among the great crowds it was those groups from Navarra who were the most prominent, storming the Bastille of cycling, filling the solemn atmosphere of the final day of the Tour with happiness, songs and swigs of wine.

On Monday, 30th July, just like on 29th September 1986, the whole of Villava received Induráin. Only on this occasion there were more than 15,000 people sharing in his success. It surpassed all expectations. Miguel arrived at Noain airport from Madrid, got into a Navarrese Government helicopter and touched down at 4.23pm on the football field of the Villava farming college where he was received by his family, and the town council. It was impossible to control the thousands of countrymen and fans who wanted to see and embrace their idol, and the rider was suddenly surrounded by the young and the old.

After the first nervous moments, Induráin was led to an open-topped car to be driven, accompanied by the Mayor, Vicente Sabalza, from the college to the parochial church. Flag-waving, shouts, songs and applause marked out the route, and he was escorted by dozens of cyclists from the Villava Club. The church bells were peeling, rockets were exploding. The cyclist, together with his family, was met at the doors of the church by the Archbishop of Pamplona and Tudela, José María Cirarda; there were also some of his companions from Banesto – Luquin, Unzué, and Lafargue. To the accompaniment of the choirs of San Andrés of Villava and of Santa Cecilia in Pamplona, and the dance of the *aurresku** interpreted by a local dancer, Miguel delivered the yellow jersey and bouquet of flowers from the final stage of the Tour to the Virgin of the Rosary, the patron saint of the district. The President of the Miguel Induráin Fan Club, Aitor David, and Archbishop Cirarda addressed the assembly, and offered him their congratulations.

---

* Aurresku – a traditional Basque folk dance

Under the arches formed by a group of *dantzaris** Miguel arrived from the church at the bandstand in the packed town hall square where he received commemorative plaques from the town hall and the fan club, and the champion's *txapela*** from the local branch of Beti Onak. The Mayor held forth at some length and – it had to happen – that sea of faces demanded a speech from their idol: 'I want to thank you for this enormous reception which you have given me on my return to Villava. I am also happy for all that encouragement – the applause and the spirit you gave me at Jaca, in the Pyrenees and the Alps, and in the rest of France. You have been all over France and that's very important for a cyclist who is suffering, and doing his utmost. For that, I dedicate to you, with all my heart, the victory in this Tour. Thank you all.'

Miguel was no orator, nor is he, but it hardly mattered. Every three words the applause and the emotion in their throats cut him short. Finally, Echávarri brought things to a close with a short but affectionate word of congratulation to the people of Villava for having such a champion amongst them. Then, cold drinks on the pelota court with politicians and sports personalities brought an unforgettable home-coming to an end.

Going from Villava to Pamplona, that same afternoon, the emotions, applause, speeches were repeated. Again thousands of people – 9,000 according to press reports – filled the Paseo de Sarasate and gave a huge ovation to Miguel, who waved back to them from the balcony of the Palace of the Regional Government. He signed the Gold Book of Navarra and, as best he could, dealt with 80 journalists or more, and faced the cameras of various television channels.

On that memorable day Miguel tried to remain amiable and attentive to all the journalists who descended upon him, and were perhaps pestering him. From the flood of remarks published the following day we can conclude that he was hoping that the triumph would not go to his head; the victory was due to the patience of those who had directed him, to his effort and preparation, to the help of the team, and the support of the public; he was happy with Banesto but he was a professional and therefore would be renegotiating his contract that year (later Gatorade tried to lure him, and Delgado, but

---

* Dantzaris – folk dancers: the arches would be formed by sticks
** Txapela – a traditional flat Basque beret

both remained loyal to their sponsor); what he longed for most, at that moment, was some rest; he was entering a new stage of cycling in which the cyclist would have to be something of an all-rounder.

That was really the final stage of his '91 Tour – the most charming and perhaps the hardest. José Miguel Echávarri, who did all he could to remain on the edge of that exhausting but equally sincere tribute, captured it all when he told the journalists: 'It's going to take Miguel a good few days to get himself together. A victory and a homage of this sort would kill anybody.'

An exhausted Miguel Induráin slept like a baby that night. In the street, in the warm summer darkness, someone was singing a new *jota*; it was a mixture of doggerel and hero-worship which a compatriot, Patxi Oroz, had proudly composed, and was handing round copies throughout the village:

> The great town of Paris
> Today is decked out for rejoicing,
> To honour a man from Villava
> For winning the Tour of France.

> The capital city of Navarra
> Gleams like the throne of Sheba
> Celebrating the victory of Miguel,
> The man who comes from Villava.

> The wheat fields of the Cuenca
> Have been clothed in yellow
> Reflecting the hue of the jersey
> Worn by its own great son.

> Today the Cuenca of Pamplona
> Is arrayed all in yellow
> To celebrate the glory
> Of the hero of Atarrabia

> Happiness and euphoria reign
> Among the population of Navarra
> Feasting and toasting the victory
> Of Mikel Atarrabiarra.

Induráin has collected
A double harvest this year
In Paris, a shirt of gold
And wheat in the Cuenca.

The most loyal and noble Iruña
Is outstanding in all its elegance
Honouring the great man from Navarra
Who has won the Tour of France.

The eagle reigns in the sierra,
The partridge on the plains,
And a farmworker from the Cuenca
In the Elysian fields of Paris.

The great town of Paris
Is decked out for rejoicing today,
To honour a man from Villava
Who has won the Tour of France.

On the banks of the Arga
A nightingale is chirping:
Bahamontes, Ocaña, Delgado ...
Induráin is better still.

Congratulations José Miguel,
Well done Miguel
Pamplona, the hive of such rich honey
Gives thanks to you both.

What can one make of it? Miguel was asleep and whatever
inspiration it was that whispered those lines to Patxi Oroz, he did his
best to set it down in verse. Who knows if the authors of those epic
ballads which then passed into literary history weren't also inspired
by nothing more than the same keen enthusiasm.

Having got to the very top, Miguel's future concern was to
stay there, not slip back, and to continue working for even greater
achievements. After conquering Paris in that wonderful year of 1991
Miguel Induráin returned to the rigour of daily training and the

strain of competition where now, as the most prominent rider, everybody would be alert to him.

He was again on the podium at the World Championships in Stuttgart, taking the bronze behind Bugno and Rooks, who were quicker in the sprint finish; and he triumphed again in Catalunya, with second place in the Trophy of the City of Barcelona, and winning the Volta a Catalunya.

Trophies, medals and nominations rained down on him: there were modest prizes like 'Most Combative Spanish Cyclist', awarded by the San Sebastián Friends of Cycling Association or 'Best Male Sportsman' awarded in the Sixth Sporting Gala of Getafe; there were the most prestigious such as 'Second Best European Sportsperson of the Year' behind the German, Karin Krabbe, in the second European Podium of Champions in which a dozen European sports papers took part; nearer to home, he was nominated 'Best Spanish Sportsman' of 1991.

From the very summit of success Miguel Induráin faced the future – a hazardous exercise which was going to provide him with glory from even more difficult ventures.

RESULTS

Ronda Criterium: first
Tour Vaucluse: first
Tour of Spain: second overall
Basque Bicycle: two stage wins
Tour de France: first overall and two time trial stage wins
World Championship road race: bronze medal
Tour of Catalunya: first overall
City of Barcelona Trophy: second
Alcobendas International Criterium: first

1992: IN A STATE OF GRACE

The new season began differently for Miguel. He was now, without question, a major figure in cycling and still nowhere near the age when cyclists normally begin to think about achieving that kind of fame. At 27 years old he still had everything in front of him.

He began early in 1992, almost impatiently. Before the end of February, in the sharp cold of winter, Echávarri sent him to race the Tour of Andalucía and the Tour of Valencia. He took part in both, aiming to warm up his muscles and get himself ready to face a season which he knew was likely to be tough, and it didn't do him any harm. Just to leave nobody in any doubt, he warned that he felt in better physical shape than the year before and he demonstrated that by his fourth place in the Tour of Aragón in April. It was known that he would not be taking part in the Vuelta a España, a race which had always been a thorn in his flesh, and that he would save himself for the Giro, and the Tour which was Echávarri's pattern with Banesto's principal leaders. Meanwhile, in May, he took second place in the Tour of Romandie and second in the Tour of l'Oise. He was definitely warming up.

GIRO '92: A FIRST PINK JERSEY

The 75th edition of the Giro de Italia began on 24th May. The Spanish press, somewhat lacking in confidence, suggested that Induráin was only using the race as preparation for the Tour; but the fact was that no Spaniard had ever won the Italian tour. The foreign press, on the other hand, believed that Miguel had the best chance; in the absence of Bugno, he was the man that the three other strong candidates, Fignon, Chiappucci and Chioccioli, would have to beat. To remove

113

any doubts about his ambitions Induráin, himself, said simply: 'I'm very motivated and I won't, therefore, be surrendering anything. Like in other great races, what happens on the road will determine the outcome for everybody, but I'll tell you beforehand that I am not here for a stroll, just to prepare for the Tour.'

The race began with a time trial in which only the specialist, Thierry Marie, put up a better time than Induráin, beating him by three seconds.

On the fourth stage, a 38-kilometre time trial between Arezzo and Sansepolcro, Miguel Induráin overwhelmed his most direct rivals, and donned the pink jersey. It was too soon, some said. There was a lot of racing still to do, Echávarri was saying. It was too soon to celebrate anything. However, during the following stages, Banesto was concerned to protect Miguel's pink jersey carefully.

The Navarra man held on to his lead, with great difficulty on some occasions, and maintained the gap over his closest pursuer, Giorgio Furlan, until the first encounter with the mountains on the 204-kilometre tenth stage from Latina to Terminillo. On this exceptionally tough day the Navarra man strengthened his chances, gaining more than half a minute on Chiappucci. Lucho Herrera won the stage with Miguel finishing fifth, two seconds back, and the other serious contender, Chioccioli, was nowhere. Paradoxically, the first climbs helped this new, mature Induráin to build up his lead: he had now put 59 seconds between himself and Roberto Conti who had moved into second place. Everything was rose-coloured.

Miguel, riding well, was responding to the attacks with both self-confidence and calmness. The fans would become used to his phlegmatic defence, his calm, predictable, sometimes boring reply as soon as some dangerous opponent tried what inevitably turned out to be a fleeting attack. Occasionally, he would even permit himself the luxury of stepping up the pace, as on stage thirteen, right in the heart of the Dolomites, when, after controlling almost the entire stage, he took off in an exhibition of climbing strength. Always watching him, always marking him, his main rival, Claudio Chiappucci, laboriously tacked on to his wheel. Miguel came in second at the summit and the gap over Conti went up to 1-59.

This Giro was proving to be extremely hard and, as a result of falls, injuries and exhaustion, Echávarri's team collapsed. Miguel was still there, but it was clear that he would only have himself to rely on, and that's what he did.

The Dolomites' second and definitive offering was on stage fourteen with its finish on Monte Bondone: wet from rain and cold Miguel endured with enough strength to finish among the leading group. In that last week, having worn the pink jersey almost from the start, there wasn't a moment's respite and, although he had to put up with it, all he wanted was for time to fly so that he could reach the finish.

Giovanetti had slipped back in the overall classification so it was now Claudio Chiappucci, 2-14 down, who pursued Miguel as the man from Navarra fought to hang on to the lead through three more mountain stages. Stage eighteen finished at the top of Monviso and it was here that they went for him. For much of the stage he practised that annoying, almost boring, restraint which we now recognise as Induráin on the defensive; then, at the critical moment, when Chiappucci and Vona threw everything to the wind, Miguel went past them both, and held them off at the finish. Giovanetti took the stage, but Induráin finished third, leaving his advantage over Chiappucci at 2-18 and over Vona at 3-14. There were rockets in the sky above Villava; his countrymen were preparing their final, noisy celebrations with three coachloads bound for Milan; and the Induráin family, who had now learnt their lesson, were not agreeing to any interviews with journalists.

He had to hold on and hold on he did. At the finish in Verbania, on stage twenty, most of his problems were over. Franco Chioccioli gave everything and won the stage that day, but Miguel shadowed him right through to the finish.

Only two days remained. The first of these was flat and monotonous, and ended with a bunch finish won by Cipollini, demonstrating that he was the quickest sprinter in this Giro. Then came the final day, a 66-kilometre time trial which brought the Giro to its conclusion in Milan and, there, Miguel Induráin was merciless. He swept the board, chasing down Chiappucci who had set off three minutes in front of him and effortlessly recorded the best time, 2-46 quicker than Bontempi who got closest to him.

All Italy was at his feet on that Sunday, 13th June. He had put on the leader's pink jersey on the third day and finished, without losing it, twenty days later, a gap of 5-12 separating him from Chiappucci, who commented: 'To end up second behind Induráin is an honour.' He was 7-16 ahead of the third man, Chioccioli, who remarked: 'Induráin won in the manner of a great champion.' And to crown it all Induráin summed up his victory, saying, without vanity, 'It was easier than I expected.' Echávarri didn't hide his satisfaction: 'I thought that Miguel was capable of this, but I didn't expect it in his first year.' All the European papers were unanimous in their praise of Induráin and were putting their money on him for the Tour.

Miguel returned to Villava on Monday 14th June to an atmosphere more familiar now than on previous occasions. His countrymen were getting accustomed to seeing him win and, from all over Navarra, they turned out to welcome him . But there was little opportunity for Miguel to relax, or be idle, with the Tour just around the corner: 'Right now, rather than celebrating, I have to make certain that I recover my strength to prevent any problems with my muscles and physical fatigue. One can't take preparation lightly because the Tour will soon be here and there are many unexpected rivals who are going to make this a very hard Tour.' He was looking forward, then, to an active rest.

TOUR '92: A METEOR ON A BICYCLE

For the first time in his life Miguel began one of the major tours in a yellow jersey, after winning the Spanish professional championship just the week before. The Tour of '92, the 79th edition of the biggest race of all, was peculiar in that its starting point was San Sebastián, a city where knowledgeable and enthusiastic followers were ready to cheer on their sporting idol. Without doubt Induráin was the favourite and the Italian, Gianni Bugno, was seen as the only one capable of challenging him; there was also some talk of Breukink, Lemond, and Leblanc, but they were given an even more remote chance.

On the start line Miguel Induráin appeared as calm as usual and he was not hiding his ambitions: 'I am going to try to win again,' he said, 'although I know I am going to have to face the pressure of being favourite.' For his part, Echávarri was wary: 'Miguel's rivals don't think they're capable of getting the better of him in those places where it's possible to make time – neither in the time trials, nor on the climbs nor on the descents. They know that and, for that very reason, I imagine they will want to take advantage of more unusual opportunities to attack.'

116

Miguel Induráin set off in yellow and he remained in yellow after the eight kilometres of the San Sebastián prologue stage. The man from Villava simply flew: he was invincible. He had begun well and what his supporters wanted was for him to finish equally well. The Tour went back into France and time bonuses handed the yellow jersey over to Alex Zülle. Very soon the peloton was into its short passage through the Pyrenees, with the race broken up and Richard Virenque wearing the leader's jersey in Pau. This was on stage two and the Villava man was in there, occupying second place at 4-34. Virenque's lead only lasted one day when, in Bordeaux at the end of the third stage, Pascal Lino took over the yellow jersey.

The Tour was becoming somewhat strange: Lino seemed to be establishing himself and, by the fifth stage, Miguel Induráin recognised that it was going badly. It had been an excessively hard beginning and, while he was maintaining a position among the leading ten overall, the mutual marking between him and Bugno was almost obsessive. The flat stages followed each other, at dizzy speed, full of frightening moments and cobblestones.

Then came the ninth stage, 65 kilometres against the clock in which Miguel overwhelmed everybody, especially his archrival, Bugno, whom he beat by 3-41. Lino held on to the lead, but 'Induráin the Rocket', as L'Equipe called him after the time trial, was now breathing down his neck, a mere 1-27 behind. It was his twenty-eighth birthday and, as they reached the Alps, that high-speed Tour slowed down.

Miguel gave fair warning: he was not thinking of attacking in the mountains but he would follow the wheel of anyone who did. On stage thirteen – a tough mountain stage, pure and simple – between Mont Blanc and Sestrières, he was true to his word. Chiappucci got away on the final climb, pursued by the strong men – Bugno, Induráin, Hampsten, Vona – with the Navarra man in control. Chiappucci won, after a truly great ride, and Miguel was third behind Vona, 1-45 down, but he finally saw off Bugno who lost a further minute and eight seconds. Lino finished way down the list and it was Induráin now in the yellow jersey, with Chiappucci in second place, 1-42 back.

What Induráin now had to do was the very thing he was an expert at – hanging on, not allowing his lead to slip. On those highest parts of the route Chiappucci was his only rival, and Induráin stuck to his wheel on the climb up Alpe d'Huez the following day, when the pair of them had blown the Tour open, and stayed there until they left the Alps behind.

On the flat stages that followed there was a lot of anxiety, but few overall changes. Everything was hanging on stage nineteen, the 64-kilometre time trial from Tours to Blois. It was likely to prove decisive and, indeed, it was: Induráin was crushing, recording the best time with superb authority. He overtook Chiappucci and only Bugno, 40 seconds slower, could get anywhere near him. Only two days remained for Chiappucci, still second but now 4-35 down, and more than 500 fans from Navarra were arriving in Paris.

So, on the Champs Elysées, Miguel proved that the previous year had not been a fluke. After the triumphant, stately ride of the final stage, Paris surrendered before him. A sea of fans saw out the fastest ever Tour; once again Induráin's countrymen cheered as he stepped on to the podium while, back home in Villava, the San Andrés Choir sang the hymn composed by the local musician, José Luis del Burgo:

> In France, Italy and Spain,
> on every road,
> there pedals a great cyclist
> who has amazed the whole of Europe.
> He flies along its great plains,
> climbs its highest mountains,
> descends to its deepest valleys,
> everybody sings of his exploits.
> His rivals fear him,
> admire him, respect him,
> fight to chase after
> his speedy bicycle.
> All the people applaud you
> the whole world cheers you
> and proclaims you –
> Miguel, King of the Road.
> In the streets there is a great clamour
> when you arrive crowned in laurels.
> Miguel, Miguel, great champion
> all your people acclaim you, Miguel.
> Miguel, Miguel Induráin
> famous son of Villava

118

you carry throughout the whole world
the name of your Navarra.

These well-intentioned verses were sung to celebrate Miguel
Induráin's second Tour. In Villava the champagne ran once more,
the rockets exploded in the summer air and the church bells
announced – quite unnecessarily since everybody was hanging on
the news of it – Miguel's latest victory. Tuesday, 27th July was a
rerun of what had taken place the previous year: excitement in the
streets, the appearance of various dignitaries, floral tributes, formal
receptions – although perhaps it lacked the emotional spontaneity
that had followed the first victory. Miguel said little and smiled a lot.
Unquestionably, he had learned how to perform the role.

Miguel Induráin was now acquiring an almost mythical
status – for good or ill – because in the World Championships which
took place in Benidorm in September everybody forecast that he
would win. In fact, it was Bugno who won, with Miguel back in sixth
place, although in the same time as the winner. This was not a
disaster, nor was anything lost by it. In any case, he came back to win
the Tour of Catalunya, in its 75th edition, for the second year
running.

During September and October Induráin took part in various
national criteriums as an 'invited star'. He easily won them all, apart
from the Community of Navarra race, where he finished second
behind his eternal rival, Chiappucci. Success still eluded him on
home ground.

HIS BEST VICTORY

For Miguel Induráin 1992 was a year full of awards, prizes and an
intense social life. On 2nd September he was granted the 'Prince of
Asturias Prize for Sport'. On 28th October he was received by Pope
John Paul II, to whom he presented a mountain bike, and the pink
and yellow leader's jerseys from the Giro, and the Tour. On 7th
November he was given the highest score of 2023 by the International
Cycling Federation. He also received the 'World Golden Bicycle' by
the publication *Vèlo-Sprint 2000*; the 'Mendrisio de Oro' awarded by
Italian sports fans; the 'Best Sportsman of the Year' award by *Corriere
dello Sport*; the 'Best Cyclist of the Year' award by *L'Equipe*; the 'Best

National Sportsman' and 'Most International Spaniard' awards by *El Mundo Deportivo*; and the 'Most Distinguished Sportsman of 1992' by the Spanish Association of Sports Press.

However, none of these prizes touched his heart so much as the event that really completed his 1992 season: on the afternoon of 14th November he was married in the Church of the Oblation in Pamplona to Marisa López de Goikoetxea, a Basque girl from Lazkao, and the second daughter of a family of six. She was 28 years old – the same age as Miguel – and worked as an administrator in the University Clinic of Pamplona.

The couple entered the church accompanied by Miguel's mother and Marisa's father and, just behind them, Marisa's mother and Miguel's father. Immediately after came the 225 wedding guests, among them José Miguel Echávarri and almost the whole of the Banesto team. During the ceremony friends of the bride attached to the Chamber Chorus of Pamplona sang a number of pieces, among them Schubert's *Ave Maria*.

After the wedding banquet the newly weds spent a fortnight in the United States where they visited Orlando, Miami and the Bahamas. A total of 34 radio and television channels, four of them from Italy and one from Colombia, were given special permission to broadcast live coverage of the event.

If that wasn't enough, from this moment onwards Miguel started to feature in the glossy 'pink' press.

RESULTS

Tour of Valencia: participated
Tour of Andalucía: participated
Tour of Aragón: fourth
Tour of Romandie: second
Tour de L'Oise: third
Spanish National Championship: first
Giro de Italia: first overall
Tour de France: first overall (at record speed – 39.504 kph) and
      three stage wins
World Championship: sixth
Tour of Catalunya: first

1993: IN A STATE OF GLORY

By 1993 Miguel Induráin had acquired mythical status. Never before, as far as memory and records served, had any Spanish sportsman achieved so much, but there was a danger in all that: living legends have a reputation to live up to: they have to keep on performing those deeds, or else they let everybody down. So, Miguel began the season shouldering the burden of names like 'Hurricane Induráin', 'Extra-terrestrial', 'Cybernetic Man', and other similar hyperboles that extravagant journalists or his adoring fans had put upon him. Trophies overflowed from the display cabinets in his house in Olatz; he had been nominated the favourite son of Villava and a street had been named after him; and his name was now regularly chanted by thousands of voices at sunset during the Feast of San Fermín.

His own preference was for the training and the effort rather than the applause, and he cycled the roads of Navarra getting his legs ready for whatever 1993 was going to throw at him. 'We all want more,' goes the song. 'Nobody wants less' would be a better way of putting it, bearing in mind that even 'less' still meant performing at the very highest level.

Simply to get some racing miles into his legs he competed in a number of minor races, including the Tour of Murcia in which he won the time-trial stage and the Tour of Valencia where he finished third. The Tour of Romandie, in May, got him fully fit for his first major race of the season.

GIRO '93: TWO OUT OF TWO

Miguel Induráin went to his second Giro convinced that this time it was bound to be different. On the eve of the previous year's race he

121

had been nothing more than a not-particularly renowned cyclist who, perhaps more by luck, had won the previous Tour and who was a complete novice in the Italian race. He won that Giro and, then, to dispel any remaining doubts, he won the Tour for a second time. Now he was returning to the Giro as favourite, with all the Italians ranged against him: Chiappucci, Bugno and Chioccioli, idols of the home crowd, would set about putting him in his place.

It wasn't just for something to say, but something he really felt, that, on the start line, Miguel declared: 'It is not essential to win the Giro but that's what I am going to try to do. I know the Italians need the win more than I do, but I feel in good shape. Whatever happens, the Tour is still the most important race.'

Miguel went comfortably through the first few, fairly uneventful, stages. Moreno Argentin, who had taken the first stage, held on to the pink jersey up to stage nine, while Induráin, always in the top five, was content to control affairs and let his team carry him along. The only thing that caused him any worry was the stupidity of one Italian television presenter who was bent on puncturing his tyre at every stage finish and taking advantage of that to make a kind of candid camera film of the best cyclist in the peloton getting thoroughly annoyed. In the race itself Miguel was doing no more than necessary – keeping a watchful eye on events – and some impatient Spanish journalists began to suggest he was not fully fit.

That diagnosis, offered by the worried commentators, was proved wrong: on stage ten, a 28-kilometre time trial, he destroyed the entire peloton, taking almost a minute out of the second man, his team colleague, Armand de las Cuevas. One of the three Italians who could have troubled him, Bugno, had retired from the fight, 1-58 slower on the day than Miguel who was now in the pink jersey. He would lose it the following day to Leali after a crazy escape, but, with the mountains now on top of them, he was in no great hurry.

Stage fourteen was thought to be the crucial stage and here Miguel was devastating. On the steepest climbs of the Dolomites he forced the pace such that only Claudio Chiappucci could stay with him; the Italian stayed resolutely glued to his wheel and, in the end, he was able to finish in front. Miguel didn't make too much effort to deprive him of this pleasure: he was back in the pink jersey, and the Giro, according to the Italian journalists, was becoming a two-man duel between Induráin and Chiappucci, back in third spot, 1-18 down. They were forgetting that between these two was second-place Peter Ugrumov, 49 seconds behind the leader.

There were no further changes at the top of the overall classification until stage nineteen, a 55-kilometre mountain time trial again, from Pinerolo to Sestrières, where Induráin dispelled all remaining doubts. He made the best time, 45 seconds quicker than Ugrumov, and took 4-15 out of Chiappucci who now went 5-33 down on Induráin in the overall classification. Two days away from glory and, judging by the astuteness Miguel had shown defending his lead up to that point, they would be the least difficult.

Miguel came into Milan wearing the leader's pink jersey and ended up the idol of the Italian fans. He knew how to win their affection and admiration just as he knew how to win the race itself. It was his fourth victory in one of the great stage-races and it meant another Sunday of celebration in Villava. So many consecutive triumphs meant that this was becoming an enjoyable custom.

The press were also passing judgement:

Who will be capable of stopping him? (*La Libre Belgique*)

King Induráin is still the maestro … he will again win the Tour … in the Italian tour he does not know the meaning of defeat. (*L'Equipe*)

He has no serious rivals, not because they have no class but because he is in a superclass. (*France-Info*)

Enthusiastic Milan again crowns Induráin. (*La Gazzetta dello Sport*)

Induráin, another Merckx. (*Corriere dello Sport*)

The name on the pink jersey is always Induráin. (*Corriere della Sera*)

Induráin has no rival. (*La Stampa*)

It was the Tour that Miguel now set his sights on, and the majority of the French papers saw him coming and unanimously forecast: 'He will win the Tour again.'

Opinion among cycling fans had reached the point of such fixation on Induráin that there was general upset when he suffered an unexpected reversal on one stage of the Tour of the Mining Valleys in the middle of June. The Asturian race was Miguel's final preparation for the Tour: he had won the second stage and then slumped so dramatically on the final climb of stage three that the worried commentators feared he might break down in the Tour. On the following day, however, everything returned to normal with Induráin winning the stage.

TOUR '93: AS FORECAST

The 80th edition of *la Grande Boucle* began on Saturday 3rd of July with the French cycling press pronouncing Induráin hot favourite. Once again everybody would be ranged against him – such is the lot of the leader – but his most dangerous opponents would be Tony Rominger, winner of the previous two Vueltas a España, Alex Zülle, Claudio Chiappucci and Gianni Bugno. The race looked as if it would be hard, with some merciless climbs in the Alps and the Pyrenees, and plenty of kilometres against the clock.

Miguel started the prologue stage in the yellow jersey and was still wearing it after the finish. When everyone was thinking that the time put up by Alex Zülle was unbeatable, the Navarra man ruined it. He had completed the 6.8 kilometres in 8-12, eight seconds inside Zülle's time.

From the second stage onwards, as the race warmed up, the yellow jersey was worn on a number of different bodies – Nelissen, Cipollini and Museeuw – over a number of uneventful days. Miguel came to the ninth stage without having expended too much energy. He was 27th overall and 3-20 down on the then leader, Johan Museeuw, a gap that it was sensible to attack over the 59 kilometres of the Lac Madine time trial. Once again, Induráin obliterated the peloton over this long distance against the clock, beating the second best time, set by Bugno, by 2-11. Miguel was back in the yellow jersey with Breukink closest to him, at 1-35. Now it was the Alps that awaited them.

Miguel came through the Alps well and celebrated his twenty-ninth birthday at the same time. With Chiappucci sunk, and Bugno, Breukink and Zülle all in poor state, the Tour, from now on, was going to be a four-way battle between Miguel Induráin, Alvaro Mejía, Zenon Jaskula, and Tony Rominger. These were the four best placed and every fan who followed the race, either there on the spot, or up on the television screen, was once again treated to the sight of Induráin monotonously present in every attempted break. Some journalists complained about the Navarra man's unspectacular style: they accused him of simply taking advantage of the work of other riders. Miguel, who knew the effort he felt in his own legs every time he caught the wheel of his closest rivals, replied that it was up to them to take the risks, not him. It was obvious to anyone that that was a reasonable enough strategy.

They arrived at the Pyrenees with Induráin leading; Mejía second at 3-23; Jaskula third at 4-45; Rominger fourth at 5-44. There were three decisive days and on the first, finishing in Andorra, the four came in together. On the second day, with a summit finish at the ski station of Lary Soulan, Jaskula and Rominger worked themselves to death, Mejía dropped back, and Miguel followed the two leaders as best he could: 'I believe I couldn't have done more,' he would say later, and by the finish they had only taken three seconds out of him. On the third day they again reached the finish, at Pau, together, thanks to an invaluable stint by Julián Gorospe which brought Induráin up the slopes of the Tourmalet. The Pyrenees were now behind them and the gaps remained practically the same as they had been before they entered the mountains: Induráin still first; Mejía second at 4-28; Jaskula third at 4-42; Rominger fourth at 5-41. There were just two stages left and it was now clear who would be on the podium in Paris, but at that moment there was one too many, and it wasn't Induráin who, along with all the commentators, now regarded himself as the Tour winner for the third consecutive year.

On the nineteenth stage, against every prediction, Rominger beat Induráin in the 48-kilometre time trial from Bretigny to Monthery. He beat him by 42 seconds in a race in which Induráin admitted he had gone out 'to do a good time and nothing else'. With just the final jaunt left and with the Colombian, Mejía, displaced after the time trial, everything was settled.

The following day, after the ritual of the Parisian stage, Induráin, Rominger and Jaskula stepped on to the podium on the Champs Elysées. At the sight of his son's triumph, Miguel Induráin Senior, there with the family, jumped spontaneously from the stand into the road where the teams were filing out and took Rominger in his arms, just as he had embraced Chiappucci the year before. 'It came from the heart,' he said, emotionally. 'That's why I did it. He has been a worthy rival to my son.' At the climax of that third victory it was revealed that Miguel was suffering from a bout of flu, a fact which had been kept secret from his rivals.

As had now become customary over the previous three years, the members of the Induráin Supporters Club cheered those final, triumphant laps of their idol – this time in the rain. Four coachloads had gone off to the French capital and those who couldn't make the journey again filled the air above Villava with the roar of exploding rockets and the ringing of church bells, while the walls of the Jaizki bar, where the club had its headquarters, echoed the rowdy sound of the *jota*, and the popping of champagne corks.

That year, 1993, was the Year of Saint James and Villava, just off the Compostela road which came down from Roncevalles, was finding itself visited by European pilgrims who, passing by on their way to Santiago de Compostela, wanted to see the birthplace of the world's number-one cyclist.

In Oslo, on 29th August, the World Championship road race took place and all eyes again turned towards Miguel Induráin. It was a terrible day, pouring with rain, windy and cold; Miguel hadn't gone to Norway to fight against the elements, and, as is well known, he ties up in such bleak weather. The whole team worked for him, on a circuit made extremely dangerous, and Miguel did just enough not to lose sight of the head of the peloton, and to avoid the constant falls of other riders. With three laps to go the team had been dropped; Miguel carried on, getting himself among the leaders and, leaving it to the last lap, made a now-or-never attack. Those who still had strength left followed him: Armstrong, Ludwiig, Museeuw, Fondriest, Tchmile, Lauritzen, Rue, Riis, Maasen, Chiappucci and Giovanetti. At the very death, the American, Lance Armstrong, came through to win and Miguel, in an incredible effort on a punctured tyre, took the silver, out-sprinting the sprint finishers who were with him.

That second place in the World Championships was his farewell to top competition that season. Almost as soon as he came down from the podium he was off for an audience with the King and Queen of Spain. He ended this glorious year by participating, more symbolically than for any other reason, in the Tour of Catalunya and the Naranco hill climb. On 20th November the French President,

François Mitterrand, on a visit to Madrid, awarded him the Legion of Honour.

RESULTS

Tour of Murcia: one stage win
Tour of Valencia: third
Tour of Romandie: fifteenth
Giro de Italia: first overall and two stage wins
Tour of the Mining Valleys: two stage wins
Tour de France: first overall and two stage wins
World Championship Road Race: second
Tour of Catalunya: sixth
Subida al Naranco: participated

1994: HEAD TO HEAD

There's truth in the assertion that things come in threes as Miguel, at the pinnacle of success, had shown by the end of the previous season. It was hardly necessary to say that 1993 had been his year – after all, he'd been celebrating the best year of his life every year since he wore the yellow jersey into Paris in 1990. But three consecutive victories was too much, and the usual prophets of doom began predicting calamities as if Miguel didn't have the guts and the resolution to keep going. Whether it came from some morbid pleasure, or simple malevolence, who knows, but certain know-alls began to conjure up the idea that it had been fine while it lasted, but all legends meet their downfall and Miguel's time was now due. From the very beginning of the season tongues began to wag, warning that a competitor had arrived on the scene who would end the reign of Induráin. The Swiss rider, Tony Rominger, was the one man capable of taking him out of the limelight and he was set on doing so.

EVERYTHING UP IN THE AIR

It looked as though 1994 was going to bring bad luck. The previous year had ended on an alarming note when Mario Conde, the Godfather of the Banesto bank, faced financial ruin, and this threatened to drag down the cycling team and everyone else associated with him. It was presumed that the new directors, urgently appointed to try to save the bank from the disaster which the meteoric tycoon had left in his wake, were under pressure to reduce expenses. At first glance it seemed an extravagant luxury to maintain the team, at enormous expense for an organisation on the edge of ruin, with nothing other than that intangible 'goodwill' which the effort of some men pedalling bicycles could provide as compensation. The year began, then, in a spirit of fearful anxiety.

The new directors, however, were concerned to calm everyone down, especially the technical staff. There was even talk of reinforcing the team, of offering contracts to new riders to achieve greater success. Manolo Sainz, Director of the ONCE team, which had been outstandingly successful in 1993, commented ironically: 'They say that Banesto is going to sign more riders, that it is going to destabilise the present situation with other teams. Banesto's reinforcements are not going to destabilise anything. Banesto will carry on being Induráin and ONCE will carry on being the best team in the world.' This was Manolo Sainz talking tough; he even remarked sarcastically about the reported increase in the budget for the new season that Banesto would be less cost effective than it had been in 1993, bearing in mind that 30 per cent of the budget would be going to the technical staff.

The new year had hardly started and everyone seemed to be totally in the dark. For his part, José Miguel Echávarri preferred to carry on as if nothing had happened and on 28th December, together with Eusebio Unzué, he had a meeting in Pamplona with Arturo Romaní, one of Conde's right-hand men, who, although now out of a job, was still in a position to offer some assistance. As a precaution against things going badly, and very possibly on the advice of Romaní, they presented the majority of their new season's contracts to the Spanish Cycling Federation on 2nd January. Those for Miguel Induráin, Marino Alonso and José Ramón Uriarte were excluded since they were the three riders sufficiently secure not to fear any cuts by the new directors whom the bank had appointed. Furthermore, Echávarri proposed the appointment of a new doctor, to be nominated by Sabino Padilla, who would share the work in view of the extensive programme planned for the coming season. With the acquisition of a number of members from the defunct Amaya team, the new Banesto could count on a squad of 26 men.

In truth, the titbits of news which did come the way of Echávarri and the rest of the technical staff were optimistic: it looked as though no decision had been taken which would affect the operations of the professional cycling squad. Induráin, during the change of ownership, announced that he was willing to take part in the Giro. Perico Delgado, the patriarch of the team, took it for granted that the Banesto Sports Group would continue with the same set-up as before and that everyone should calmly wait for the decision which would be made known, at the latest, that very week.

Although everything was still up in the air, the 26 members of the team were called to attend a team meeting in Almería which would last several days. Echávarri was clearly acting as if Mario Conde had not disappeared from the glossy pages of all the popular magazines: it seemed not to concern him at all. Meanwhile, the fans were getting used to finding out about the uncertain future of the cycling team by reading the economics pages of the daily papers.

The new bosses of the bank made a series of reassuring statements: they gave Echávarri their full blessing to take his boys off to Almería; they even mentioned the possibility of the team having a press launch in Madrid on 31st January, before going off to compete in Mallorca.

Not letting the opportunity pass, the team had its meeting in El Ejido, the winter resort of Almería, on 11th January; they aimed to stay there until the end of the month. There were some new faces: Guillermo Cuesta was the doctor who would be helping Padilla; the Navarra presence was augmented by two newly appointed cyclists, Santi Crespo and José Luis Arrieta; and the highly promising Basque rider, Aitor Garmendia, also joined the group. The 26 were all there, even Pruden Induráin who was still slightly injured after an accident the previous week: a driver had not stopped at a stop sign and Pruden had suffered a sprained left wrist, a blow to the elbow, and a cracked rib. It was no joke, but, on the other hand, he was hardly likely to wear himself out at a team meeting.

It was rumoured that the new directors of the bank would be coming to El Ejido; it was rumoured that they would give a press conference to confirm the continuation of the team; it was rumoured that all the signed contracts would be honoured. All the same, there's no denying that the atmosphere of that meeting was more tense than it had ever been.

DISTRACTING MANOEUVRES

An unexpected piece of news did arrive to relieve the tension. The 43-year-old veteran, Francesco Moser, announced his intention to beat the one-hour record. He had established his own magnificent record, of course, in Mexico, in January 1984, setting it at 51 kilometres and 151 metres. Then somebody, somewhere, initiated the rumour that Induráin might also have a go. Miguel, at the team get-together in Almería, was neither affirming nor denying it; Spanish commentators, however, reckoned it was a sure bet that if Moser did break the record Induráin would make his own attempt on it.

Throughout this time, rather as if someone wanted to stir things up, the media persisted in reporting cycling news: Rominger had given assurances that he would be in the Vuelta; he would definitely prepare for the Tour in the United States and this time he would beat Induráin; he would take part in the Tour of the Basque Country to test his physical fitness. Then they carried on again with Moser's one-hour record attempt. Induráin, himself, as usual, was training hard in response to Moser's challenge and, at the same time, seemed to want it both ways as far as the eternal business of the Vuelta was concerned: 'Well, the truth is that I am hopeful and fearful at the same time about beating the one-hour record. I could attempt it at the end of 1994 or in 1995 instead of the Vuelta. Everything depends on how the Tour finishes and on the equipment I would need, like a wind tunnel, strength tests, and other procedures for the preliminary trials. I don't have much experience in a velodrome and to go for it, with any chance of success, I would have to give up something. If it was this year, I wouldn't be at the World Championship and if it was next year I'd lose out on the Vuelta. What is clear is that I have to do it within the next two years. Greg Lemond, who was tempted, has already warned me that it is best to do it when you are at the top of your form and not when you're on the point of retiring. If I had to be honest I'd say I was hopeful but not obsessed by it. The preparations, all the paraphernalia that's needed, the aerodynamic studies and the medical side of things, that's Echávarri's business. Really, what I have to do is concentrate on the season which is now just beginning. Some years ago, in Paris, I carried out some wind-tunnel tests and it was complicated. I had problems hiding my back due to my size. I don't know what the best position would be; I do know that neither the machine used by the British rider, Obree, nor the one which Moser is going to use, would suit me.' Taking advantage of the situation, Echávarri remarked: 'We are all very hopeful about the adventure; up to now no Spaniard has ever had a go at it. We have to seize the chance now that we have Miguel.'

Echávarri didn't give any clues as to whether Miguel would ride the Vuelta, but the possibility that he would beat the one-hour world record in a Banesto jersey was too tempting for those who scarcely needed any more persuasion. On 12th January, Martín Rivas Fernández, the bank's new representative for the Banesto Sports Group, publicly confirmed that all the contracts would continue, that the name of the team would be maintained and that he had full confidence in those who would be making the sporting decisions.

The Banesto cycling team had been saved. Happily, it had kept to the edge of the tidal wave that would land the omnipotent Mario Conde in Carabanchel prison.

MOSER'S IMPOSSIBLE HOUR

Things got back to normal. On 15th January Francesco Moser raised his own one-hour mark from 51.151 kilometres to 51.840 kilometres, but failed by a considerable margin to match the 52.270 set by Chris Boardman. Moser blamed the wind, forgetting, perhaps, that he was 43 years old.

This didn't let Miguel Induráin off the hook and, in the absence of any other novelties, he was concentrating on the new challenge that Moser had set him. The team gathering at El Ejido was now altogether more relaxed and full of pleasant conversation. Miguel told *L'Equipe*: 'I am afraid of the hour record, but I'm thinking of seriously training for it. I've decided to do it, but it will depend on the time I can devote to getting myself prepared for it. I will have to concentrate my training not on performing in a stage-race of some six hours per day, but on a one-hour race, where the pedalling is different and which needs a different kind of bicycle. Although it might not seem very important, the ideal riding position is the key and I'm still not sure what that ideal position is.'

An old hand now, Induráin was preparing silently and secretly to face a challenge which he intuitively knew he would be well prepared for. While all this was going on, Moser abandoned during his second attempt, this time in Bordeaux. Then, just to add fuel to the fire, Jean François Bernard, a Banesto team-mate, indicated that he, too, was going to have a go. This would be no bad thing for Miguel: he could learn something from it.

The very end of January saw a stubborn confrontation between the Spanish cycling teams and Unipublic, the organisers of the Vuelta a España. The reasons behind this disagreeable row were the terms demanded for participating in the race. It was obvious that what was really at stake was the whole business of publicity: they wanted to force Miguel to ride. So often it had been expected that he would participate, and so often he had sacrificed the Vuelta for the Tour.

Induráin, himself, dropped all his restraint at a meeting in Pamplona: 'Only Echávarri,' he insisted, 'can make me ride the Vuelta. At worst, I could get tendinitis in the prologue stage. I realise that my presence would give it a major interest, but I can also see what's in it for Unipublic. I think they are insisting on my taking part for their own interests because it would be good for publicity, and they will do everything they can to get me there. But I have to weigh up what's going to be most helpful to me to win the Tour again – the Vuelta or the Giro. I want the freedom to chose what I want to do, since they'll soon demand explanations from me for whatever I do. I have to have that freedom, without being pressurised. And, with regard to the one-hour record, I don't need to beat it to improve my list of achievements, but I'm very much looking forward to it. If I can, I aim to attempt it at the end of the season.'

As always, Miguel Induráin made it clear that he knew what he wanted. Meanwhile, Moser made another attack on the one-hour record, this time in Mexico, but with no success. This, it would seem, was his final attempt.

BACK WITH THE VUELTA

The 1994 season was beginning and Banesto was the team to beat. The link with Amaya, or rather, the take-over, had brought in some new names, and even a joint technical director, Mínguez. Vuelta, Giro or Tour, they would, out of necessity, have Induráin as their leading rider, for good or ill. Judging by their success in 1993, it was obvious that ONCE was the more complete team, but the presence of Induráin more than compensated for that.

Miguel's start to the season was brief: he made his first appearance on 2nd February in the Tour of Mallorca, only to retire on stage two. He was seen, but not seen for long.

133

Meanwhile the Spanish teams were still unable to reach an agreement over the quantity of ICU points that Unipublic were demanding each team had to have accumulated if they were to take part in the Vuelta. On 4th February, with Miguel's retirement from the Mallorcan race still a sore point, Echávarri faced a press conference on the island and announced that Induráin would not ride in the Vuelta a España. He was certainly restrained in what he said: 'It is not because we want to pick a fight with the organisers of the Vuelta, only that our objective for Induráin is, as in previous years, to secure the Tour. Because of that we have analysed the routes meticulously, and the dates, the weather and Miguel's previous experiences both in the Vuelta and in the Giro, and we have concluded that the best preparation for the Tour is definitely the Giro. If Induráin rode the Vuelta his first encounter with the mountains would be on 30th April, while it would be a month later, the beginning of June, if he did the Giro. What's more, I don't want to say that Induráin will necessarily be at full strength in the Giro, and if he has to ease off so as not to waste his strength, he'll do so – and don't let anybody go around trying to find financial reasons for this decision: they'd be wrong. We're going for the Tour and everything will be organised around that objective.' Echávarri had had his say.

The Tour of Andalucía, the traditional opening to the season on the peninsula, began on 8th February with a tough route and some menacing stages chosen for the Sierra Nevada. On the second stage Miguel's frantic attack, five kilometres from the finish, caught the astonished sprinters by surprise. It was just to test himself out, but, the following day, he cramped their style again. He seemed to be thoroughly enjoying himself, when the Banesto squad was stunned by the news that Antonio Martín, one of their team members, was dead – run over by a lorry while out training near Madrid. This was on 11th February, the fourth stage of the Tour of Andalucía, and, understandably, the team took the decision to withdraw from the race. They had just lost a truly bright hope who was being called the successor to Perico Delgado and Miguel Induráin in the Banesto team, and in the Tour. Miguel remembered him with great sadness: 'Before the Tour last year I hardly knew him; even after that I didn't know much about him, but when he joined the team I saw a great deal of him. He was an impressive young man, as a person, and he knew where he was going as a sportsman. It's a terrible shame for the whole of Spanish cycling.'

But life goes on and the team-mates of that wasted young cyclist who had shown so much promise swallowed their tears and their grief, and went back to pedalling. The 22nd February saw the start of the Tour of Valencia and the first of the head-to-head confrontations which, if only in the minds of some commentators, would be the essential theme of the year: this was to be the first Induráin–Rominger encounter. In fact, it turned out to be a lot of talk about nothing: Banesto turned up with Julián Gorospe as team leader, and with Induráin there to get some quality training and kilometres in his legs.

Miguel worked hard, but didn't seem to be concerned about winning since he was particularly active in the everyday work of the peloton, performing that valiant and indispensable role of support rider. He took advantage of the situation to get in some effective training by driving the peloton along, which is, after all, the lot of the domestique. However, perhaps so as not to disappoint, in the sixth and final stage – a 23-kilometre time trial – Induráin did make an effort. He won it ahead of Rominger and very nearly gave the leader, Ekimov, a fright, finishing the race in second place behind the Russian. That, then, was the first test, if that's what it was, and first blood went to the Navarra man.

Meanwhile, the newspapers continued complaining about Induráin's absence from the Vuelta. García Candau was blaming Echávarri and his astronomic financial demands for Induráin's non-appearance. Echávarri insisted this was a complete lie, and the three-times winner of the Tour was finally forced to break his silence: 'If this business with the Vuelta was about money, I could live very contentedly on what I've already got. I repeat, once and for all: I have elected to fight for the Tour. I studied the route of the Vuelta and decided that I would not compete in it however much they offered me.'

It was something of an anticlimax when, on 2nd March, Banesto and Unipublic reached an agreement whereby the team would ride the '94 Vuelta without Induráin, on the understanding that they would compete in the '95 race with him as team leader. You can trust me to pay up eventually, Echávarri would say, bearing in mind that the following year's Vuelta would be run in September with an international peloton ready to retire for the season.

MORE SAND THAN CEMENT

The 61st edition of the Paris–Nice began on 6th March with Induráin and Rominger the stars of the race. Zülle offered some possibilities for ONCE and Ekimov, riding for WordPerfect, was capable of making the podium. From the very first day Rominger seemed very sure of himself, almost to the point of being provocative: 'I shall be in the Tour to beat Induráin. In this race or in any other he can beat me, every day if he so wishes, but only up to the eve of the Tour. After that, this year's Tour will be mine.'

Induráin, meanwhile, was trying not to be too far behind the winners of the early stages of this classic – pure sprinters like Cipollini, Baldato or Abdoujaparov. He appeared to be in reasonable form, but less determined, less fluent, than Rominger. The moment of truth came over the last two stages: on stage seven Miguel, suffering from an allergy, was left at the back of the peloton; and, against the clock, on the eighth and final stage he had to put up with a crushing win by Rominger, and the sight of his principal rival on the podium. The man from Switzerland had given his first warning.

There was more anticipation on 14th March when it was announced that they would both be taking part in the Tour of the Basque Country. This would be another golden duel at the beginning of April, in the knowledge that the Swiss had won the two previous editions of the Basque classic. Rominger was back to his bravado again, like a boxer just before entering the ring: 'If I ride like I did in the '93 race, I'm sure I'll win two stages and the race overall.' He was so confident and, as usually happens, some journalists were egging him on, keen for the confrontation with Induráin.

In the Milan–San Remo on 19th March, by way of compensation, Rominger finished behind Induráin, although they were both some distance behind the winner, Furlan. Perhaps this rivalry was fictitious: at this moment in time, at least, Miguel didn't seem to be too obsessed with it. He took advantage of being in Italy to spy out the route of the Giro, undertake some wind-tunnel tests and have a quick look at the special bike that was being prepared for his attack on the one-hour record. From his magisterial position, the all-time champion, Eddy Merckx, was putting his money on the Navarra man: 'They can say what they like, the only rival Induráin will have in the coming Tour will be Alvaro Mejía.' In saying this, the Belgian was going completely against the grain of other commentators.

On 2nd April Miguel rode the Star Trophy to continue his training programme, and the weather was so awful that he got a touch of bronchitis, and arrived late and feeling unwell at the finish. With the Tour of the Basque Country getting closer Miguel was in better health: 'The route is hard and they say that the end of the Balmaseda stage could even be dangerous. And the Ibardin stage, if there is a split the day before, could be worse. I believe Gorospe and Zarrabeitia are in better form than I am; Rominger is very strong, as always; Furlan I saw in the Milan–San Remo, and he was doing a lot of attacking; Chiappucci was quiet, but he was there. I want to do a good race, as best I can. We'll see what happens.'

After that restrained comment, Eusebio Unzué, who would be managing the team in the race, added an even more cautious note: 'The race will be decided between half a dozen riders in the time trial, unless Furlan tries to put on a show. The most likely person to win is Rominger, who is in better form than anybody right now. Induráin is currently in reasonable form, but both Rominger and the Gewis team are better. If Miguel gets through the first three stages without any problems, he can make the podium.'

The press was adding fuel to the fire and in the Basque Country, where there is perhaps the greatest enthusiasm for cycling, they were holding their breath, anticipating the duel between the two iron men which began on 4th April in Arrasate. But it was all over as soon as it started. On the second stage, in appalling weather, Induráin was coughing, and the peloton was sneezing and barely pedalling. Then came a fierce attack from the Navarra man which destroyed everybody's calculations and messed up the forecasts until he decided to ease up, leaving things just as they had been: it had perhaps been nothing more than a little experiment. On the following day the unexpected happened: twenty kilometres into the stage which would finish at Balmaseda, Miguel steered his bike towards Unzué's car and, pedalling gently, returned to the hotel: he had retired from the race. It was the Director, not he, who explained to the journalists what had happened: a pulled muscle, just above the right knee.

Rominger won the Tour of the Basque Country without having to fight the duel. 'The King is dead. Long live the King' some headlines seemed to be saying. Others, equally pompous, were now talking about 'the Rominger era'.

ROMINGER: A KNOCK-OUT VICTORY

On 25th April a much-devalued Vuelta a España began, with the forecasts predicting it would be an entirely Swiss affair: Rominger or Zülle would be the most obvious candidates in a race which featured very few major figures. First to make his mark was Tony Rominger, winning the opening stage.

In a different context altogether, the British rider, Obree, was recovering the one-hour record which Boardman had stolen from him, recording 52.713 kilometres on the Bordeaux track.

Back in the world of the epic stage-race, Rominger had pulled on the yellow jersey after the first stage of the Vuelta and would hold on to it through to the finish. It was like a dream. In fact, from 25th April to 15th May, it was impossible to see any conceivable winner other than the shy, slim Swiss who, at 33, still had ambitions of reaching the very top.

Rominger won the Vuelta and six stages along the way. It was a monotonous, military like procession in which Tony Rominger dominated on the flat, in the mountains and against the clock. He did whatever he wanted, when and how. The '94 Vuelta a España was all Rominger and it was only possible to see something of Jalabert, who didn't match his promise, or Zarrabeitia, who finished second, a full 7-28 behind the Swiss, when he condescended to allow it. The veteran, Pedro Delgado, who had been there before, also made the podium, 9-27 down. Rominger wanted everything and took everything in that Vuelta. He pulverised the race and, after his lap of honour, had every right to say: 'I don't know what form Induráin will be in. If he is at his peak, I'll only be a minute away from him, but he only has to slip a tiny amount and we'll be exchanging positions on the podium of the Tour.'

Rominger was euphoric and he had good reason to be: he had been devastating in the Vuelta; he had just had a son, and now he had prepared his praetorian guard for the Tour. It would be formed by Etxabe, Escartín, Arsenio González, Sierra, Leanizbarrutia, Mauleón, Unzaga and Olano, an extremely powerful Mapei–Clas squad, under his orders, for the assault against Induráin. Meanwhile, Banesto was licking its wounds with the compensation of coming first overall in the team competition. This was thanks largely to Zarrabeitia and Delgado, but, although they made the podium, they didn't get anywhere near the Swiss.

And Miguel? After his strange retirement from the Tour of the Basque Country and his absence from the Vuelta, the media scarcely seemed to remember him, in spite of his reappearance, on 1st May, in the Grand Prix of the Canton d'Argovie in Switzerland. He finished 24th in what was a fairly ordinary race, 25 seconds behind the winner, Pascal Richard. It passed almost unnoticed that the International Federation of Professional Cycling had issued its classification which put Induráin first, on 2564 points, 378 above Rominger.

Miguel stayed in Switzerland to start the Tour of Romandie, on 3rd May, in a freezing downpour. He was third in the prologue time trial, 3 seconds back from Armand de las Cuevas. The unkind weather made him lose minutes over the following stages and he finished the race, again won by Pascal Richard, in a pretty modest 36th place, and a full 16-19 down.

With the Romandie over Miguel stayed in France with his masseur, Juan Pujol, so that he was on hand to go over several of the stages that he would be facing in the Giro and the Tour. In Madrid Echávarri had announced that Banesto would be competing in the Giro and, if nothing surprising cropped up, Induráin would be team leader. Working for him would be his brother, Pruden; Santi Crespo; the Frenchman, Rue; José Luis Arrieta; González Arrieta; José Ramón Uriarte; Jesús Montoya; and Heulot.

Still in France, Induráin recovered his colour and his spirits with a conspicuous showing in the Tour of l'Oise where he ended up a clear winner. He had not tasted victory since that almost forgotten stage of the Tour of Valencia. Miguel's supporters, weighed down by Tony Rominger's sweeping successes, found new hope. The Giro was imminent and they wanted to believe, needed to believe, that in Italy he was going to make it three wins in a row. Just to set the record straight, however, Induráin was issuing a warning: 'This time I am only going to the Giro to get fully prepared for the Tour. I am not here with the same conviction, nor in the same physical condition, as in previous years. I am concentrating on the Tour and, after the Tour, on the hour record. All the same, I don't want to suggest that, if I happened to be well placed in the first part of the race, things wouldn't change. I have chosen to ride the Giro for technical reasons. In Spain the organisers of the Vuelta and television made me a very generous offer but if I was just riding for the money I could have retired already, and be living the life of a wealthy man. In Italy I will ride under much less pressure and, what's more, I like the Italian style of racing, with fast riders who keep up a high speed on the flat. I believe that, at the present moment, the best cycling is to be found in Italy.'

NOT THREE IN A ROW

There was bad news on the eve of the Giro: Rominger had got to within a mere 62 points of Induráin in the classification of the International Federation of Professional Cycling. Much worse still, on 19th May, Luis Ocaña was found dead in his house at Caupenne d'Armagnac. Recently separated from his wife, he had committed suicide with a shotgun. He was 49 years old with all the glory of his cycling days still in his memory. In the world of cycling the news was deeply felt, but things had to carry on and the Giro was on the doorstep.

Banesto would be managed in the Giro by Unzué and, in his opinion, Induráin had found his old form in the Tours of Romandie and l'Oise. But Unzué was also an old scout, with an eye for promising young riders, and the rival he feared was just such a man – Eugeni Berzin, a lanky Russian émigré, with the looks of someone who'd been abandoned, and who had just signed for Gewis.

Miguel, for his part, continued to make it very clear as to what he was prepared to give of himself: 'The first weeks are very hard, so I shall wait for the last stages before deciding whether or not I shall fight for the overall classification. The injury has left my knee weak, but I still have hopes about winning. The race will prove whether or not my strength is there. The route puts more emphasis on the mountains than against the clock, but I don't believe they have done that to prejudice anybody. It will be hard for everybody, not just for me.'

Clearly, Miguel was now a graduate in diplomacy, but what was undeniable was that he had arrived at the Giro having done 1,000 kilometres less riding than in previous years. However, from among the seventeen teams of nine riders who were going to take the start in Bologna, he was still counted as one of the joint favourites, together with Ugrumov, Chiappucci, Bugno and Tonkov.

The time-trial section of the first stage put Armand De las Cuevas into the pink jersey; that man, Berzin, was second, two seconds back; and Miguel was third at five seconds. It was only over seven kilometres and Induráin needed a couple more to recover the seconds he had lost over the cobblestones of the first few kilometres. Miguel was going better as the finish got closer.

On the second stage, 232 kilometres between Bologna and Osimo, the Gewis team had it all their own way, ensuring that Moreno Argentin crossed the line first. The important men – Furlan, Della Santa, Berzin, Bugno and Ugrumov – got into Argentin's slipstream, and took a precious nine seconds out of Induráin at the finish. He was not too worried by that gap, he said: they had only just begun and he was feeling fine. Overall he was fifth, 21 seconds behind the pink jersey.

The third stage, from Osimo to Loreto, was steadily uphill. It was ridden at a crazy pace, with the peloton ambushed by the unexpected flight of the Italian idol, Gianni Bugno. Induráin put everything into controlling the escape and had the peloton flying to restrict Bugno to just two seconds at the finish. Miguel was pleased: 'I'm still feeling good and, if the weather lasts, I hope to be back in form at the first time trial. These days are a Gewis benefit: they are on their home ground and they know how to raise the tempo in the closing stages. As for my rivals, I haven't seen Chiappucci looking very sharp, Bugno's good but nervous and, of all of them, the most dangerous seems to be Ugrumov. I shall need to watch him and not give him so much freedom as last year.'

This time Miguel was not so far-sighted: on the fourth stage he found himself facing a challenge that he hadn't counted on – Eugeni Berzin. The 24-year-old Russian, brave on the climbs and excellent in the time trials, put on the pink jersey and, following Rominger's example in the Vuelta, didn't lose it throughout the remainder of the race. 'He's going to be a difficult man to beat,' confessed Induráin. He didn't know just how difficult.

In the following stages Miguel fought: he was strong and his other major rivals had missed out in a selection which was as early as it was ruthless. Induráin prevented the 1-05 gap which Berzin had opened up from widening and held on until they reached his eagerly awaited time trial – 44 kilometres against the clock, an ideal distance for him. But that 29th May was agony for Induráin who failed to live up to what was expected of him and what he expected of himself: Berzin wiped him off the map: he won the stage, taking 2-34 out of him, and two of Induráin's other main rivals, De las Cuevas and

Bugno, also finished ahead of him. An unrecognisable Induráin, who had been thoroughly routed on his own terrain, was virtually saying goodbye to his hopes by the eighth stage.

The headlines in the Spanish press reporting that disastrous day were cruel. There's nothing he can do here now, they said, so let's look towards the Tour. Induráin was hurt: for the first time since he had come to the Giro he had lost a long time trial that suited him perfectly. The doctor, Padilla, said disconsolately: 'I want to believe that Miguel's slump in the time trial was due to an allergy. In fact, he is still under treatment.' Induráin, however, perhaps a little tired of them scratching round for excuses, preferred the straightforward explanation: 'I didn't ride a good time trial, full stop. The truth is it was not something I expected. I did the same as on other occasions: the same food, the normal routine. I soon saw that I was not going to recover time and that it was going to get worse. But, I'm in good health, sleeping perfectly well, and I don't have any problems. I realised that I was going badly and I couldn't turn it round.'

Induráin, never short on graciousness, took the opportunity to congratulate Berzin on his victory. Meanwhile, opinion in the papers was hardening that nobody would be able to take the pink jersey away from Berzin, and some were malevolently adding another forecast – that the Tour would be Rominger's. Miguel, in spite of everything, remained confident that the Russian's youth and inexperience could trip him up, and he was waiting for the mountains to see if there would be another opportunity that he would be able to take advantage of. He was holding fourth place overall, 3-39 down on the leader, and was still hoping for a place on the podium.

They came to the dreaded Dolomites – pure, hard mountains – and with them came a new hero who livened up the race and, in the process, broke the peloton: lean, small, and balding, Marco Pantani from the Carrera team left everybody behind. Induráin was perhaps one of the few who managed to catch a glimpse of his wheel although at the expense of practically exhausting himself. But on the Mortirolo stage he did succeed in getting on to his wheel and hanging on, putting distance between himself and Berzin, Bugno, and De las Cuevas. On the last climb Pantani nailed it and Miguel, his reserves now draining away, went backwards. Pantani and three others had disappeared from sight when he reached the finishing line with just 36 seconds over Berzin.

There was still hope on stage eighteen, the 35-kilometre hill climb from Chiavari to Passo del Bocco where the road rose steadily and strongly after the 20-kilometre mark. But again Berzin was too strong: the pink jersey gave him wings and he improved on Miguel's time by twenty seconds. The Navarra man finished second and gained one place overall: he was hoping, at least, for a place on the podium.

However, Induráin had not given up the Giro for lost. He expected Carrera would take the final battle to Berzin by trying the Pantani option and he would take advantage of that by latching on to the Italian's wheel. Carrera certainly attacked in the Alps and Pantani got clear but, in following him, Induráin brought Berzin flying up, and, try as he might, he couldn't drop him. Up, too, came the Gewis veteran, Moreno Argentin, to protect his team-mate who was fighting tooth and nail in defence of his pink jersey.

Miguel didn't weaken: he was still hanging on for the last stage in the Alps, stage 21 from Les Deux Alpes to Sestrière, and the last opportunity. When it came it was hell. In the midst of a snowstorm the riders, all more or less together, could barely stay upright; they were forced to call a truce in the blizzard, and leave things as they were as they bade farewell to the mountains. It was, as Eusebio Unzué would say, a matter of survival. Induráin could only be realistic: 'It was all we could do to keep our balance. I have fought right up to the end and this is not a bad result. Now I've got to think about some rest and get some strength back before I face the Tour.'

He did step on to the podium in Milan on 12th July, but never before in the Giro had he been on the bottom step. From the top, Berzin was beaming at him and, from the second step, Pantani was not letting him see his bald patch. Marisa was there, together with the Mayor of Villava and some Spanish sporting authorities. It was imperative to prevent his morale from slumping, for Miguel had ended the Giro in a very serious mood: it was a race he was accustomed to winning–as he always said, it was his best preparation for the Tour – and third place was something he had never known before. An even darker shadow was cast the following day when the ICU gave out its current classification: Rominger, 2518 points; Induráin, 2175.

On 17th June a silly season story appeared in the papers: Banesto, it was reported, was planning to get rid of its cycling team the following year. Induráin and all the others, therefore, would be able to wear the colours of Festina. The news item was neither refuted nor confirmed, but anyone interested in following it up would know just how difficult such a change would be since the majority of the riders had signed for two years, and breaking their contracts would result in huge expense for a revived company which was scrutinising every last scrap of expenditure.

Meanwhile, the cycling season went ahead while Miguel was drawing breath and recovering his spirits after the Giro. Berzin gave a demonstration of the fine form he was in by finishing second in the Bicicleta Vasca, behind Della Santa.

Induráin's rest lasted until 26th June when he took part in the Spanish Road Championship. It was a race of 239.4 very tough kilometres and the forecasters had Miguel down as favourite, but with certain reservations. Nobody could have anticipated, however, what actually happened: it was a true experiment by the Villava champion. Induráin planned to make the race as hard as possible by taking the lead and driving on with relentless power. No one was capable of following such a crazy pace and, for 150 kilometres, the Navarra man was out in front, eventually opening up a gap of almost six minutes. Then he stopped. He waited and, when the exhausted, disconsolate leading survivors were on top of him, he abandoned the race at kilometre 191. Abraham Olano was proclaimed Champion of Spain and received the cheers from the podium, while Miguel was explaining to the press: 'The strategy which we had marked out was to make the race tough and so, when I was about to be neutralised, there was no sense in carrying on.'

It was a tactical experiment, an eccentricity perhaps, but the fact was that Miguel gave a demonstration of extraordinary strength which would give more than one person who believed he was now finished cause to think – and to shudder.

TOUR '94: TRIUMPHS NEVER COME IN ODD NUMBERS

At the end of June the press published the names of the 189 riders who, in 21 teams, were going to take the start of the 81st edition of the Tour de France. The atmosphere was warming up: this, it was forecast, would be a fight to the death between Banesto and Mapei, or, to put it another way, between Induráin and Rominger. The

144

route, made for climbers, gave an advantage to the Mapei team which was stronger in the mountains than Banesto.

Miguel Induráin, triple winner of the world's most important cycle race, was preparing himself for the fray with some intensive massage sessions to tone up his legs which had troubled him in the Giro. His masseur, Vicente Iza, described the anatomy of those legs: 'On stages where he has to make a great effort, Induráin usually suffers in his quadriceps. Now they are fine and I am concentrating, particularly, on the lumbar region and the neck muscles. He has magnificent legs because, with the passage of time, they have become more fibrous, without an atom of fat on them.'

The '95 Tour had a preponderance of mountains: five summit finishes, the last of these the hill climb at Avoriaz. The organisers, obviously, had no intention of making things easy for the triple-champion, but, rather, to avoid monotony and give an incentive to the others. Present at the Induráin–Rominger duel would be some illustrious guests who, themselves, had a chance of making the podium – Alvaro Mejía, Alex Zülle, Bugno, Chiappucci, De las Cuevas and Ugrumov. The rest simply didn't count.

Miguel reassured the fans: 'I know I have come to the Tour in good form. What happened in the Giro doesn't worry me. The Tour is different.' Juan Fernández, Director of Mapei and Rominger's manager, wanted to have it both ways: 'Rominger is in the right frame of mind to win. The route favours him, but it's not bad for Induráin either.'

The grand old men of French cycling didn't seem keen on another victory for the Navarra man and, in the days before the race, Guimard, Hinault, and even Eddy Merckx were offering advice on how to beat Induráin. They all agreed it was simple: because he weighed twelve and a half stone, the secret was to attack him in the mountains – a platitude scarcely worthy of such wise Sanhedrins.

On 2nd July the Lille prologue went according to forecast: the meteoric Boardman flew over the course, averaging more than 55 kph. Induráin, as if reluctant to go for the yellow jersey, made the second-best time, but he took four seconds out of Rominger which was enough to give him the first psychological victory.

From the first road stage it was clear that there would be no respite. Nerves were on edge; there was urgency, elbow nudging in the struggle to snatch time bonuses, furious sprints and falls – this was the pattern of the opening days. In one huge, dramatic crash, at the finish in Armentières, Jalabert came down and ended up in hospital, taking his dreams with him. He was the most-celebrated victim of the imprudence of a gendarme who stepped away from the barrier just when the massive, jostling bunch came sprinting in. Many French hopes had been riding on him.

The four seconds that Induráin had over Rominger went up to 28 seconds after the 66.5-kilometre team time trial between Calais and Eurotunnel. The Italian GB–MG squad flew, putting Museeuw in yellow, while Banesto, thanks to great work by Induráin, Alonso, Bernard and Mauri picked up an unexpected third place. They say 'He who strikes first strikes twice' and, in his particular battle, Miguel held on to second overall, while Rominger dropped back to tenth.

For the first time in its history the Tour crossed the English Channel. After two hellish days on narrow roads with sharp little leg-breaking climbs, it returned to the Continent with GB's Vancella in the yellow jersey, Miguel third at 14 seconds and Rominger eighth at 42 seconds. The man from Switzerland had certainly been seen struggling and grumbling about his left knee.

The flat stages, as is normal in the Tour, were furiously busy and full of scary incidents. There were the usual escapes, breaks, jockeying for position, a frantic pace and riders bickering among themselves. All of this could put lead in the legs of the less well prepared. On stage six the legendary Greg Lemond, the only American ever to have won the Tour, abandoned.

At the start of the seventh stage, in Rennes, two little nuns from Burlada left their convent to greet their countryman, Induráin, and promised to say a prayer for him – in case he needed it. The press was back with the business of Rominger's knee, but Miguel was not so convinced: 'I believe there's nothing wrong with Rominger. We were together in the peloton and I didn't notice him having any problem. If he says so, it must be true, but I don't trust it.'

Curiously, rereading the press coverage of that Tour, the comments of the two rivals after every stage stand out. On the eve of the ninth stage, a 64-kilometre time trial between Perigueux and Bergerac, the Swiss was feeling strong in spite of the 28 seconds Induráin had taken out of him: 'Starting from tomorrow the race will change. My knee? I haven't had a single moment's trouble with my knee; it's never worried me. Tomorrow I can concede a minute, or a minute and a half, to Induráin because if I'm fit I can easily take two minutes out of him on the Avoriaz hill climb.' The Navarra man, by contrast, preferred caution and called on the voice of experience: 'The time trial tomorrow is over a long distance so there could be some big time differences. Over such a distance, if you don't hold on to your rhythm you can lose a lot of time. It only takes a second a kilometre for you to realise that you're not going well.'

So to the ninth stage, the 64-kilometre time trial on 11th July, and they were still in the middle of the San Fermín fiesta. Up till then it was the rouleurs and the sprinters who had been on top, but Induráin ended all that. Averaging over 50 kph, he demolished everyone, taking more than two minutes out of Rominger, 4-22 from De las Cuevas, more than eight minutes from Chiappucci, more than nine minutes from Zülle and more than eleven minutes from Bugno. In the moment of truth Induráin was Induráin and he continued to make history: 'I was not expecting to open up such big gaps. The further I went the more lively I felt. My reference was Rominger and I was thinking I'd take a minute from him, but I've gone way beyond my expectations. I have faith in the team to face the mountains without any anxiety.'

The other man, the only one the forecasters had reckoned on as a rival to Miguel, came back to earth and admitted: 'You have to accept it: Induráin was stronger. But it hurts to have to accept a defeat like that. I intend to attack him in the mountains, but it will not be easy. Now all he has to do is control things.' As if Induráin needed telling.

Miguel now pulled on the yellow jersey and the whole of Banesto was in party mood, all except him. With the mountains now immediately upon them, Sabino Padilla had decided that he should reduce his diet to carbohydrates: pasta, rice cereals mixed with fruit juice and yoghurt. Currently Induráin was losing between two and three pounds on the flat stages, and some four to six pounds in the mountains.

L'Equipe, which described Induráin as 'extra-terrestrial' after his extraordinary ride at Bergerac, confirmed that the organisers were annoyed because, with such a huge gap between Miguel and the rest, the race would lose its interest. On its front page it published a cartoon: 'Le Tour est-il fini?' with a desperate organiser, a hangmen's rope tied around his neck, answering: 'Pas du tout' (without doubt).

In the first encounter with the vastness of the Pyrenees Induráin, having seen Rominger flagging, took off up the imposing

147

final climb towards the stage finish of Hautacam with only Leblanc for company. Miguel allowed him to cross the line first: all he wanted was the 2-19 that he was going to gain on the Swiss which would strengthen his hold on the yellow jersey. Now there were no constraints on him: he didn't have to worry about responding to attacks: he was the one giving the orders.

For Tony Rominger things were not going at all well in the Pyrenees. He was 7-56 behind Miguel after the Aspin–Peyresourde–Tourmalet stage where thousands of Basque and Navarra fans were waiting at the roadside with their transistor radios playing, and their pans of fish casserole and potato omelette. Suffering from severe stomach trouble Rominger didn't make the start of stage thirteen in Bagnères de Bigorre; he was desolate: 'It's very difficult to explain what I feel. The fact is my stomach has been troubling me ever since Hautacam.' Induráin could only show his sympathy: 'He was obviously not well; it made no sense to carry on racing. In one sense his retirement is a relief to me, but he was no longer the man who was troubling me most. Those that I'm most concerned about are Pantani, Leblanc, Virenque, De las Cuevas.'

Induráin held the yellow jersey from the Pyrenees to the Alps without any major scares. Bravely supported by the whole of his team, he used his habitual tactic of rigidly controlling the race and not conceding the slightest chance to his closest rivals. Marisa, his wife, had been there on the podium at Albi, surprising him as she handed over the bouquet of flowers: that day was his thirtieth birthday.

Cautiously, modestly, on the very day before the finish on the Champs Elysées, with a lead of 5-39 over second-place Ugrumov, he explained: 'I am going to try to win a fourth Tour. It has been harder this year, which is why so many have abandoned. This has been a different year for me, a bad year, but I have no wish to crow at those who said I wasn't going to win.'

On the following day, 24th July, Miguel Induráin won his fourth Tour by a bigger margin than on any previous occasion. He won after the traditional promenade of the final stage, a tradition only broken by the Gan rider, Seigneur, who got to the finish first after an unexpected solo break when the peloton stopped under a bridge to shelter from the pouring rain. Paris was enthusiastic, but in Villava the bells rang out, the exploding rockets created their din and the champagne flowed. In the Induráin Supporters Club members and non-members alike packed together in front of the television, hugged each other and burst into song: 'Miguel is nowhere near finished', they shouted into the microphones of the broadcasters who were there. There wasn't enough room in the club for everybody so they jubilantly spilled out into the streets and announced there'd be a party in the village until Miguel returned home.

In Paris, meanwhile, his parents, his sisters, Marisa, and the 400 villagers, led by the Mayor, who had travelled there in six coaches were full of pride and affection once again. And once again it was a moment of delight for the sports administrators, and the President of Navarra.

Down from the podium, and with his lap of honour completed, Miguel began the celebrations after his fourth victory: 'Now to enjoy it. I suppose they'll be having a party already in my village. I can honestly say that in this fourth Tour I have not had a single really bad day so what I've got to do now is get myself ready, hopefully, for the fifth. It's not easy to get used to this and I must say that winning the fourth Tour has been a moving experience. It's always the same, that strange, special sensation on the podium – you just find yourself not thinking about anything. Now I'm waiting for another kind of tough stage – the party, the reception in the Spanish Embassy, dinner with the journalists. And, from eleven o'clock onwards, the body is exhausted.'

True to form the reception was held that night in the Spanish Embassy, presided over by Princess Elena, and attended by the top officials in Spanish sport. Induráin received congratulatory telegrams from Prime Minister Felipe González, and, for the first time, and as a hint of things to come, from the leader of the opposition, José María Aznar.

The following day it was officially announced that, all being well, Induráin would prepare for an attempt on the one-hour record, in Bordeaux, before the end of the year. The French journalists who had cast so much doubt on the triple champion before this last Tour had to bow to the evidence before them:

Induráin will be the first cyclist to win five consecutive Tours. The rest cannot touch him. His victory has been the most convincing because he was better than ever in the mountains and has turned the tables on those who spoke about his decline. (*L'Equipe*)

Who could stop him winning a fifth Tour? The fact is there is nobody with a chance of doing that. He is number-one favourite for the '95 Tour, and already he has equalled Anquetil and Merckx. (*L'Humanité*)

He has become legendary, through his serenity, his class and his domination on every type of terrain. (*Le Parisien*)

With six mountain stages, five stage finishes at altitude, and one of those a hill climb against the clock, the '94 Tour should have brought Induráin to his knees, according to what some people were predicting. They were wrong because Induráin brought everybody else to their knees. (*Libération*).

On 26th July, like a replay of previous occasions, Miguel was given a royal welcome back in Villava and in the Navarra regional parliament. He arrived at the village town hall in a Banesto car, escorted by the local police. There his mother, his wife and half the corporation were waiting for him. Once again the Mayor, Vicente Sabalza, delivered the congratulatory speech which he had now given three times before: 'You continue to bring about these triumphs which we enjoy, and which make the whole of Villava and Navarra happy.' And then came Miguel's reply, with no less sincerity for its repetition: 'After so much suffering I am grateful for this reception from my countrymen who helped me so much, not only on the route of the race, but also those supporting me at home. I am delighted that I can carry on doing well. It has been a difficult year. It wasn't possible to win the Giro, but at least we were on the podium.' And, then, joking: 'And that's a good thing, also, so that we don't get used to too many victories.'

After the welcome home in Villava, the solemn event in the Palace in Pamplona was also repeated for the fourth consecutive year. Here the President of Navarra, Juan Cruz Alli, read the declaration by which the Regional Government recognised 'his perseverance and effort in the search for important goals, and purposes'. A commemorative plaque was presented to him; he again put his signature in the Book of Honour and handed a yellow jersey to the President. Once more he appeared on the main balcony to thank the thousands of supporters for their presence and their allegiance, and he threw them a promise: 'The fifth Tour will be difficult, but for my people, and the team, we will do everything possible to achieve it.'

THE MAGICAL HOUR

Miguel Induráin was front-page news a few days later, on 6th August. Journalists and autograph hunters crowded round him on the start line of the San Sebastián classic. It was a race he had won in 1990, before most of his major achievements, and again he was back in front of the San Sebastián fans, along with the best riders in the world: Rominger, Berzin, Bugno, Chiappucci, and De las Cuevas – the Induráin generation – and Pantani, Virenque, and Olano of the new wave, but still of the Induráin era. Induráin did little more than polish up his form and finish comfortably in the middle of the peloton, two minutes behind the winner, Armand de las Cuevas. He hadn't intended to do anything more strenuous. In fact, he was really only taking part to please the fans and to improve the prestige of the race.

At this precise moment the race was something of an interruption to the intense training he was undertaking in Italy for his attempt on the hour record. He had already begun adjusting his position on the bike some days before – altering the extent to which he was leaning, and moving his saddle backwards and forwards, searching for what was most comfortable.

The intensity of media interest in Miguel's preparations made it clear how serious the attempt was. 'Induráin wins everything; have no fear', some bright sparks stated simply. Miguel, on the other hand, who knew only too well what he was dealing with, preferred to be more humble: 'Nobody should think that beating the record will be easy. I have done time-trial stages which might make you think this will be a simple challenge, within easy reach, but on the road you can get help from a following wind or the route can be advantageous. The track is a more complicated thing: it requires a difficult technique because you've got to go close to the line to avoid doing extra distance, but the banking always has a tendency to take you away from it. It's a technique which I haven't mastered and it's difficult to master. Even your position on the bicycle is different. It's certainly not going to be easy. It's not just that my form has dropped off since the Tour; my real enemy is inexperience.'

151

To intensify his preparation Miguel made a fleeting appearance in the Tour of Castille and León, and retired after winning the time-trial third stage. It was obvious that he was completely focused on one thing, although nobody had yet officially announced when it would take place.

In the middle of August he tested his strength for almost three hours behind closed doors in San Sebastián's Anoeta velodrome with eager fans packed outside the walls of the building. Miguel blamed the secrecy on his own inadequacies: 'I've still got so many things to sort out: wheel testing; changes to the handlebars; adjustments to the forks – and for that I need to concentrate. My right shoulder is hurting through the effort I make on the bends and it really isn't easy to control the bicycle.'

After the second test at Anoeta, on 20th August, the Banesto managers warned that Induráin would only make an attempt on the hour record if he had some guarantee of success. What he did have, after that second test in which he rode at 53 kph, was a new set of pains, now in his arms.

On the 22nd he had his first ride in Bordeaux at the speed he would need to ride to break the record and on the track he had selected for the attempt. They were now talking about the very beginning of September, without being any more concrete than that. It was also known that Channel Plus TV would be paying more than £400,000 to transmit it live. Entry tickets to the velodrome would cost between £16 and £20. The President of the Induráin Supporters Club, Aitor David, who was going to be there whenever it took place, had already hired three coaches and had requested at least 150 seats from the organisers.

Moser, who had made his unsuccessful bid some months earlier, was doubtful about Induráin's chances: 'After the Tour is not a good time,' he said. 'What's more, he has had little chance to get used to the track.' Berzin wasn't betting on Miguel, either, because of his lack of velodrome experience. Eddy Merckx, someone who ought to know, disagreed with those gloomy forecasts: 'Induráin can certainly break the record if he's in good physical shape: track experience isn't that important.'

On 29th August, when Induráin most needed to concentrate on the record attempt, the press revealed that the French Cycling Federation had brought a charge against him, citing an allegedly positive drug test in one stage of the Tour of L'Oise. An anti-asthma medicine, Salbutamol, might have been the cause. The ICU immediately refuted any suggestion of drug taking, but the damage had already been done. On top of all this, on that same day, his father started showing symptoms of a heart attack; fortunately, it proved only to be a warning, but it required a spell of preventative hospital care.

Miguel showed great fortitude in the face of these adversities and calmed everybody down, assuring them that he had not lost his concentration. He continued testing in Bordeaux and hopes rose again when Sabino Padilla announced that 'after checking the medical analysis we have to say that Miguel Induráin is on the verge of beating the hour record'. An animated Echávarri added: 'I am hoping to wake up from this bad dream with the record. The latest training rides proved to us that he could break it on 2nd September in the Bordeaux velodrome.'

All the tickets were sold within three hours and the organisers warned that spectators would have to enter the arena promptly, twenty minutes before the attempt, in order to prevent a rise in temperature: heat would be his greatest enemy. The maintenance staff of the velodrome had tried, unsuccessfully, to cool the track.

It was important to remember the data: the existing record, put up by the Scotsman, Graeme Obree, was 52.713, thus Induráin needed to aim for 53. That meant a minute and eight seconds for every kilometre, or every four laps. Miguel would turn the pedals a total of 6,000 times and would use a 59x14 gear. The machine itself was a testimony to the future – a bicycle from the stars, baptised 'The Sword', purpose built in Italy in carbon-fibre, at an incalculable price, and weighing less than seven kilos.

On 2nd September 1994, in front of a tightly packed velodrome and more than 200 journalists, Miguel Induráin did it. The hour was exactly up as the electronic score-board indicated the distance – 53.040 kilometres!

He dismounted 'The Sword' with aching legs and without any feeling down the right side of his body, and a strange tingling in his arms. The velodrome was an absolute explosion of all the jubilation which had been suppressed after his promising start: he had been level with Obree by kilometre nineteen and had continued pedalling powerfully through to the finish, leaving you with the feeling that he could have gone further, perhaps even 55 kilometres in the hour.

Miguel Induráin, however, acknowledged how terribly hard the trial had been: 'I began well, I felt comfortable and then it was a matter of keeping up the rhythm. But it really hurt. I was not at one with the bicycle; my position was causing me pain and I noticed something out of place on my right side. By kilometre 30 it was painful all over and it felt bad through to the end. As for the event, I didn't hear anything, nor did I see the velodrome score-board, but I sensed that I was up on time. The experience teaches you that the most reliable thing is what your legs are telling you.'

Worn out, but serene, Miguel Induráin smiled tolerantly through a full fifteen minutes of congratulations, half an hour in the anti-doping control – God forbid – and then an exuberant press conference in which he insisted that it had been a triumph of the whole team of technicians and mechanics who had helped him.

To one side, without taking any attention away from him, was an emotional Marisa: 'I never doubted. Miguel always seemed to me to be very confident, very sure that he could do it.' Echávarri was overjoyed and, with the tension broken, he couldn't hold himself back: 'That's Miguel. Miguel is magic. What, next year again? At the present moment I just want to enjoy a little of this. And then? God knows. For Miguel? A bit of peace and a holiday after this.'

The President of the International Olympic Committee, Samaranch, proclaimed Induráin one of the great sportsmen of the twentieth century. And that was no exaggeration. The media pointed out the overwhelming presence of Navarra people in Bordeaux and the barely contained excitement of Marisa, accompanied by Miguel's mother, Isabel, by his brother, Pruden, and their sisters. His father was not fit for all this emotion: he was convalescing in Villava after his heart murmur, but he was happy and thankful to be allowed to catch a glimpse of it on television. Once he recovered he was able to show his pleasure in what his son had accomplished, and just what he had accomplished occupied the front pages and their emphatic headlines:

53.040. He has done it! (*L'Equipe*)

That's it! (*Marca*)

Induráin flies in Bordeaux. 53.040. Bravo! (*As*)

Congratulations! (*El Mundo Deportivo*)

Induráin pulverised the record. (*El País*)

Induráin takes the hour. (*Libération*)

Induráin's best hour. (*Le Figaro*)

He has rounded Cape Horn. (*Le Parisien*)

He broke the 53 kilometre barrier. (*L'Humanité*)

On 6th September, perhaps by way of an apology, the French Federation dropped the case of Induráin's alleged doping. Someone had wanted to play dirty and it hadn't worked.

Miguel continued, for as long as he could, fulfilling his racing commitments: he took part in, and won, the City of Salamanca Criterium; he put in an appearance at the International Criterium of Gandía; and at Fuenlabrada; at Alcobendas; and at Zaragoza. These rather ordinary races were magnified by the singular presence of the King of the Tour. As the season was drawing to a close he started in the Tour of La Rioja but didn't complete it.

With the end of the season came the announcement of the retirements – the sad toll that all cyclists one day have to pay: the maestro, Perico Delgado; the Mexican, Raúl Alcalá; San Sebastián's Pello Ruiz Cabestany; the Australian, Phil Anderson; the American, Greg Lemond; Iñaki Gastón from Alava; the Irishman, Sean Kelly; the French prologue specialist, Moreno Argentin; the Italian sprinter, Franco Chioccioli; Marco Giovanetti, the recent winner of the Vuelta; the eternal French promise, Charlie Mottet. All of them, companions of the peloton, who would never again turn a pedal in anger. They were a generation of great men who were giving way to newer, younger men with whom Miguel Induráin would continue to share the struggles and the glory.

ROMINGER: THE HOUR OF THE CENTURY

The season ended, just as it had begun, with confirmation that its essential theme had been the rivalry between two men. Tony

Rominger won the Grand Prix de Nations with great authority and then there came a worrying announcement: an exclusive report in *La Gazzetta dello Sport* told of his intention to make an attempt on Induráin's hour record in Mexico. The Swiss, having lost the duel with the Navarra man, was returning to the fight.

On 11th October the route of the 1995 Tour was presented and, attending the presentation as an invited star, was Miguel who surprised everybody with his unusual attire: black suit, black and white checked shirt, and a huge tie which reproduced, in black and white, Michelangelo's frescos in the Cistine Chapel. The Tour of '95 would spread out the mountain stages more and would include 171 kilometres against the clock. Someone voiced the view that they had made things more difficult for the four-times champion, but he didn't seem to see it that way: 'I like the route. The Pyrenees and the Alps are not following immediately after each other and there is one time trial before the mountains, and another one after. The fact that I'm the only favourite? That's normal after winning the last one, but you can be sure that throughout the season new aspiring riders will come forward. Obviously they will have to be all-rounders, men who can climb well in the mountains and time trial well.' All the same, both Echávarri and Perurena, as well as Juan Fernández and Manolo Sainz, were agreed that the '95 Tour would again be won by Induráin.

On 22nd of October a shiver ran down the spines of Miguel's most fervent followers. Tony Rominger made a surprise attack on the hour record and, behind half-closed doors in Bordeaux, he beat Induráin's mark. To the amazement of the 80 guests and journalists who were present, he demolished the record – 53.832! He had gone 792 metres further. 'Rominger has done a great ride,' declared the Villava man, courteous as ever, 'and it will be difficult to beat it. It is good for cycling. Naturally, I have no intention of trying it again, at least for the moment.'

The Swiss rider had certainly benefited from being able to refer to Miguel's times and he had chosen Bordeaux to avoid any risks, and to ride on the same track, but it was far from certain that Rominger, at the age of 34, could do it. However, in case there were any lingering doubts, he made another attack on 5th November and upset everybody's calculations by breaking the 55-kilometre barrier. Nobody in the twentieth century had managed to ride a bicycle 55 kilometres and 291 metres in the course of 60 minutes. This was two kilometres, two hundred and fifty one metres more than Induráin, who humbly said: 'I am amazed by the record and by Rominger's performance. I didn't think he could get beyond 55 kilometres and he has achieved it. For that I warmly congratulate him and the whole of his team for that achievement; it's the fruit of some excellent work.'

They were both honourable men. The ICU published its final list: first was Rominger with 2,034 points; second was Induráin, with 1,880 points. It could just as easily have been either one of them. The year was ending and, with it, the duel between these two great men who, without foul play and without intrigue, had dominated the podium. The year was ending, and the 'Devil', Chiappucci, who was off to the muddy pleasures of cyclo-cross, said farewell to it with a prophecy that was a mixture of admiration and resignation: 'For me, the next season will continue to be marked by the sight of Induráin's back; it's the thing I've seen most in the eleven years since I turned professional. But Miguel is, without doubt, the best.'

RESULTS

Tour of Valencia: one stage win
Tour de L'Oise: first
Giro de Italia: third
Tour de France: first overall and one stage win
Tour of Castilla-León: one stage win
City of Salamanca Criterium: first
World One-hour record (later beaten by Rominger)

1995: FIVE WITHOUT STOPPING

The previous season had been very hard for Miguel: it hadn't begun well and he'd arrived at the Giro without many kilometres in his legs. His most ardent followers were surprised by the taste of defeat, but he knew the reasons for it only too well. On top of that, he hadn't shone in his increasingly infrequent competitive appearances; his closest rival, Tony Rominger, had numbed the joy of the hour record he'd laboured so hard to achieve; and his team-mates, from whom he'd learned so much and to whom he owed so much for his many triumphs, had moved on. But the Tour! The Tour had been and continued to be something unique for Miguel Induráin. Now it was four in a row and the approaching season was going to be shaped by a single unanswered question: would Miguel Induráin be capable of winning the Tour once more? Or would this be demanding the impossible? Disappointment was always a possibility, but the fans continued to have complete faith in him and were once more betting on the man from Navarra.

A SINGLE OBJECTIVE

Miguel began serious preparation for the new season half-way through January, training three hours a day. He was a stone above his ideal weight after Christmas – his mother's fried eggs and ham made him look more like a human being, and less like a machine. From time to time he would interrupt his pedalling, and get talking with some neighbour or other, about cycling, of course. Miguel insisted that, in his view, Berzin had been the previous season's best rider. True, he still hadn't put in an appearance in the Tour and the Giro, but, well, the Giro is different, a different kind of racing. The

Tour is more draining; more pressurised. It remained to be seen how Berzin would perform in the Tour and only then would it be possible to judge his quality.

The Tour was always his yardstick and it was the only clear objective he had at the beginning of 1995. He was expecting to have some 50 days of racing in his legs by the time the Tour came round, but what he didn't know was how those 50 days would be divided out: Giro or Vuelta? Giro and Vuelta? You could rule that out. Giro and Tour of Switzerland? Tour of Catalunya and Tour of Switzerland? It was not only Miguel who was weighing up the multiple combinations: the Directors of the Banesto team were also having to face up to the new year.

Meanwhile, out on the roads of Navarra, Miguel would join up with groups of club cyclists, charitably ride with them for a few kilometres, Indian file, next to the kerb, and chat about the complications of beating Rominger's record.

The new Banesto team was officially presented in Palma de Mallorca on 1st February and Echávarri made it clear that, with regard to Induráin, the one certainty was that he would be riding the Tour. He started in the Tour of Mallorca, put in a few hundred kilometres, and then abandoned, but remained on the island so that he could take advantage of the warm winter sun to train at his leisure.

The press launch of the Vuelta which, for the first time, would take place in September didn't seem to concern Miguel. He carried on tuning up his legs and adding a measure of prestige to a number of relatively modest races where he was more concerned about testing himself than going all out to win. The Luis Puig Trophy, the Tour of Murcia, the Catalan Week were, for him, an efficient method of training; he had no intention of taking on the Italians who were winning all these early season races.

On 21st February the whole of the international peloton was shocked by news of the death of three middle-rank, but pugnacious, Colombians who had been knocked down by a lorry while out training near Bogotá: Néstor Mora, Augusto Triana and Hernán Patiño had fought out their final sprint.

With spring just about to break Miguel was soon about to have his first serious encounter in the Milan–San Remo. The cycling press, as in the previous year, was determined to play him down. A Frenchman from the ONCE team who, until then, had been well known as a sprinter and a tough rider on the flat, began sweeping the board in all the major early season races: Laurent Jalabert would be to Induráin in 1995 what Rominger had been in 1994 – Rominger permitting, of course – and Induráin, too! Meanwhile, Jalabert deservedly won the Paris–Nice, the Milan–San Remo and the International Criterium – all before the end of March.

Sticking to his own rhythm Miguel continued to put more kilometres into his legs during the April races. He was apparently going at half speed in the Gran Premio de Estella, in the Gran Premio de Amorebieta, in the Tour of Aragón and in the Dutch Amstel Gold Race. He was absent from the Tour of the Basque Country, a spectator at the battle between Jalabert and Rominger which, surprisingly, ended up with Zülle winning. Unquestionably, however, ONCE's Jalabert continued to be the cycling revelation of the year, topping the podium in Amorebieta and the Flèche Wallonne.

Half-way through April Echávarri and Induráin gave the press conference everybody was waiting for, and here the uncertainties were removed: Miguel, who was just getting over a cold and was still suffering from an allergy, would not ride the Giro. How he emerged, physically, from the Tour would determine whether he would take part in the Vuelta or the World Championships, or go for another attempt on the one-hour record, this time at altitude.

TUNED

He was visibly more aggressive in the Tour of Aragón, where he took one stage, and well on the way back to form in the Tour of the Mining Valleys where he again had a stage win. He was going better still in the Tour of la Rioja: he was overall winner and there were encouraging signs that he was getting strong in readiness for the Tour.

With the tension of previous years resurfacing, Banesto decided to ease matters with Unipublic by provisionally nominating Induráin for the Vuelta. This would satisfy the organisation, for the moment, although the decision would not be officially confirmed until after the Tour. At least the argument would be postponed until August.

Eddy Merckx, who had closely followed Miguel's career, was, perhaps, on this occasion, too critical of the racing programme that had been worked out for him: 'It's a great mistake for Induráin not to be riding the Giro which has always been his best preparation for the Tour. The alternative schedule he'll be undertaking is just not the same. Nevertheless,' he almost corrected himself, 'in spite of that, Miguel can win one or two more Tours. It depends on how he maintains his form and how his rivals are. Rominger is definitely my candidate for the Giro and, if he wins it, his morale will be sky high for the Tour. Because of that I still see Rominger as Induráin's most obvious challenger.'

Perhaps in response to the Belgian's forecast, the cycling press were predicting that 'everybody would be against Rominger' in the Giro. That was just how it turned out, for all the good it did them. Tony took the pink jersey on the second stage and never let go of it. It was a victory, as they said, 'the Induráin way'.

By the middle of May Miguel was beginning to feel good, comfortable, and in form. In the Tour of Asturias he destroyed everybody on the climb of the Naranco and, although he again suffered a set-back on the road up to the Lakes of Covadonga, he won a further stage, and finished third overall.

Rominger's victory in Italy again had the experts endlessly pondering the comparisons. They were comparing chalk and cheese, Echávarri got round to telling them: 'It's a pointless debate. We are judging two personalities, two different philosophies. Both deserve great respect: they are both great champions. With regard to their performance Rominger is possibly similar to Merckx and Induráin could be compared to Anquetil. In other words, one wants to monopolise everything and the other does his own thing.'

Other members of the peloton also took part in the discussion. Thus, Fondriest definitely preferred Induráin for the Giro; Breukink spoke up for Rominger, reckoning he had more ambition that the Navarra man; Chiappucci continued to defend Induráin's greater all-round class. The ICU, for its part, simply added up the points obtained so far that season and gave a clear advantage to Rominger: 2,183, against Induráin's 1,725. And Miguel, just to prove a point, carried off the Midi Libre in the last week of May.

In Italy, *La Gazzetta dello Sport* also entered the fray, putting its money on Rominger who had just won the Giro ahead of Berzin and Ugrumov. Somebody was kind enough to translate the article in the Italian daily sports paper for Miguel, who commented: 'The Tour will tell if Rominger is the stronger. Tony has done a great Giro, because, as the article itself says, "he has ridden á la Induráin". I'll be waiting for him in the Tour, which is the world's most important race. I don't believe he can maintain his present level of performance but, if he can, I'll be the first to congratulate him.'

Then, once again, he blazoned his confidence in the Dauphiné Libéré, easily taking the time-trial stage and ending up winner overall. Other opponents were also staking their claims: Berzin won the Bicicleta Vasca and Jalabert came out on top in the Tour of Catalunya. Despite all this the media couldn't get away from its fascination with the idea of an Induráin–Rominger duel. They published data on each man's physical capacities:

	Induráin	Rominger
Height	6'1"	5'7"
Weight	12st 8 lbs	10 st 3 lbs
Lung capacity	81 litres	41.5 litres
Oxygen consumption	88 litres/min	84 litres/min
Maximum pulse rate	195	195
Average pulse rate (mountains)	160	165
Resting pulse rate	28	38

TOUR '95: MIGUEL V OF FRANCE – OR NAVARRA

On 28th June Miguel flew from Biarritz to Paris where he would get a glimpse of the route planned for the team time-trial stage. Unzué saw Rominger, Berzin, Zülle, Pantani, De las Cuevas and Virenque as the most dangerous rivals, and the trainer voiced his concern that Miguel was gambling the whole season on just twenty days, even though it was well recognised that Banesto had a team capable of redeeming any mistakes with climbers like Aparicio, Carmelo Miranda, González, Arrieta and Rué, and all-rounders like Davy, Uriarte, Garmendia, and Marino Alonso, although, for the first time, Pruden Induráin would be missing.

On 1st July you could have cut the tension in Saint Breuc with a knife. The prologue was going to release the mass of pent-up nerves in a peloton which contained the finest riders in international cycling. Moments before signing on Miguel Induráin was telling the press: 'I don't know if I'm better or worse than in other years; I do know that I'm feeling good, and that's enough for me. I accept the pressure of the Tour, which the Giro and other races can't begin to touch. Anyone who can't take that pressure will get nowhere.'

The day before, Rominger had been lamenting: 'Induráin puts pressure on us from the word go. How does he manage to be in peak form right from the prologue?' The Swiss admitted that he hadn't arrived at the Tour 100 per cent fit; he still felt dragged down by the poor health he'd suffered ever since the Giro.

The prologue stage, 7.2 kilometres against the clock around Saint Breuc, was hell. There was a torrential downpour and, on top of that, it started so late that night was closing in by the time the last riders were finishing. The best time was put up by Castorama's Jacky Durand who took the most risks. Miguel rode very cautiously, not wanting to jeopardise the Tour in the first few kilometres, and lost 38 seconds on the winning time.

Just as risky was the first full stage, 233 kilometres between Dinau and Lannion, with three fourth-category hills. Once more there were plenty of skids, false moves and riders coming a cropper. Both Induráin and Rominger spent the whole time at the back of the bunch, well guarded by their troops. The Italian, Baldato, of the MG team, finished first in a long sprint with the whole of the peloton strung out behind him.

The second stage was again an Italian affair. Mercatone's Mario Cipollini came to the front of a 37-strong group of the top riders. It seemed as if nobody really wanted to take over the yellow jersey, but, because of the time bonuses, Laurent Jalabert, one of Induráin's main rivals, found himself wearing it.

The third stage was a dangerous team time trial over 64.7 kilometres between Mayenne and Alençon; there was a lot of unease in the Banesto hotel: this was a stage the team was nervously anticipating. In the event, they didn't do badly. Thanks principally to Miguel's efforts they managed the third-best time behind the Gewis and ONCE squads. By now the Navarra man was 34 seconds up on Rominger; Jalabert was still in yellow and Miguel was eleventh overall, 58 seconds down on ONCE's Frenchman.

The hilly fourth stage from Alençon to Le Havre proved disastrous for Jalabert who lost the leader's jersey after a dramatic fall in sight of the finish. It was won once more by the sprinter, Cipollini, from the rest of the peloton. Gotti was the new leader and Miguel went up a bit, now 50 seconds down on the yellow jersey. He was satisfied with these first four days: 'Half a minute up or down is nothing at this point. The selection will come in the time trial at Lieja. I shall go out to do the best possible time. Berzin and Zülle are the ones who worry me most.'

The days that followed were equally nervous affairs, and extremely fast and dangerous. The stages were won in mass finishes by out-and-out sprinters like Blijlevens or Zabel, while Induráin kept his mind on the breaks, travelling at the head of the bunch, saying very little to the others in his team: a whistle or a gentle tap, and they knew what was required of them. Miguel, after the finish of the sixth stage at Charleroi, described the state of the peloton to the journalists: 'There are some tired people around now. De las Cuevas is not comfortable. Berzin is wearing himself out getting into every break, and I'm keeping a good eye on him all the time. Rominger looks relaxed to me, but unenthusiastic, which is not like him. Zülle is robust, with a lot of strength. Pantani is getting better each day and I think he's going to get to the mountains in very good form. I'm surprised at how well Jaskula and Mejía are going.'

From this snapshot we can see that everything was not going perfectly for Miguel: his most direct rivals were ready to attack him at any moment. For that very reason he decided to make the first move: on the seventh stage, between Charleroi and Lieja, he attacked suddenly, and in earnest, twenty kilometres short of the finish. Only the Belgian, Bruyneel, could stay with him and Miguel allowed him to cross the line first while the rest were 50 seconds back. It was the first warning shot. The overall classification was the same as the stage finished – with Bruyneel ahead of Induráin: ONCE's Bruyneel pulled on the yellow jersey and Miguel occupied second place, 31 seconds back.

The following day's eighth stage was the first individual time trial – 54 kilometres on the road from Huy to Serain. Here was the living proof of what Miguel Induráin was capable of: he rode just as he was expected to and recorded the best time. However, his strongest rivals also rose to the occasion: Riis was 12 seconds slower, Rominger at 58 seconds, Berzin at 1-38, Jalabert at 2-36 and lost somewhere in the night was a disappointing Zülle. With this win Induráin was in the yellow jersey. He hadn't inflicted a mortal blow, but it served to give him confidence as they faced the mountains with Riis, second overall at 23 seconds, the man to be watched most carefully.

From here on his concern was to control the race – something which, in Tour after Tour, Miguel had become expert at. After the rest day he would be confronting the Alps with a new generation of opponents: old rivals from so many previous Tours like Bugno, Chiappucci and Jaskula were giving way, in the perpetual battle against Induráin, to newly emerging men like Riis, Berzin, and Jalabert. The first Alpine stage, from Le Grand Bornaud to the summit finish at La Plagne, was won by Zülle after a 90-kilometre lone break. Miguel's colleagues, Rue and Aparicio, worked hard to bring him up to the lower slopes of La Plagne, and there he left them to drive on upwards in Zülle's tyre-tracks. The Swiss rider won while Induráin, second at 2-02, sealed the fate of the Tour. His major rivals were out of sight: Riis came in at 5-58, Rominger at 6-35, Chiappucci at 12-32, Pantani at 14-02, Virenque at 14-20, while Berzin collapsed completely, crossing the line more than seventeen minutes back.

Miguel was quite unusually exuberant. With the yellow jersey on his back and with Zülle 2-27 back in second place, he declared: 'For me, it's been tremendous. Rather than getting back to Zülle what I really wanted was to open up gaps on the others. The team's work was excellent and everything turned out better than we were expecting.' And he repeated his usual remark: 'Now the important thing is not to fall back, but to stay in front.' The media, equally enthusiastic, was now speculating on who would be second on the podium because it was clear who the winner of this Tour was going to be.

The tenth stage threatened with the legendary 21 hairpin bends of l'Alpe d'Huez. Pantani put on a wonderful display for the fans and finished alone, the first of an agonising string of exhausted cyclists. Induráin was second, 1-24 behind the Italian: having been paced by his team-mates to the foot of the final climb towards l'Alpe, Miguel ascended at his own pace: in other words, he put everything into it and all those who couldn't hang on were left behind. Only Zülle and Riis were able to stick to his wheel, and finish in the same time as the Navarra man. Berzin, completely wrecked, abandoned the race. As on the previous day Miguel's concern was to widen the gaps, not to hold on to Pantani: 'If I follow Pantani on his own terrain, I'll burst', he would confess at the finish.

It must have been a twisted mind who devised the '95 Tour: the torture went on from the Alps to the Pyrenees, practically without a break, with the three intermediate stages almost as tough as those in the highest mountains: as if the cyclists were even more than superhuman. The end of the Alps and the beginning of the Pyrenees gave a fleeting glimpse of the one thing that could alter the general classification: in this all-out war ONCE rode itself into the ground on Zülle behalf, and Banesto exhausted itself in a back-against-the-wall defence of Induráin's lead. There was definitely an external factor which Sainz had not foreseen and which to some extent thwarted the ONCE Director's plans: such was the reciprocal marking between Riis, Pantani and Zülle that the Swiss was left shackled because of the need to control so many diverse fronts.

Banesto, it has to be said, were in a pretty poor state by the time they got to the Pyrenees. However, Induráin was able to lift their spirits: 'I have always done well in the Pyrenees,' he said. 'The cols are long and I climb them better than the short steep ones. Physically, I am better than in other years: I feel I'm stronger.'

There was one note of warning. The French, after Jalabert won the final Alpine stage, were wildly singing the praises of their countryman and were pointing to him as the one to take over from Induráin. Chiappucci had less faith in the Frenchman, commenting with some irony: 'Jalabert has as much chance of winning the Tour as Cipollini has of winning on Alpe d'Huez.'

On stage fourteen Pantani confirmed that he was the best climber, easily winning at Guzet Neige. It was 16th July, and Miguel's 31st birthday, and he celebrated it by taking a couple more seconds out of Zülle, and, on top of that, leaving Rominger with no chance of winning the Tour or even making the podium in Paris. After the finish at Guzet Neige, even before he had taken off his yellow jersey, Miguel could be seen shovelling down a lavish salami sandwich. He was, perhaps, over-indulging on his birthday.

On 17th July, a rest day prior to the major Pyrenean stage, Miguel reflected: 'I would always want to be at the top level in cycling. I am 31, and riders like Merckx and Hinault quit when they were 32. It all depends on how you want to carry on, whether it's winning or just riding well. I know that I'm strong and in the right frame of mind this year. Next year we'll see what we can hope for. I intend to carry on, but I know that one day all this has to come to an end.'

The Farmers' Association in this region had the nice idea of presenting him with a calf, which created a problem for the team

166

because they couldn't carry it in the mechanics' van, and they had to explain that to their generous admirers. They decided, therefore, that, for the time being, they would leave it in a stable in Saint Girons and would send someone to take it back to Villava later on. It's not known if it ever arrived.

The queen of stages, as it was called, between Saint Girons and Cauterets, with the agony of the three legendary cols, the Peyresourde, Aspin, and Tourmalet, turned into a tragedy. On the descent from the Aspin, long before the battle for the stage would be taken up, five riders piled into each other and came down on a bend at more than 70 kph with the awful result that Motorola's Italian, Fabio Casartelli, smashed his skull against a parapet. It was the death of an ordinary rider which froze the peloton as it learned of it. Virenque eventually won the stage, ahead of a painful trickle of riders. Induráin came in 2-34 behind, with Riis and Zülle stuck to his wheel. But on the summit of Cauterets the principal figure was the body of Casartelli, a 'work-mate' as Miguel defined him to the journalists – a work-mate, but a dead one.

Meanwhile, the Tour organisers decided not to interrupt the race, not even for a single day as a mark of respect. The hullabaloo of the publicity caravan would arrive at Pau the following day as if nothing had happened. José Miguel Echávarri was indignant: 'This is like the running of the bulls during San Fermín. Nothing ever happens, but when it does happen everybody is sorry. The difference is that you go to the feast of San Fermín because you want to; this is a way of earning a living.'

The following day a collective decision of the riders saw the peloton enter Pau in one group leaving the way clear for the six survivors of the Motorola team to cross the finishing line in tribute to their companion, Casartelli.

After all this trauma came stage seventeen, between Pau and Bordeaux, which at 246 kilometres, was the longest stage in the race. It was won by Zabel of the Telekom squad, and the rest came in together, worn out by the dead-flat road and a temperature of 45 degrees in the shade. Induráin remained overall leader with an advantage of 2-46 over Zülle and 5-59 over Riis.

Armstrong dedicated his victory on the eighteenth stage to his colleague, Casartelli. The stage, which went from Montpon to Limoges, saw Induráin quiet, but watchful. Rominger, who no longer had an interest in the race, was resigned to his fate: 'Now I will never win the Tour. I am content with what I have achieved – three Vueltas and two Giros, but I know now that I will never win the Tour.'

There remained a 46.5-kilometre time trial, almost tailor-made for showing off Induráin's brilliance, and he did so quite mercilessly. This was the Miguel of old, as he was in his prime, recording a devastating time around the Auphelle circuit. He consolidated his overall lead, extending the gap to 4-35 on Zülle and to 6-47 over Riis. Once again the cycling journalists found themselves wondering who would succeed Induráin and they couldn't come up with an answer. There was nobody like him – no one who could win the Tour with such assurance.

Five coaches faithfully left Villava that night bound for the fifth fiesta in Paris. In the Embassy, too, as had become customary, they were getting ready for the victory reception.

The ride from Sainte Geneviève to the Champs Elysées, where Abdoujaparov decided the outcome of an impressive sprint finish, was also triumphal: Miguel Induráin had just equalled Anquetil, Merckx and Hinault in the total number of Tour victories, but only he had achieved the even more difficult task of winning the five consecutively.

Some newspapers produced a full-page headline that read – 'Quintourain!' – and the *Journal de Dimanche* baptised him 'Miguel V of Spain'. To cap it all, an enormous banner on the Champs Elysées claimed Villava to be the capital of France and compared Induráin with Napoleon. While the presentations on the podium and the laps of honour were taking place, the commentators were explaining the key elements of the '95 Tour: Induráin's domination over his direct rivals on every kind of terrain; the retirement of an exhausted Berzin; the weak part that Rominger played; and the inability of Zülle to attack Miguel in the high mountains.

On the other side of the barrier, impatient to embrace him, was Marisa, now unable to hide her pregnancy, together with his parents and his sisters; the President of the Navarra Government; the President of the regional parliament; the Mayor of Villava; the tireless occupants of the 30 coaches hired by the Induráin Supporters Club from Irún and Villava; friends, and acquaintances. Present also at the culmination of that Tour was Princess Elena and her husband, Jaime de Marichalar, the Directors of Banesto, and various Spanish sporting authorities.

In the Maica café, the new headquarters of the Supporters Club, the whole of Villava was crowded around the television chanting, 'We can't wait. We're counting the days to the sixth Tour', while the champagne ran, the rockets exploded, the bells peeled and a cry went out that a monument to Miguel should be set up in the middle of the village square. Just like the year before, and the year before that, and the year before that; just like the first time.

The International Olympic Committee awarded Induráin the Olympic Order 'for his sporting spirit, modesty and exemplary bearing'. He had now taken part in eleven Tours, three Giros and six Vueltas, and, only citing his major races, he had ridden more than 300,000 kilometres. During the party in the Embassy he had a moment of openness with the journalists, who wouldn't stop asking him questions about his future plans, even though he'd just given himself a caning on the pedals: 'Every year I have taken a week off after the Tour to recuperate. Then I'll think about what I'm going to do. This is a tough job, but it's when you're young that it changes your life most. You have to leave your friends, your hobbies and entertainments. Now it's not such a sacrifice. The Tour? It's a race that's won day by day. I haven't thought about the sixth Tour, but now I'll have time. I don't have any special feelings because this is the fifth. Winning the Tour is what makes it worthwhile – and I don't believe there's any need to make a lot of fuss: I've done some great things, but my record can't be compared with that of Merckx or Hinault.'

It was Hinault, in fact, who was pondering Miguel's epic achievement that very day: 'The immediate future is Induráin. I believe he can win a sixth Tour because right now there isn't a challenger in sight who could trouble him.' Eddy Merckx joined in the praise: 'Bike racing is simple: you have to pedal stronger than everybody else and nobody knows how to do that better than Induráin. He can win a sixth Tour because he is so enormously consistent. Induráin is the only person who trains exclusively for the Tour, and it shows.'

Once again, on 24th July, the hardest, and, at the same time, the most appreciative stage was awaiting Miguel. Sun-tanned, and smiling like he was returning from holidays, slimmer, and rather informally dressed, he arrived at the Palace of Navarra in one of Banesto's Mercedes. Thousands of Pamplonese were willing to put up with a temperature of 38 degrees on the Paseo de Sarasate to see

169

their idol, Miguel Induráin, appear on the main balcony at eight o'clock in the evening. The President, Alli, greeted 'the best cyclist of all time, Miguel V of Navarra' while from below came the popular chant, 'Induráin–Induráin–Induráin'.

There's no doubt that Miguel would always prefer climbing the Tourmalet to the agony of speaking into a microphone. Emotionally, and rapidly, he said what he had to say, which was not much – not for lack of feeling, but because he was no great orator: 'As you wanted, last year, when we were celebrating the fourth Tour, I have fought for it and have been able to get it. The fact that you are able to celebrate it, and also that you have enjoyed all the effort, seems wonderful to me.'

It was not a display of eloquence, but it would do. Inside the Palace, after signing his name in the Book of Gold for the umpteenth time, he joined Marisa who was being questioned by the reporters about her pregnancy. 'The best news of the year,' she was saying, and then added: 'My pregnancy has managed to do what none of Miguel's opponents could do: when we first learned the news, and it was confirmed, both our legs were shaking. Miguel is ever so excited, although he'll pretend he's not.' But Miguel didn't really hide, and promised: 'I'll dedicate the sixth Tour to my son.'

Miguel, senior, was delighted at the thought that he was soon to be a grandfather: 'They kept it a bit secret and when he went off to the Tour we were not sure about it; we saw some indication, but nobody said anything. This news is more important than the Tour.'

Before Miguel left the Palace of Navarra for the second part of the hardest stage – the reception and tribute in Villava – President Alli joked: 'They're saying around here that if you don't win the sixth Tour Marisa will not let you in the house.' And, in the same spirit, Miguel replied: 'Yes, they are saying that; I've heard it, too.'

In Villava, where everybody was waiting impatiently, they would repeat the programme of the last five years. Finally, after he had fulfilled his duty and properly thanked them, it would be almost dawn before Miguel was able to sleep.

A VERY SPECIAL WORLD CHAMPIONSHIP

Miguel was certainly given the royal welcome during his brief rest: the summer criteriums were clamouring for him, since his presence greatly added to their attraction. In the heat of August he won the first edition of the Rominger Classic in Switzerland; he appeared in the San Sebastián Classic; he carried off overall victory, together with a stage win, in the Tour of Galicia; he put in a brief appearance in the Tour of Cuenca; and he rode the Tour of the Madrid Cols.

On 18th August, in a short press conference, Induráin announced what was already an open secret: 'I am not going to ride the Vuelta. I'm not in the form that I'd need to be in and, as such, I couldn't do the race with any chance of winning. So we have decided to prepare properly for the World Championships in Colombia where we hope to make a decent impression.' Enrique Franco, the President of Unipublic which was organising the Vuelta a España, commented angrily about Miguel's absence from the race: 'Oranges are grown in Spain and exported to France; and here we eat mandarins.'

Away from the row in which Franco and Echávarri would later get embroiled, Miguel was preparing for his trip to the United States where, with his eye on the World Championships, he would train thoroughly; and he was hopeful.

On 2nd September the Vuelta inaugurated its controversial change of date. It saw Jalabert wearing the yellow jersey from stage two through to the finish. The ONCE rider won with the same ease as Induráin or Rominger. It seemed pretty clear that the school of Echávarri and Unzué was having its imitators in the search for the complete cyclist.

While Jalabert was celebrating his first Vuelta victory and the whole of the press was speaking warmly of the only man in the race capable of putting the Basque rider, Abraham Olano, in the shade, Miguel was training with his brother Pruden, Santi Blanco, José María Jiménez, and Andy Hampsten at altitude in Colorado Springs under the medical eye of Sabino Padilla. It was thought likely that the Championship would be a very tough and Miguel's view was that the principal enemies would be the altitude of the Diutama circuit, the Colombian riders, and Bugno. When he arrived in Bogotá, on 1st October, he confirmed that the heat, the humidity and the difficulty of the route itself would have to be added to the problems he had already identified.

Induráin was staying at the Hotel Dann in the town of Paipa, an idyllic setting in the Boyacá region, 200 kilometres from Bogotá, and he discovered immediately that he was going to be protected by

171

the police, and members of the special operations unit right up to the door of his room. Because of the multitude of admirers swarming around the hotel he was unable to step outside without the guards almost physically having to prise open the way for him.

On 4th October the championships began with the individual time trial. In an impressive demonstration of speed Miguel won the gold medal at an average of 46 kph. Olano, 49 seconds behind him, took the silver. It was a sensational performance by the two Spanish cyclists, achieving what had never been done before, while all the others who had set out as favourites – Fondriest, Breukink, Obree and Thierry Marie – were nowhere. Stepping down from the top of the podium, Induráin explained, without a hint of self-importance: 'I was thinking about winning here when I decided not to compete in the Vuelta. The race has been very tough, but I felt strong and I can almost say that I enjoyed the ride.'

Sabino Padilla, full of pride in his own work, was once more singing Miguel's praises: 'Induráin continues to surprise me. He is unique. When we learned about the circuit for the Worlds he said to me: "Sabino, I'm going to have to slim down a lot; this is a course for lightweights." And he has got his weight down; he has gone without meals; he has trained to the limit. When a sportsman has a brain and is fit, all you have to do is guide him.'

On 7th October, facing the start line for the World road race, Miguel was excited: 'We are going to fight for the gold. We're going to give it everything', he said, and the journalists agreed with him. Merckx, present among the organisers, commented: 'The more I think about the circuit, the more convinced I am that Induráin will win.'

Missing from the race were Rominger, Zülle, Leblanc, Riis and Jalabert, worn out from the demands of the season. Miguel's rivals, at least according to the betting, would be the Italians, the Colombians and Richard, but it was Abraham Olano who won, in an epic race on a fiendish circuit. In the final kilometres Olano, Induráin, Pantani and Gianetti made a terrific effort, and hit the front. The Basque rider, taking advantage of the fact that the other three were apprehensively watching each other, suddenly accelerated. He caught out Gianetti, the best sprinter in the group, who already saw himself winning the sprint. With Olano away off the front Induráin didn't want to respond to his countryman's attack; instead, he devoted himself to a splendid piece of team work on Olano's behalf.

172

With a rear wheel punctured, Olano rode the last two kilometres without looking back, or in front, or at anything. He reached the line first, followed by Induráin who had returned to the job of supporting rider, and had held off the group gaining on him at the end. It was gold and silver again, in reverse order.

On the podium, this time beneath his team-mate, Miguel listened to the wild cheering of his countrymen who had come from Villava. The commentators were speculating about whether or not Induráin had done the right thing helping Olano to his victory. The Austrian journal *Kronenzeitug* was emphatic: 'Only a king like him gives away the gold. A Merckx would never have done what Induráin did for his colleague; Induráin is an historic sporting figure.' Pantani, who finished third and shared the podium with the two Spaniards, was almost complaining: 'Olano was lucky having Induráin as a super-protector.' In the Colombian papers, too, people were offering their opinions: Paco Galdos, ex-cyclist: 'Olano attacked very intelligently, at exactly the right moment, but it was a magnificent gesture of companionship by Induráin'; José Nazábal, ex-cyclist: 'Miguel showed that he is a complete gentleman'; Juan Fernández, Director of Mapei: 'Induráin didn't let Olano win. It was a masterly piece of team work'; Mikel Zarrabeitia of Banesto: 'Olano won on his own merits and Induráin was a great team-mate'; Miguel María Lasa, ex-Director: 'Olano would have done the same for Induráin.'

All that apart, what really mattered about this dream-ending was what Olano, himself, said about Induráin, one month later, in the cold light of day: 'I will always remember the embrace Induráin gave me just before going up on the podium in Diutama. That moment is something I'll always remember. I was in front of him and he gave me an embrace. It makes me tremble every time I talk about it. He has always been honest with me; the others – I don't know.'

Induráin stayed on in Colombia, taking advantage of the altitude to make another attempt on the world one-hour record. As soon as it was known that he was training in the Bogotá velodrome, people from Induráin's supporters clubs in Irún and Villava flew there. On 15th October, in front of thousands of spectators, Miguel failed, against the wind and against himself. He didn't get up to full pedalling speed and the attempt came to an end at 31 kilometres. He took it serenely: 'I've had a bad day, that's all. I was simply not going well.' At the end of that same month there were some secret trials in Bordeaux, but Induráin would make no further attempt.

On the last day of October it became known that Sabino Padilla, the medical wizard who had played such a part in Miguel's development, had been signed by Athlétic Bilbao F.C. for three seasons. Relations between Padilla and the new managers of Banesto had not exactly been smooth of late, and they were even more tense during the attempt on the hour record in Colombia. To pacify the cycling fans the directors of the Bilbao team were pressurised into announcing that they had no objection to Padilla sharing his new duties in the club with looking after the best cyclist of all time.

After his fifth win in the Tour, honours and prizes continued to shower down on Miguel. The Cabinet awarded him the Grand Cross of Civil Merit 'to reward his sporting and personal excellence', and later he, together with Abraham Olano, would be received by King Juan Carlos. He was granted the Grand Prize of the French Academy of Sport in recognition of those same qualities.

When he was interviewed about all this by the journalist Carlos Reigosa, Miguel spoke more eloquently than usual:

'And how do you cope with the success?'
'There are good things and bad things about success. Up to now it has been alright for me, but I have assumed that some day it will end. I attach some importance to success, but not as much as the media, which only sees complete success and total failure.'
'Do you always have to win?'
'I'm not afraid of losing but the more I win the more relaxed I am.'
'Will you win two more Tours?'
'I think that's complicated. The Tour is always difficult. I've done five already and I believe that is difficult to repeat, you know? If I win two more it would be unrepeatable.'
'And if you don't win, would you try again?'
'Certainly. I can definitely see myself losing a Tour and trying to win the following year. That wouldn't interrupt my career: I've already lost a Giro and my morale collapsed, but then I carried on working with my morale the same as normal.'
'Has Olano thanked you?'
'I haven't been with him yet. He thanked me when we were there, and the congratulations and that, and we talked for a while.'

Miguel had got the hang of it and he now knew how to disentangle himself easily enough in front of the microphone, even though he would never like it.

MIGUEL III

On 7th December Miguel received the prize he wanted most of all. Some days later than the predicted date his son, Miguel, was born. These things are difficult to describe, firstly because the emotion of fatherhood is different for everyone, and even more so when it's the first-born. For that reason, it is sensible simply to transcribe the typical society announcement which the press agencies released:

> The wife of Miguel Induráin, Marisa López de Goicoechea, gave birth to a boy, weighing 4.1 kilos and measuring 50 cms, on the afternoon of the 7th in the University Clinic of Navarra. The birth took place naturally and without complications at 5.25 pm.

> Both Marisa and Miguel – who remained with his wife throughout – were obviously delighted at the birth, and said they were enormously happy. The new mother also said that being able to count on her husband's presence during the birth had greatly helped her.

> Marisa López de Goicoechea entered the University Clinic at 10 am, and occupied one of the four dilation rooms where she continued to be monitored right up until the birth which was assisted by the Director of the Department of Gynaecology and Obstrectics, Dr Guillermo López. At his side were two specialist helpers, two matrons, an anaesthetist and several auxiliaries. According to Dr López 'the birth took place without incident, and both mother and child are doing well'.

> Immediately after he was born, the child was given the tests that are given to all the newly born; the results were perfectly satisfactory.

> After the birth, Marisa was moved to a room in the delivery area, accompanied by her husband, who announced he intended to spend the night at the centre.

And here ends, with apologies, what the agencies said about the happy event. By the following day the press already knew that the child would be named Miguel, that Marisa was on her feet and that Miguel – the cyclist, of course – had suspended training. What else would he do? It was also known that they were receiving visits, calls and continuous congratulations, and – something more remarkable in a world so dominated by tatty commercialism – they had rejected a multimillion-peseta offer from a magazine in return for exclusive colour photographs of the family. Thank goodness. Perhaps they even wanted the umbilical cord included!

The calendar of 1995 was at an end, the boy and his mother were now at home, and Miguel was returning to hard reality: the press launch for the '96 Tour took place in Pamplona which, perhaps in honour of the five-times champion, was going to host a stage finish for the first time ever. Miguel was asked the simple-minded question as to whether he hoped to be wearing the yellow jersey when he arrived in the Navarra capital. He sensibly replied: 'I'd sooner be wearing the yellow jersey when I arrive in Paris than in Pamplona.'

While the experts were discussing whether or not Miguel would definitely retire at the end of the 1996 season, as one Catalan newspaper had claimed, and while the Banesto team gathered together in Pamplona, its executives announcing that in 1996 they would only be going for the Tour and the Vuelta, 1995 was quietly slipping away. The fuss was not going to wake baby Miguel.

RESULTS

Tour of Aragón: one stage win
Tour of La Rioja: first
Tour of Asturias: two stage wins
Midi-Libre: first
Dauphiné-Liberé: first overall and one stage win
Tour de France: first overall and two stage wins
Rominger Classic: first
Tour of Galicia: first overall and one stage win
World Championship Time Trial: first
World Championship Road Race: second
Olympic Order awarded by the IOC
Civil Merit Award from the Spanish Government
Grand Prix of the French Academy of Sports

1996: THERE WAS THE WILL
BUT NOT THE WAY

By the turn of the 1995 season there was no doubt in anybody's mind that, for all his triumphs, age was catching up with Miguel Induráin. What's more, life had changed for him, as it does for all of us when a son arrives. He found himself facing the new year with more responsibilities and affections than simply those of being a cyclist, and more to yearn for, perhaps. There can be no doubt, either – and this could have been predicted easily enough – that Miguel would be under great pressure in the 1996 season to win a sixth Tour. Win that and then he could do whatever he wanted. If, to achieve that, he had to forgo other races which might deplete his strength, then so be it. He could surrender the Giro and the Vuelta, and anything else.

More than that, it began to be suggested in certain circles that with a sixth Tour victory, which would have beaten all records, Induráin would perhaps do well to retire while he was at the very peak of his success – like an aristocrat or, rather, like a God in the history of the sport.

The fact is that Miguel had already been enthroned as a hero and a legend. Just to take one example: at an auction in Valencia a firm paid over £9,000 for an old bicycle Induráin used to ride during his time at Reynolds! At least the benefits were destined to go to the Valencia Association of Health Care which offered free services to those in need.

THE TOUR AND ONLY THE TOUR

Banesto began the season by signing on a new doctor to replace Sabino Padilla, who was now looking after the footballers of Athlétic

Bilbao. He was 37-year-old Iñaki Arratíbel, born in Tolosa and with a degree from the University of the Basque Country; he had spent two years working hard in the University Clinic at Friebourg and had a very good manner with sportsmen, as he had shown with Olano, and many others. In the middle of January he took over his new post and liaised with Induráin in order to bring his services into line with those that Sabino Padilla was still providing.

Miguel was training, as he always was by this time of the year, on the roads of Navarra and in Benidorm where he usually spent a period of time with his family. The journalists were asking his opinion of what was being said about Rominger and Riis – that they were only going to prepare for the Tour: 'It seems fine to me that everyone prepares in whatever way they want, although obviously to prepare for only one race has its risks. In any case, I'm sure that Rominger is getting ready for something more than that. In the end I think we'll be pretty much on the same level.'

The first race was the Basque Six Hours, on 3rd February, in which an extraordinary duel between Induráin and Olano had the crowd on its feet. There was enormous enthusiasm and they ended up in a dead heat. They were equal on applause, too, and both agreed that 'the best part of the race had been the supporters'.

At Banesto's public presentation, in Madrid on 6th February, Echávarri admitted that the whole team was thinking about its duties in the Tour. Miguel listed those who would be his closest rivals this year: Zülle, Riis, Olano, Pantani, Jalabert and Bugno. It was not clear whether or not he had listed them in order of greatest danger to him. Neither did he clarify his post-Tour commitments which left the question of his participation in the Vuelta still up in the air. On the other hand, there was nothing new in that, and some of the journalists were inclined to believe that Induráin was hinting at retiring: 'I haven't decided whether or not I'll hang up the bike at the end of this season. It depends on how the campaign goes. If I believe I'm not in good form, and things don't go well, I'll quit.'

During this time it became known that Abraham Olano, whom the press had already crowned the natural successor to Induráin, had decided to move his tax residence to Monaco. From all sides criticism rained down on the world champion, and interest turned towards Miguel's financial affairs. He had already expressed his opinion about one's tax obligations in the economics paper, *Expansion*: 'Paying the tax office is as hard as winning the Tour.

178

Preparing yourself for the Tour is tough, but then comes the suffering of having to hand over almost half of what you've earned with your own sweat to the taxman, although this is something I now accept. If you see that the country improves because of what you contribute, and nobody cheats in the black economy, then you agree with it.'

Miguel admitted that he, too, had contemplated changing his tax residence, but that it wouldn't compensate him for having to leave, and then return to the country. Money, he said, was not everything: 'I value money for what it's worth, but I don't have an exaggerated view of it. It permits you to live well. The amount of money you need depends on the style of life you lead. For my lifestyle I have more than enough.'

He also spoke of another little problem other than the tax itself: 'The Navarra tax office investigates me every year and there are always details that have to be sorted out, according to the people who deal with my affairs.' And his investments: 'I only have a couple of small businesses with people from the team: a car concession and a sports shop. The rest I have put by, but I don't know what it's invested in, whether it's in investment bonds or in pension plans. I don't know.'

In passing, he finished off with a social comment: 'Recently it has become very fashionable to be on the front page of the papers every day or in the magazines, and anyone who is a bit more relaxed about things is not thought to be worth much. We have to change how we think. I believe there is far too much tension in our society and it's necessary to live life – which is the sweetest thing – and to keep work in perspective. There is so much anxiety in this country, just as in the rest of Europe and the world. If we could achieve tranquillity we would all be better off.' And this was the Miguel who, after his first victories when he was a youngster, used to tremble at the thought of speaking.

Returning to what really concerns us, for the remainder of February he carried on with his training programme, putting the kilometres into his legs, just as he'd planned. So, he made his first appearance in the Tour of Mallorca, took it calmly and retired in the second stage. He rode no more than that in the XI Almería Classic. Flu forced him to retire from the Tour of Andalucía and also prevented him from meeting his commitment to participate in the Luis Puig Trophy.

Jalabert, for his part, began March by winning the Tour of Andalucía and showed himself very much an opponent to be taken seriously when he swept the board in the Paris–Nice.

Miguel, half-recovered from his flu attack, took part in the Tour of Murcia, very gently and carefully. He put more kilometres into his legs, but nothing else, in the Milan–San Remo and, in the same easy style, rode a couple of relaxed days in the Catalan Week. While Zülle – another serious rival – was winning the race, the man from Villava went off to visit his family in Benidorm and from there to Pamplona for a general medical examination. The results of that would determine whether or not he would fulfil his next commitment, the Tour of the Basque Country.

April began and Zülle secured another victory, this time in the Estella Trophy; Induráin took part just to continue testing himself. He announced, in passing, that he would not ride the Tour of the Basque Country, a race that was won by the Italian, Francesco Casagrande.

Miguel appeared to be quicker and more lively in the Gran Premio of Amorebieta, which Gianetti won, and, half-way through the month, Echávarri announced that he was beginning to find his form. That improvement was visible in the Tour of Aragón: the race was won by Mauri, but Miguel was frequently prominent at the head of the bunch.

At the very end of April it became obvious that Miguel Induráin was well on the way to being his old self. From start to finish he livened up the Amstel Gold Cup Race, which Zanini won, and he completely dominated the picturesque Tour of Alemtejo, in Portugal, winning outright, along with two stages. Interestingly, Pruden won the other two stages and finished second overall, behind his brother. The Induráins certainly ruled the Portuguese race.

May begins and Miguel is continuing his preparation for the Tour without any upsets. The new doctor, Arratíbel, comments that 'he is still nine pounds overweight'. Eusebio Unzué calms everything down: 'He is at 85 per cent of his true form.' And the man himself, as the moment of truth gets closer, speaks about it all with complete calmness: 'I've still got to climb some of the long cols to see how I am on that terrain. I'm already at the same level of form as in other years. Pressure? The same as ever. Two months before the Tour people always start to talk more about the race; it's normal, but it doesn't affect me.' And he continues citing the names of his biggest threats: Riis, Rominger, Berzin, Zülle, Jalabert. He forgot about Olano who would go on to win the Tour of Romandie.

His good form was apparent in the Tour of Asturias. He had gone there insisting: 'I intend to fight for victory and to test myself to the limit.' He gave everybody a lesson on the Naranco stage and, what's more, won the race.

On 18th May the Giro once again began without Induráin. 'The King is dead; long live the King', so the saying goes, and the Spanish press turned its hopes towards Abraham Olano, the natural heir, to bring off the victory that the Navarra man had failed to achieve the previous season. And Olano truly worked for it: right at the very end he managed to capture the pink jersey, only to lose it on the penultimate stage because of the fierce slopes of Mortirolo. The Russian, Tonkov, showed, without a doubt, that the route of the '96 Giro would ensure victory for one of the specialist climbers.

While the Giro was in progress, the remaining top international cyclists pitted themselves against each other in the tough Bicicleta Vasca. Miguel was there and aiming to cause trouble. He remained watchful during the first two stages, then, on stage three, he stirred things up, forcing such an exhausting pace that only Zülle and Marcelino García, the eventual stage winner, could hang on. He won the fifth stage on the ascent of Arrate and ended the race on top of the podium with a comfortable, well-deserved victory.

On 1st June, in the Classic of the Alps, Jalabert gave a new warning, showing that he was going better and better in the mountains every time. Miguel ended up eighth; he didn't have to dig too deep, but he did confirm one thing – Jalabert was going to be an especially dangerous rival in the Tour.

The Dauphiné Libéré began the following day and, to judge by the results, it seemed that Induráin had gone there to finally sort everything out. He won the time trial, won the Alpine stage and won the race. He gained a moral advantage over Jalabert who had to abandon on the extremely tough final day's climbs. He also made use of the race to diagnose his own form and that of his rivals: 'I don't think I've progressed that much in the mountains, although I'm on the right track. My opponents have got better in the time trials, but they seem to me to be worse on the big climbs.' The Navarra man appeared secure: 'Now I'll prepare for the Tour and only take part in the Spanish Championship at Sabiñánigo on the 23rd.'

After his victory in the Dauphiné Libéré, the French papers were reiterating their praise of Induráin:

Always God and the maestro. (*L'Equipe*)

He continues to be the boss of the international peloton. (*Le Parisien*)

The ICU classification had Jalabert first with 2,989 points; second, Induráin with 2,063 points; third, Olano with 1,565 points.

TOUR 1996: THE LAW OF LIFE

With the date of the Tour, the object of the entire year's work, getting ever closer, Banesto announced the team which would help Miguel Induráin achieve what no one else had ever achieved – a sixth victory. At his disposal would be Marino Alonso, Vicente Aparicio, José Luis Arrieta, Carmelo Miranda, José María Jiménez, Orlando Rodriguez and José Ramón Uriarte. Echávarri was still in some doubt as to whether Pruden Induráin or Erwin Nijboer would complete the group.

The Spanish Road Race Championship took place on 23rd July at Sabiñánigo, and again the journalists were insisting the race would be a head-to-head confrontation between Olano and Induráin. It didn't turn out that way: Miguel worked for the team and didn't challenge for victory, coming in 37th, 2-04 down on Fernando Gínes who won the sprint from second-placed Olano.

The 26th June was Induráin's last chance to train on the roads of Navarra. The day before, accompanied by several members of the team, he had tried to ride the route of the Pamplona–Hendaye stage in earnest, but they had been surrounded by cars full of journalists and photographers who wouldn't leave them alone. So, early on the 26th, Miguel and his brother, Pruden, left his house in Olatz to climb the Col of Erro, as he has done thousands of times before: it is an obligatory route on his training rides: Zunzarren, Monreal, Campanas, Esparza, Cizur, Ororbia, Orcoyen, Pamplona, Olatz – a well-known circuit which has everything: mountains, straights, bends, wide roads, narrow roads, light and shade: four hours, and 120 kilometres.

Arriving back at the house, the kids shout, 'Here he comes. Here he comes!' and Miguel and Pruden wave, and then, when they see the journalists closing in, it's a case of slamming the door, and into the shower. The bags are already packed.

On 27th June, almost as if it were a gesture of reconciliation, Induráin happened to find himself on the same flight as the ONCE team from Barcelona to Brussels. From the Belgian capital he travelled on to the starting point of the '96 Tour, the Dutch town of Hertogenbosch.

Now we reach a critical moment in the all-time history of cycling. Throughout all these pages we have gone around with Miguel Induráin, the man and the sportsman, to the point where we feel we're almost on intimate terms. Now the Tour de France was about to begin, as it had always done at the beginning of July since its inception 93 years ago, but this time it was different, for Induráin and for cycling itself.

His most avid supporters doubtless took Miguel's victory for granted, perhaps without stopping to think; for them there was no argument: it simply couldn't be any other way. Doubtless, too, every cycling fan, whether an Induráin supporter or not, was going to follow this edition of the Tour with special excitement. Either Induráin would win and we would all become part of history – he for achieving what nobody had done before and we for living through it – or he wouldn't win, and so not only would he lose, we would all lose. That truism transformed the event more into an epic than a sporting occasion: only the top step on the podium would mean anything. One day Miguel Induráin would have to stop and all of us – whether committed or impartial – knew that, but it was this Tour of '96 which would determine whether Miguel, and all of us with him, would go down in history in one glorious fanfare, or whether we would look back, not in anger, but more in a spirit of resignation than pride. We all wanted to hang on to that first possibility, even though the consequences would mean Miguel Induráin's farewell or perhaps the remote chance of him going for a seventh.

It couldn't have escaped anybody's attention that the '96 Tour was going to be different from all the others. The hour had come for Banesto to call in its six-million-pound investment which maintained the best cyclist in history, and all the infrastructure that was needed to support him: a general manager, two team directors, three mechanics, a doctor and a public-relations man accompanied Induráin, and the other eight cyclists. All the planning revolved around the Tour, and all the human and technical resources of the team revolved around Miguel Induráin. The Director drove a Mercedes, equipped with a television monitor and a radio transmitter to send the appropriate orders according to the situation in the race. 'Miguel,' Unzué said, 'has an intuitive nose for sniffing out all that's going on in the peloton. As well as a heart, he has a head.'

In the Banesto team everything has to go like clockwork. The masseurs – Manuel Arrieta, Vicente Iza, Juan Pujol, Manolo Arizkorreta and Iñaki Aragón – get up first each morning to prepare the food and liquids that the cyclists will consume, each one according to the diet that the doctor, Iñaki Arratíbel, has determined. After breakfast the massage session continues and, after that, the mechanics are given their instructions, and the strategy for the riders is planned. Doctor Sabino Padilla takes exclusive care of Miguel, and gets each one of his muscles working perfectly. Pruden, his brother, gives him psychological support: he works for him as a domestique, protects him from falls and also provides a listening ear. Michel Lafargue handles relations with the press and ensures that he is not plagued by interviews. The machine, then, is fully tuned.

During this time, the daily, El País, published a supplement designed to calm everybody's nerves which contained an interview report with Induráin in which he spoke of his complete serenity before this momentous Tour. Nothing was distracting him, not his son, nor the scenery, nor tomorrow, nor the future: 'Right now, only the Tour exists, those 3,835 kilometres which go from the prologue at Hertogenbosch to the Arc de Triumph in Paris.' He also indicated that he was relaxed in the knowledge that he had trained fully for the race: 'I prepare myself to the utmost over two or three months to win the Tour. It's the way I've done it for a good many years. It's also important not to be carrying any injuries, to be well physically, to take care of yourself. With the kind of preparation I do, it's possible to last a lot longer.' And everybody crossed their fingers.

On the day before the prologue stage Miguel spoke to an exuberant press conference and repeated what he had always said: 'The Tour has to be won day by day. You shouldn't lose any sleep before the start. What has been done before doesn't mean a thing: one starts at zero.' In the face of the journalists' insistence, he reiterated that he had not been thinking at all about his future: that would depend entirely on how strongly he finished this race. Miguel respected his opponents, ranked by commentators' forecasts: Zülle, Riis, Rominger, Virenque, Olano, Gotti, Armstrong, Berzin and, above all, Jalabert. He preferred not to be specific: 'What they want is to beat you – all of them. And for one to win, another has to lose. The one who wins will be the best.'

Asked for his opinion about the route and the danger of the prologue stage, he replied: 'All stages are dangerous. It is essential to be alert every day, but this Tour will begin to be decided in the time trial and at Sestrière. Then we'll see who will be strong at the end and who will not. The three days in the Alps could decide it.' Now he had said enough. From here on he would let his bicycle do the talking, which was, after all, his way.

José Miguel Echávarri, true to form, was complaining about the race route which, he maintained, 'isn't very favourable to the qualities of our champion'. The fans preferred just to take it as it came.

On Saturday 29th June that historic *Grande Boucle* set off with a 9.4-kilometre prologue time trial in the Dutch region of Hertogen-bosch. It was a dangerous ride with sharp bends made riskier still by the rain. The best time was Zülle's, who averaged 51.822 kph, upsetting the forecasters who had, unanimously, given Boardman as the winner. He, in fact, was two seconds slower and Induráin, twelve seconds behind Zülle, was in seventh place. The Navarra man had ridden flat out on the straights, but chose to take the bends cautiously. He was satisfied with the outcome: 'The essential thing was not to fall and not to take unnecessary risks. Four or five seconds overall are of no importance, and I imagine that prudence will have been the common factor among all those who needed to be at the front.'

The Tour continued in Holland on the following day, with the first stage a lengthy 209-kilometre route around Hertogenbosch. The stage was not so much flat as dead level, but it was dangerous territory with 120 roundabouts, and more than 500 awkward points where the wind and the rain became a real ordeal. It was a high-speed, panicky day in which everybody was hustling for bonus seconds and, in the process, aiming to get it over with as soon as possible. The narrowness of the roads and the invasion of spectators on to the road brought things to the brink of tragedy. There were falls, punches, elbow nudges; in short, it was hell, decided in the end by a sprint dominated by Gan's Frederic Moncassin ahead of a large group from which a number of riders, Rominger and Virenque among them, had lost a few seconds.

Induráin stayed where he was, seventh overall and twelve seconds down on Zülle's yellow jersey. He avoided the falls and didn't lose his concentration. He could see the peloton was on edge, and nervous: 'People are very wound up and highly strung. Everybody wants to be in front, but we can't all fit. Making up lost time is always a worry, but the Tour is going to be decided by more than ten seconds.' With that he had to cycle away from the Hertogenbosch finish because he was engulfed by hundreds of fans who followed him, waving flags and banners.

The long second stage, between Hertogenbosch and Wasquehal, ran for 247.5 kilometres over Dutch, Belgian, and, finally, French soil. Again it was flat, with complicated twisting sections, and, again, it was a fast, nervy affair culminating in a sprint finish by the whole peloton. It was won by Saeco's specialist, the uncompromising Mario Cipollini. Induráin had gone up to sixth overall, as a result of Buenahora's retirement, but remained twelve seconds behind Zülle. He had ridden carefully, without taking any risks. Survival was the main thing in these stages: 'It doesn't matter about gaining any time in these opening stages; what you must do is not lose any or, if the worst comes to the worst, lose as little as possible.'

The third stage, 195 kilometres from Wasquehal to Nogent-sur-Oise, was also flat, and appropriated by the quick men so they could amass their points and time bonuses. The seconds Moncassin gained in those brief sprints served him handsomely: he was able to take over the yellow jersey from Zülle. Again the stage came down to a mass sprint, won by the German, Erik Zabel, of the Telekom team, much to the astonishment of Cipollini who thought he'd won. Induráin remained sixth overall, although the bonuses widened the gap between him and Moncassin to nineteen seconds. The Navarra man, of course, was unperturbed and told people to stay calm: 'There are lots of riders trying to make their mark and so they're stirring things up in the last part of the stage. There's nothing to be said for taking the lead now because, if you do get the yellow jersey, you'll have to work twice as hard and it's just not worth the effort. Although, if you're not the leader you have to be equally attentive, so, in the end, it works out pretty much the same.'

Sabino Padilla, who was with the Tour exclusively to attend to Induráin, was brimming with confidence: 'Physically, Miguel is much the same as he was in 1991, when he won his first Tour. He has not suffered any wear and tear, and he has gained in experience. At the present moment his form is close to 100 per cent and he has more resistance than ever.'

The 232 kilometres of the fourth stage, between Soissons and Lac de Madine, took the race over increasingly undulating terrain, including a couple of small hills that were capable of causing a bit of trouble, and that's just what they did: at kilometre 38 a group of five riders went off the front – Stephan Heulot, the French champion, along with four other, lesser-known riders. The escape reached alarming proportions, the gap stretching to more than seventeen minutes. Nobody seemed inclined to take them seriously until ONCE and Banesto decided to put the brakes on this extravagance. At the end the fugitives came in, headed by the Frenchman, Cyril Saugrain, with their lead reduced to a more reasonable 4-33. Heulot, of the Gan team, took the yellow jersey from Moncassin and, because the five men in the escape group had cornered the first five positions overall, Induráin was now down to eleventh place on general classification, 4-17 behind the French champion.

It was very windy and, with the anxiety of cutting down the lead of the five up ahead, the lines of riders frequently fanned across the road producing numerous falls and breaks in the peloton. Miguel Induráin stayed calm, and equally calmly received the news that he and Olano had been chosen by José Grande, the Spanish Cycling Manager, to lead the Spanish team at the Atlanta Olympics, beginning on 31st July.

According to those most in the know the race would be better controlled by the favourites from now on. Heulot was seen as only a temporary leader, although his gap could give him a sufficient buffer for two or three days. The fifth stage, the 242 kilometres from Lac de Madine to Besançon, passed through a hilly region and included a fourth-category climb twelve kilometres from the end. This was too far out to prevent the mass finish that took place after the long-suffering riders had had to put up with the persistent, trying rain of the sort that you don't mind on your face, but which soaks through to your bones. The race was run cautiously, and steadily – there was no alternative – and after Giusseppe Calcaterra had made one headstrong attempt to get clear, with 30 kilometres to go, everything ended in a compact group, the sprint going to the Dutch, TVM rider, Jeroen Blijlevens. Those who were following the stage on television had a fright when Induráin punctured, and the ONCE and Mapei teams began to press hard, but his Banesto companions had no difficulty in bringing him rapidly back into the peloton.

A mere five stages had been covered and the pessimistic weather forecasts seemed to have thoroughly disheartened the peloton, and filled the riders' legs with lead. Some, including some of the top riders, had been unable to put up with it and had gone home. Cipollini, Gotti and Svorada were among those who would no longer be part of the final story of this very tough, nerve-wracking '96 Tour.

The same appalling weather was set to torture the riders on the sixth stage, 207 kilometres between Arc-et-Senans and Aix-les-Bains, now on the very edge of the Alps. A second-category, a third-category and three fourth-category climbs wore down still further the 183 survivors who had taken the start that day: only 169 of them would reach the finish of the stage. Pedalling in the rain could have been the title of the film of the stage, with the rain, the cold, the wind and all of nature's fury venting its anger against the fragility of a few men on their lightweight machines. Another Dutchman, Rabobank's Michael Boogerd, upset the sprint which the speed-men were carefully preparing and slipped in first, ahead of the big group containing all the main figures.

The alarm bells rang after one ferocious attack by ONCE which caught Induráin alone, without help. Almost all the Banesto riders had missed the break and been left behind, and Miguel had to control the attack himself. This was an unusual Tour we were witnessing where the principal candidates were being almost exaggeratedly vigilant, and where the tension was adding to the daily punishment inflicted by the violent downpours. Echávarri was in a sombre mood at the finish in Aix-les-Bains: 'It has been much tougher than we were expecting. Really, the stage was like something out of Dante; it has damaged everybody, especially those who have the most to lose, logically enough. We hope that our men recover, first with a shower, then with a quick massage and then by putting on plenty of clothes to try to keep warm. And, even so, we shall just have to wait and see how everyone is feeling after this terrible day.'

Up to this moment the Tour had been extremely harsh, but this was nothing compared to what it was going to be like from stage seven onwards. The Alps began with the 199-kilometre stretch between Chambery and Les Arcs, with the legendary, special-category Col de la Madeleine in the middle, the first-category Cormet de Roselend in the last third of the stage, and, finally, the climb to Les Arcs.

From that seventh stage the uncertainty as to how Induráin would fare in the mountains, without a prior long time trial, would start to be resolved. It was the change of menu which the organisers had presented him with this year and it remained to be seen how he would cope with it. At first Miguel felt optimistic, although he admitted his uncertainty: 'The mountains we've been through so far have been very easy, and so the change is all the more apparent. These are the first hard mountains of this Tour and they can do a lot of damage, especially if the weather carries on punishing us. The Les Arcs stage, however, is not the hardest; the hardest is the three Alpine stages as a whole. In previous years, when I got to the mountains, I had to be concerned, more than anything else, with defending; on this occasion it's just as important that I attack.'

He didn't attack. He couldn't. On Saturday 6th July, the day before the festival of San Fermín, with the whole of Navarra in the middle of its fiesta, Miguel Induráin suffered, on the first stage of the Alps, the most cruel *pájara** of all those he has suffered in his long cycling career. The mother of all *pájaras* suddenly overwhelmed the five-times champion on the final col, up towards Les Arcs. He had controlled things on the Col de la Madeleine, going over the top second behind Virenque; he had held out on the climbs of Méraillet and Roselend, bereft of help because his team-mates (and also a laboured Jalabert) had dropped back due to the severity of the route. Then his strength drained away. It was the same ill omen that forced Heulot, who until that moment had been in the yellow jersey, to dismount from his bicycle. Miguel rode on, unprotected, but, to all appearances resolute, along with the group of favourites who were chasing down the fleeing Udo Bolts. Together with a number of second-rank riders, there was also Rominger, Olano, Riis, Ugrumov, Berzin and Zülle who was being pulled along by Aitor Garmendia

---

*Spanish cycling jargon meaning a sudden, quite unexpected and overwhelming exhaustion; a slang expression equivalent to the 'bonk' in English cycling argot, but with more dramatic overtones.

after twice hitting the ground in spectacular falls. Here, then, was the *crème de la crème* all riding, watching and scrutinising Induráin. The Mapei men must have seen something – some gesture, some empty turn of the pedals – and away they went, Olano and Rominger bringing down the hammer with five kilometres still to go to the summit of Les Arcs.

And there began his calvary and the drama of a defeated Miguel Induráin – a tight-pressed, distorted expression on his face, and painful, robotic pedalling. Miguel was nailed, while his closest rivals did what they had to do, get away from him and make up minutes on him that he would never recover. This is what the Tour is. Only a man as remarkable as Miguel Induráin was capable of pushing on upwards, with blurred vision and legs as heavy as lead. Only an exceptional rider like Miguel Induráin could swallow his pride and drag his five depleted senses over the finishing line on the wretched pinnacle of Les Arcs. Only someone as unique as Miguel Induráin would refuse to dismount and say enough was enough. The diehard supporters of Induráin, staring at the television with their hearts in a knot, wanted to put wings on their wounded eagle and magically cut short those interminable four kilometres which broke open the Tour.

Whoever it was among that select group who had the sense to glance at Miguel and, because they knew him well, could see how he was, gave the *coup de grâce*. It was Rominger who, at a particular moment, saw in Miguel's face the signs of collapse and ordered Olano to throw everything to the wind. Later, at the finish, he would say: 'Perhaps I am not the best cyclist in the peloton, but I am the sharpest.'

Luc Leblanc, who took off on his own at the foot of the col, won the stage for Polti. Rominger, with a little flourish 100 metres from the line, took second place in front of a group containing Virenque, Olano, Riis, Ugrumov and Berzin, all of them inside a minute of the winner's time. Zülle finished 3-29 down and, finally, in sixteenth place, 4-19 behind Leblanc, came Miguel Induráin, completely shattered. No sooner had he reached the finish than he disappeared into the Banesto van. The result gave the yellow jersey to Berzin; Olano, with the same overall time, was second; Rominger was seven seconds back and, at eight seconds, came Riis.

Miguel got to his hotel in Les Arcs and went to his room. He showered, had a massage and came down to dinner.

After the fall came the speculation. It was a case of a huge physical collapse – that much was obvious. People were asking themselves why, as if such a sudden loss of strength didn't occur in the best of cycling circles, as if it was the first time Miguel had suffered something similar. Those with good memories cited the Sestrières stage in 1992, the Mortirolo stage in the Giro or the Tour of the Mining Valleys.

The curious thing was that, initially, there was no logical explanation forthcoming because, up to that very moment, Miguel had been riding absolutely normally. Doctor Padilla himself expressed his astonishment: 'He told me that he hadn't been able to see anything, that there was a cloud in front of his eyes. He didn't even know who had given him the first water bottle. There's no logical explanation; there's no information that tells us the reason for his collapse.'

This is just what a *pájara* is like, according to those who have suffered it. Echávarri recognised it for what it was and ventured: 'he was asking us for mineral drinks time and again. The climb was difficult to control and by the look of it he hadn't been sensible enough to feed himself properly. Fortunately it was not a physical problem, but a matter of faintness. This has been a negative warning for us, but we'll have to see how he reacts.'

Some experts were suggesting that Miguel had ridden for too long in his racing cape which, coupled with the fact that he hadn't eaten enough, had caused him to dehydrate. Who knows? What we do know is that hours after the disaster Miguel confirmed that he had really suffered on the slopes of Les Arcs: 'I only just got to the finish. They've gained a little time on me, but, the way I was going, I could have lost much more. I had signs of dehydration and I had to ask for bottles of mineral drink during the climb.' In addition to the time he lost, Induráin was fined twenty seconds for taking unauthorised drinks.

He admitted that he'd been taken completely by surprise and that things had become complicated: 'There were two parts to the stage: in the first, up to five kilometres from the finish, I was thinking about attacking; in the second I realised that I couldn't and I only just made it to the finish. I was feeling very good on the cols of La Madeleine and Roselend, but then I got worse without knowing why. It's a big set-back, but in the next few days I'll have to try to get back the time.'

Echávarri also offered a measure of hope: 'I believe that Miguel can demonstrate that what happened is a small aggravation and that it doesn't in any way alter our aspirations. The bad weather has put its stamp on this Tour and that's something everybody else will have to pay for as well.'

The sudden collapse of form which had seized Miguel Induráin changed the meaning of the race. For the moment, the leader was Eugeni Berzin, whom everybody remembered winning the 1994 Giro, when he took over the pink jersey on the fourth stage and resolutely defended it to the end.

The eighth stage was nothing less than a 30.6-kilometre hill climb between Bourg-Saint-Maurice and Val d'Isere. Hoping that San Fermín would protect him, Miguel had to overcome the adversity of the previous day and face up to a stretch of road which, even in normal circumstances, would not have been entirely propitious for him. Having seen what had happened, the experts thought he'd do well if he finished no more that a minute and a half outside the best time.

With their fingers crossed, Induráin's most enthusiastic supporters saw their idol give his utmost on the climb against the clock to Val d'Isere. He didn't begin well and his intermediate times couldn't match those of his main rivals, much less those he would have been making in normal circumstances. He was by no means fully recovered from the disaster of the day before, but, in the last third of the course, he summoned up everything and managed to stop the watch at 52-54. It was the fourth-best time, 1-01 slower than the quickest set by Berzin who had set off in the yellow jersey.

Miguel was recovering. Considering just how bad things had been 24 hours earlier, he could be said to have put in a reasonable performance: with strength of purpose he'd overcome what had previously seemed irreversible. After his ride he was relaxed and even optimistic: 'I feel pretty good and I'm pleased about that. I was up there with Riis, Rominger and Olano, and after a collapse like yesterday's that's important. I was pretty much on a par with everyone except Berzin who, along with Olano, has come out of the Giro in top form; the morale of both of them is high. They finished in much better shape than I did – that was obvious. For the time being I shall be looking to see how things go and hoping for a change in the weather – that it'll warm up. I have made a good recovery in 24 hours, but I expect to better that over the next few days.'

José Miguel Echávarri praised Miguel's performance in the hill climb and insisted that the Tour was far from lost: 'Given what happened on Saturday, it's only natural that Miguel knew how to recover and defend his prestige. If he recovers physically and psychologically, Miguel still has a lot of fight in him. I saw him finish well; he put everything into it and it's good that he did because it showed that he has what it takes.'

There was still another day left in the Alps, nothing less than the 189.5-kilometre ninth stage, between Val d'Isere and Sestrières, with the special-category Iseran and Galibier, the second-category Montgenèvre, and the first-category climb to the summit finish at Sestrières. The dreadful weather had not stopped; on the contrary, it was getting so bad that it was doubtful if the last Alpine stage could take place.

L'Equipe, after the mountain time trial, and on the eve of the hell that was expected on the Sestrières stage, pontificated across a full page: 'We have been present at two stages which have changed an era. Goodbye Miguel. Welcome Berzin.'

On this occasion, the French paper didn't get it right. The storm over the Alps was so bad that the 'queen of stages' remained just a princess: the day was reduced to a mere 46 kilometres, the final part of the route. There was snow and ice on the 2,770-metre Iseran and on the 2,460-metre Galibier, and nearly bears, even! The Tour organisers concluded that it would have been impossible for the race to go through a virtual snowstorm and decided the only possible thing to do was to shorten it. The stage, therefore, was not going to be the agony in which the older generation would be destroyed, as L'Equipe had predicted. It was also wrong with its slogan 'Au revoir Miguel, bienvenu Berzin': Miguel remained alive, and very much alive, while Berzin lost the yellow jersey.

With such a short stage, only 46 kilometres, finishing on the slopes of Sestrières, it was obvious that it was going to be fiercely contested by the strongest men. It would not be a race for the faint-hearted. Very quickly the Dane, Bjarne Riis, was stoking the pace out in front, fully intent on doing damage. He opened up an unbridge-able gap, despite the predictable best efforts of Berzin and Olano who were dragging best of the peloton behind them in their effort to stay in contact. Among them was Miguel Induráin: he seemed to be calm and, from the back of the group, he seemed to be watching for whatever reaction was going to take place.

Riis's ascent to Sestrières was an epic, amazingly quick. He was playing for the yellow jersey, as was Berzin – but the Dane was to win it and the Russian to lose it. While Olano was setting the pace for Rominger, glued to Berzin's wheel, three kilometres from the finish Induráin's enthusiastic supporters felt a sense of euphoria: they could see how he was showing what he was made of, going past an astonished Olano, Berzin, Ugrumov, Bruyneel and others in that top group. Riis finished first to take the overall lead and those who survived Induráin's attack reduced the gap, crossing the finishing line one after the other: Leblanc at 24 seconds, Virenque at 26 seconds, and Rominger at 28 seconds profited the most. Miguel's effort had cut Riis's lead which, five kilometres from the line, had been over a minute. Riis now wore the yellow jersey, with an advantage of 40 seconds on Berzin, and 53 seconds over third-placed Rominger. Miguel was up to eighth overall, at 4-38. Suddenly it wasn't raining so hard.

Induráin was satisfied at the finish: 'It was an important day to see how strong the others are. We have all paid for the effort we made on the mountain time trial. I'm still not fully recovered; I'm lacking a bit of spark, but I'm content at how I'm picking up. I hope it will soon get hotter, not only because it suites me better, but also to enable me to recuperate fully day by day. Riis is full of strength and confidence, and, what's more, he's got a strong team to help him, which Berzin doesn't have. He and Rominger are the most dangerous, and now it is my turn to hope that they, too, weaken like Berzin did today.'

Miguel's demonstration of strength was filling the leader with trepidation: 'I believe Induráin has already recovered and I shall watch him', said Riis, adding, in perfect Spanish: 'He's soon going to make us all recharge our batteries.' The sun had begun to come out and the Tour was still wide open, although the Dane had made it clear that he was going to give it his all.

Stage ten, between Turin and Gap, brought the race back into France. Over its 208.5 kilometres there were the last two Alpine cols – the first-category Montgenèvre, at half distance, and the third-category Col de la Sentinelle which would be the more dangerous because it was at the end of the route.

It was a day with plenty of skirmishes stirred up by second-string riders, but they failed through their own ability, or lack of it, to get anywhere. Ullrich, Madouas, Ugrumov and Virenque also made attempts on the Montgenèvre pass, and the Mapei and Gewis teams prevented things getting out of hand. Fifty kilometres from the end, when the peloton had already learned of the retirement of Jalabert, Bruyneel and Lino, along with other lesser-known names, Sorensen got clean away. A group of the top 40 riders which had nullified any number of attempted escapes, only managed to get its hands on the Dane – much to his misfortune – just 200 metres from the finishing line. Telekom's Erik Zabel again won the sprint, a few millimetres in front of that sprinter *par excellence*, Abdoujaparov. Of the leading figures in the bunch, Miguel Induráin finished quietly and comfortably, and remained in eighth position, still 4-38 down on the Dane.

Nothing had changed in the overall classification and Riis was feeling secure, and declared ecstatically: 'I can see myself wearing the yellow jersey in Paris.' The commentators thought he had an excellent chance of carrying off the world's greatest stage-race but, curiously, there was always reference to Induráin and his steady recovery. Nobody was daring to discount the Navarra man's chances completely.

The rest day in Gap would, on the other hand, benefit Miguel, speeding up his return to form. In general, the riders occupied themselves with training, massage and a bit of sightseeing. Certain riders, those who had a point to make, those in the top rank, had more to do: they found themselves facing the media and giving their opinions on the first part of the Tour. For Miguel Induráin this meant a swarm of television cameras, photographers and journalists from all round the world. The Navarra man was not at his best, but he answered all their questions

Regarding his tactics over the next few days: 'Obviously the way I ride after the Alps will have to be different from other years. I've lost time and I must make the most of it when those ahead of me are on the move. It's the first time that I find myself in this situation, so the first thing will be to recover physically and get my morale back.'

Perhaps it was going to get hot: 'If the weather had been good from the beginning, it would have been much better. But, in any case, even if it warms up, there are some very tough days left: the Massive Central, Hautacam, Pamplona and the 60-kilometre time trial. The opportunities are there; the problem is having the strength to recover.'

On the question of the help he expected from his team: 'If you attack, the important thing is to go clear. This has to be a battle between the team leaders. The team can make the race quick for you. If any team makes a move it has to be the leader's, not mine.'

Some help from ONCE was hinted at, now they had no aspirations for themselves: 'If I'm the only one who attacks, it's tough on me. If there are others, and we can both benefit, it's better for us all, naturally.'

And there is always the time trial: 'The time trial is good for them, too. I'm not thinking about the time they can take out of me. It would be better to reach it with time in hand than having to make up time. The least time they've got on me the better, but I'm not contemplating how much. My hope is to win. Four of five minutes can be pulled back and, of course, I'm going to be working with that hope in mind.'

A glance back to the set-back on Les Arcs: 'It was the same in the mountain time trial, in that I was not yet fully recovered. The Sestrières stage was too short and, for me, the long stages are better. To pull back the four or five minutes they've got on me will not be easy. In a single day it's impossible unless I gain a lot and the others nothing.'

But was he now recovered, or not? 'Normally I'm not good in the cold and the wet. It's some time now since the sun was out and my muscles are not fully recovered. After a collapse the muscles remain empty and it's necessary to fill them. The main thing is that I am getting better, bit by bit.'

And, for the ghoulish delight of some, he had to recount the events on the climb to Les Arcs: 'It has not affected me too much – psychologically. Throughout the whole of the stage I felt fine; I was intending to attack. It was a matter of three minutes. If I'd had the problems throughout the stage, it would have been irretrievable. I haven't found an explanation for what happened to me. On the Sestrières stage in the '92 Tour I hadn't eaten well. On the Mortirolo, in the Giro, I went too hard on the climbs. I put it down more to the cold: the muscles don't recoup all the energy they need. With the cold, being a well-built rider, you expend more energy than a smaller rider.'

And he had to forecast: 'The big favourite is Riis, but if he concerns himself too much with me he could have problems. There is also Olano, Rominger, Berzin and Virenque. The Telekom team are in form, with good morale , and they could make it simple for Riis.'

On that brief rest day cycling heroes from previous eras were also giving their opinions. They all agreed: the Tour was still not lost for Miguel. Bernard Hinault: 'A collapse is something that can happen to anybody, but it can be fixed. He has to get his head down on the bars and launch his attack. This is not the time for refined tactics. Induráin can only do one thing – attack'; Perico Delgado: 'It's difficult for him, not because of himself – he is sure to go well – but because of his rivals, above all Riis, who seems to me to be very strong, as is his team. There are too many people ahead of him who would need to fail'; Eddy Merckx: 'Miguel can still win the Tour although he's a long way back on Riis. We are in the middle of the race and he can still attack, which is what he has to do. Induráin will always be dangerous'; Felice Gimondi: 'If he can get back to being the Induráin of last year, he'll still have plenty to say in this Tour'; Roger Pingeon: 'If the weather stays good, Induráin is still capable of doing great things'; Lucien Van Impe: 'I don't see a clear winner of this race'; Stephen Roche: 'Induráin still has an excellent chance of winning the Tour. The hot weather has returned and that is his best ally. Many of those who are in front of him are going to blow up. With the stage finish at Pamplona and the time trial at Bordeaux, the last part of the race is very good for him.' There was clearly no lack of good wishes.

The 202-kilometre eleventh stage, between Gap and Valence, wound its way through the Massive Central over six mountain cols – three second-category, and three third-category. The race passed off without any major alterations to the top of the classification. An escape by six second-rank riders prospered, without troubling anyone unduly. The group arrived in Valence with a lead of almost three minutes and the sprint took everybody by surprise. Against all expectations it was the Colombian, 'Txepe' González, who had never been seen on the podium before, who took the honours in this uneventful stage through the Massive Central.

The Germans in the Telekom squad kept an iron grip on any manoeuvres in the big group: there, nobody moved. It was apparent from the way Induráin was riding that he was not fully recovered. The weather was still not hot; certainly not hot enough to melt the tar on the road which is the kind of weather that suits him best, always assuming he's in form, of course. Miguel was not going to attack just for the sake of it, less still when it was clear that the leader, Riis, and his team were punishing anyone who tried anything without his nod of approval. It was better to pedal on in a cold, calculated way, an activity at which Miguel is a master. The supporters – still betting on him – watched as Miguel made himself scarce for yet another day. One more opportunity to try and reduce the gap of almost five minutes that separated him from the yellow jersey had gone by – one rung of the ladder less for Induráin, one more for Riis. It was telling on the nerves of Miguel's enthusiasts who now, perhaps, had a slight feeling of resignation.

Still in the Massive Central, there was another leg-breaking stage – stage twelve – which took them from Valence to Le-Puy-en-Velay: 143.5 kilometres but full of difficulties, most conspicuously a second-category, three third-category cols and the fourth-category climb up to the finish. Again, everybody was hoping that something would happen, something to break the uncertainty. Was there any chance of that or not?

Everything remained the same for the time being. A 134-kilometre escape, organised by a group of eight minor riders, didn't cause the masters of the peloton to stir from their siesta. The fugitives were led in by MG's Pascal Richard, with a fifteen minute lead. The Telekom boys, Riis's praetorian guard, controlled whatever they had to control which, in truth, was not very much. Some of the Banesto team – Uriarte, Arrieta, Pruden – disturbed things a little, perhaps trying their luck on behalf of their team leader, but they were hardly troublesome.

Before the start, in Valence, the team leader, Induráin himself, had met with journalists who asked the million-dollar question: 'When?' 'I can't attack to gain only twenty seconds,' he said. 'That doesn't serve any purpose. The day I attack it will be to try to open a big gap, on a day that is just right. Riis is not the only one who is dangerous, just because he's the leader; all those ahead of me can also turn out to be dangerous.'

From the other side of the fence distinguished spectators who, in their time, had sweated for the yellow jersey, were also expressing their opinion about the outcome, in relation to Induráin. Marino Lejarreta had every confidence in him, and speculated on the where and the when: 'If Miguel is in good form he will try everything on the Hautacam stage. You can open big gaps on that climb. I regard the stage which finishes in Pamplona as more difficult.' Laurent Fignon was unreservedly pessimistic: 'I feel sorry for Induráin, but he won't be able to pull it back. It's the same as Delgado in the Tour of 1989 – he finished third, 3-34 down. He could be on the podium, but he won't win. To win in Paris all it takes is just one second, nothing more. Even if Induráin was just a minute behind he wouldn't take that out of Riis in the time trial. This is Riis's Tour. He has spent years learning to be a cyclist, working for others. Believe in him now, and in his chances.'

Untouched by pessimism, the Induráin Supporters Club had already organised two coaches so they could be there, on the Champs Elysées, at the end of the Tour. Needless to say they were hoping to see Miguel coming home in yellow.

For the time being the race remained in the Massive Central, perhaps with its toughest, most dangerous day – 177 kilometres between Le-Puy-en-Velay and Superbesse-Sancy with all the hills stacked in the second part of the route: a second-category, a fourth-category, and three third-category climbs, the very last one an exhausting end to the stage. Once again, much was expected of the peloton's big men in a Tour that was being fought out in a rather colourless way. The stage was not disappointing in that various skirmishes and attacks took place. It was won by Rabobank's Danish rider, Rolf Sorensen, who had already made repeated attempts on earlier stages. It was a case of 'jumping on the bandwagon'. Behind him came the Portuguese Orlando Rodrigues, for Banesto, and the always restless Virenque followed by Leblanc. At 23 seconds came Miguel Induráin, giving time to these men.

The stage developed as if things were going to happen, although in the end nothing did. On the narrow roads towards Superbesse the Banesto boys began to move up until they got themselves into single file at the front of the peloton. Marino Alonso was responsible for stringing out the bunch into a high-speed train and the push made itself felt. Everyone was waiting for Induráin's imminent attack when his companions realised the disaster that had struck: he had punctured and dropped back. Everything stopped again and the law of the peloton, which says everyone respects an opponent's misfortune, left things as they were: order was re-established without advantage being taken.

A couple of kilometres higher up the col Induráin's team tried again. This time Banesto's youngster, José María Jiménez, accelerated so violently that he went off alone with neither Miguel, nor anybody else, able to follow him. It was a useless gesture because, 200 metres higher up, he was finished.

All these efforts did little, therefore, other than show up the weakness of Rominger and Berzin at sustaining high speed uphill. Riis, well protected by his Telekom domestiques, gave no such sign of weakness. Furthermore, he, himself, would play a leading role in more than one skirmish, as if he wanted to make it clear who was in control: 'I am stronger than all the rest and I had no problems at any time during the stage', he said. 'My team has worked well and shown that it is the best in the Tour.' There were no doubts in the Dane's mind.

Meanwhile, expectation remained – perhaps against all hope – that Induráin would make the definitive attack, and Unzué was being asked about it: 'We shall have to wait and see how he is in the stages that are really hard. There were two good days: Les Arcs and Sestrières. On the first, what happened happened, and the second was cut short. We are going into the third week of the race and, at best, we will begin to see the effects of the Giro. Everybody is expecting Miguel to attack and, for some, the Tour could be lost. Miguel has to make a move but not go mad. One has to wait for the opportunity. Hautacam could be good, and Pamplona – a double-edged blade.'

Stage fourteen – Belle to Tulle – said farewell to the Massive Central, with 186.5 kilometres containing a second-category climb very near the beginning, three small fourth-category hills and a third-category just before the finish. It was France's great festival day and the roads were lined with huge crowds. It was hot, very hot – by luck or design, one never knows – but the race produced one problem after another. The peloton left Belle full of determination and there was plenty of action. After 21 kilometres, climbing the Col de la Croix Morand, an attack brought the top riders to the front, without Miguel knowing about it. If that wasn't bad enough, a fall near the back involved some of the Banesto team; already out of touch, they were delayed even further. By the time they got round to realising what was happening, the front group, lead by Riis and Olano, had put a minute between them. Banesto's effort was joined by ONCE and Kelme, until, 38 kilometres up the road, they made contact with the escape group, and the race returned to normal.

At the end, and after several attempts to get away, a solitary Abdoujaparov arrived first, to take a well-deserved victory. Miguel finished, eventually, in the group containing the major figures, 4-26 down on the Uzbekistan in the Refin colours. We wanted some heat and the temperature rose to 30 degrees, but nobody could shake off the feeling they had never had before that Induráin was riding a very insecure Tour. He was careful in what he said after the finish: 'We will try to make as good a fight of it as we can. Riis is very strong and it's going to be difficult to do anything about him. However, lots of things can still happen and I'm feeling well enough to get to the Pyrenees. Hautacam and Pamplona could be two stages for doing battle.'

Asked about his mistake – allowing himself to be left hanging after his major rivals had escaped – he commented: 'Everybody was beginning an attack on the mountain. Rominger and others were cut off, then came the fall, with Escartín and Pruden down, and the peloton was split. The best riders were in the front group and it was up to us to press on, together with the Kelme and ONCE teams, who didn't have anyone up ahead. They also had an interest in making the effort. They are professionals and they lent us a hand. I'm very grateful for it.' In fact there was a great deal of speculation that day about ONCE and Kelme helping Induráin's team.

Unzué, in turn, also gave his explanation for Miguel's absent-mindedness: 'The problem is that without the yellow jersey Miguel is more casual and is not among the leading positions at the head of the peloton. It's the only time this has happened. In any case, they must still be afraid of him, since they all worked against him, trying to take more time out of him.' Some people can see a silver lining in any cloud!

So, one more stage had gone by without anything happening. In the bars, meanwhile, there were fewer and fewer bets being placed on Induráin's chances.

The scorching heat was the worst enemy on the fifteenth stage – 176 kilometres from Brive-la-Gaillarde to Villeneuve-sur-Lot. It was a race where the terrain presented few difficulties, one of those classic transition stages, with two little fourth-category hills, a third-category and the Massive Central now behind them; it was expected to be uneventful. However, there were attacks almost from the word go – fortune hunters, with no chance in the overall classification, trying their luck for the podium on one stage. A six-man break did get away, and stayed away, and, in the end, it was Carrera's modest veteran Podenzana out in front, enjoying the greatest day of his sporting life. The rest carried on their war of nerves – plenty of sideways glances, but nobody throwing care to the wind and going for it.

Everyday seemed like a transition stage, waiting for something to happen. Something was expected to happen on stage sixteen, the following day. Here, all eyes were fixed on the summit of Hautacam; at last we were in the Pyrenees. Between Agen and Lourdes-Hautacam were 199 kilometres with a final, frightening, 13.5-kilometre climb at an average gradient of 1 in 12 where the riders would arrive with their legs already well spent. Almost all the Spanish cycling commentators were agreed that the miracle was going to happen in Lourdes, that Induráin would produce the ace which all magicians have hidden up their sleeve and everything would go back to what it had been before, to what it had been in the previous five Tours. Miguel, the best commentator on himself, was inclined to be more cautious: 'These two stages are going to be decisive and I will attempt to cut back as much time as I can, but then it depends on how my strength holds up. There are people better placed than me and I would like to get to the time trial at Bordeaux with the smallest possible amount of time against me.'

The Navarra man was not what you could really call an optimist. This was in contrast to the patriotic fervour of at least one trembling newsreader who saw, in the very slightest of Miguel's gestures, an indication of 'now you are going to find out'; it was in contrast, too, with the analysis made by the heart, with the eyes blindfolded. In reality, Miguel didn't seem to be fully recovered or, rather, he didn't seem to be the Miguel of earlier years, not just by the way he was riding, but also by his emaciated appearance.

Unzué and Echávarri agreed that Miguel was not going to walk away from the Tour without making an attempt, and they made the point that the roads over which he was to ride usually turned out to be advantageous to him. Though he tried, one had to bow before the evidence: Riis was the strongest and, on the summit of Hautacam, he had made this absolutely clear after unequivocally destroying the hopes of anyone who thought they were going to be able to put him in the shade in the '96 Tour.

There was no shade on a day which was to become exhausting because of the heat and the effort. The race arrived rapidly at the foot of Hautacam, chasing Roux, Richard and Piccoli who had got away at kilometre 29. The teams set to work for their team leaders and, after passing through Lourdes, the best of the peloton faced the great bulk of the mountain shoulder to shoulder. The painful climb began with the usual mutual vigilance until the yellow jersey made the decision. Riis suddenly accelerated as if to test the opposition. Induráin, Virenque, Olano, Berzin, Dufaux, Leblanc – the very best, in other words – followed him as well as they could. Riis went and then, cunningly, slowed right down. They all got up to him and carried on together for another half-kilometre, their eyes fixed on each other. Then Riis went again and his push broke them. All that remained was to climb quickly to arrive first at the summit. Miguel was nailed by the Dane's second attack and finished laboriously in twelfth place, at 2-28; he remained tenth overall, 7-06 back. Thankfully, this did not appear to be another collapse: it was purely and simply that he couldn't stay with the pace. It was not a major collapse, nor even a little one; he did everything he could, and that was all.

The analysis began to be made and now there was talk of something having happened to Induráin. It had to be in his physical preparation because just being one year older, which was what he was that day, hardly seemed enough to account for such a difference between this and the same day the previous year. Miguel gave his own explanation, although some were not convinced of his sincerity: 'I gambled on following Riis, but I couldn't get on to his wheel. I was able to respond to two of his attacks, but I couldn't go with the third. The fact is that at the beginning of the climb I was going well, I was there, but the pace Riis set was too much. Then, after losing Riis's wheel, I was thinking that I could stay with the pace of the others, but I couldn't do that either. I gambled and, at the end, I lost more time than I expected. I gave everything I could and I can't do more than that. Time goes on and the young come chasing after you, because that's the law of life, and just as I have taken the place of others for so many years, they have taken my place. That is what sport is and you have to accept it. Now I hope to stay as high as possible in the overall classification and, if I can, to look for something from those other two positions on the podium.'

It was a comment full of humility and sincerity. Eusebio Unzué confirmed Induráin's words: 'It wasn't to be. Today was the day when the Hautacam would reveal each person's real form, and the leader has shown us that it's not by luck that he's wearing the yellow jersey. Miguel has not been the Miguel of old and Hautacam has shown us how Induráin is inside. He has been worn down by the race, he is not recovering well and he is not capable of doing great things. As for whether he will or will not go to the Olympic Games, the final decision will be his, but I would advise him not to go.'

Unbelievably, the stubborn fans were hoping that the arch-miracle would occur on stage seventeen – the queen of stages, now, after the decimation of the biggest of the Alpine stages. This was the exceptionally hard 262 kilometres between Argeles and Pamplona, with three first-category cols, the special-category Col de Larrau, a second-category and two fourth-category climbs. That was it! The race was finishing in the home town of Miguel Induráin, on known territory; more than 300,000 people would be cheering him on throughout the whole length of the route to where his own people were waiting for him at the finish. Miguel had to do something.

He did: he got through to the finish, which produced the extraordinary sight of an indisputable hero who, without even winning the stage, was acclaimed, congratulated, applauded and embraced. Miguel reached the finish in the first group of important riders, except that this group was 8-30 down on another, much smaller group of exceptional men, led in by the Frenchman, Dufaux. Stuck to his wheel, and allowing him to take the victory, was the Emperor, Bjarne Riis. Twenty seconds back came the other six from that leading group. Miguel remained eleventh overall at the end of this day, 15-36 down on the yellow-clad Dane.

As expected, the stage was infernally hard. Only the pure climbers acquitted themselves well because the roulers, the all-round road-men, were hammered on the cols. Again it was Riis who called the tune and made certain of his first Tour. It was a beautiful spectacle, as an epic cycle race always is, and the beauty of the epic was added to by the generosity of thousands of people from Navarra chanting, encouraging a worn-out, but unbroken, Miguel Induráin. Perhaps it was Miguel Induráin that the organisers of the '96 Tour had in mind when they decided on a stage finish in Pamplona. It was Miguel Induráin who was now being acclaimed beside the roads of Navarra, even knowing that this was not going to be his Tour. It was Miguel Induráin who was now frantically cheered on for a sporting career that was in no way tarnished by his weary riding of this edition of *la Grande Boucle*.

The leader, Riis, also understood this when he insisted Miguel joined him on the podium, raised his arm and offered him the bouquet of flowers, and the honours that went with victory: 'I will win this Tour, but he is the greatest', admitted the Dane, marvelling at the fervour with which his countrymen were cheering him.

When he came into the finish Miguel Induráin still wore the smile with which he had greeted Marisa, and his son, as he passed through Villava. He finished tenth, which was no mean performance. Others who had been listed as possible favourites when they set out from Hertogenbosch had, by this juncture, already climbed off their bicycles some days earlier. Not Miguel: he knew how to lose with dignity and, with great sincerity, commented: 'I feel fine. I have no health problems: the only explanation for what has happened to me in this Tour is that my legs have not responded. Riis has been better than all of us, and that's that. It doesn't matter; one cannot always win. I came to the Tour to win for the sixth consecutive time, but I have realised that my strength has failed me and that is not because of anything strange. After the set-back at Les Arcs I planned to wait until Hautacam and to attack there, but when I wanted to make the effort my legs didn't respond. I am in the race and I can see the way things are going, but, at the hour of truth, my strength fails me. What I am certain of is that I am not going to abandon, baring a catastrophe or an illness. I will finish the Tour and I will put everything into the time trial. This is sport and the world won't come to an end if you don't go well, or don't win. This moment had to come at some time, after five years of things turning out well for me. Now what I want is to see Marisa and my son, and to try to recover for what remains of the season.'

Thus Miguel Induráin made his position clear, the prophet in his own land, the undisputed hero in a wildly excited Pamplona which, since the festival of San Fermín right up until this very moment, had been chanting at full voice the popular hymn: 'Induráin–Induráin–Induráin'. Now the legend had become just a man on a bicycle – and was perhaps the better for it.

Miguel's hour was up and, as usually happens, a certain chronicler had to prey upon the God's fall from grace, and insist on cutting him down to size, now that it had been revealed that he was just made of flesh and bone. 'In such poor form Induráin will not be able to take part in the Olympic Games' was the slanderous remark of one feature writer. In his typical fashion, Induráin admitted without embarrassment: 'Atlanta? Right now I don't know if I will be there, but if I do go it will be to fight for a medal, for sure, because if I just want to be a spectator I can see it on television.'

205

Miguel was resigned but satisfied. The Navarra stage had been physically tough but deeply moving. The whole of Villava throbbed as their countryman passed through streets which over-flowed in warm tribute. The balconies were decorated, an enormous grandstand had been erected for the multitude of villagers who were chanting the name of Induráin to the rhythm of a group of street musicians, even though they now knew he had been dropped on the terrifying Col of Larrau. Flags, caps, pennants, gloves – all with Miguel's image – were waved for two kilometres; it was only two kilometres, but for Induráin and his countrymen it went happily on for ever.

On the edge of the street, having got there early to find a good position, was the Induráin family: his father and mother, Marisa holding the baby Miguel who was sporting a small Banesto cap, and his sisters – it isn't every day that two sons, two brothers and a husband pass by your front door, riding the Tour de France. Miguel blew them a kiss as he came through. 'Go on, Miguel!' they shouted. Minutes later Pruden went past, waving to them. 'Pruden, for he's a jolly good fellow!' they shouted. It was a truly family occasion.

The 154.5-kilometre eighteenth stage took the race from Pamplona to Hendaye, with victory now decided. Three fourth-category and two second-category climbs said goodbye to the Pyrenees with the guarantee that it would be a nervous ride, full of action. Riis was assured of victory, but there still remained the fight for the other places on the podium – with Ullrich second at 3.59 and Virenque third at 4.25 – and the reward of publicity for the sponsors. Before the starting flag was raised, Induráin was still receiving the tribute from the thousands of Pamplona's citizens who were crowded into the Castillo square to bid him farewell. On an improvised platform Miguel, his parents and the whole of the Banesto squad waved to the multitude. A round of applause greeted the emotional and spontaneous kiss which Miguel senior gave to Bjarne Riis, the Viking who had taken over the yellow jersey from his son. He had done so in absolutely the right way – with class, hard work and elegance. The race was neutralised as it passed through Villava, and here Miguel dismounted, gave an affectionate kiss to Marisa, to his son, and said goodbye to his countrymen.

The rest of the stage was uneventful. A group of second-order riders went, fairly leisurely, off the front. Only Telekom's Christian Henn and TVM's Bert Voskamp, who would arrive first at the finish in Hendaye, were in a hurry. The remainder of the escape group came in more or less at their ease, and the big peloton at 16-56. That was about it – there was a kind of slackness, a kind of bitter-sweet resignation in the air. Nobody was now waiting for when, how and where the Tour would turn upside-down; nobody now had their nerves on edge, nor was anybody risking his prestige, and making promises he couldn't possibly fulfil. Miguel Induráin was not going to win the Tour for a sixth time, at least not in this 83rd edition. He just got on with the task of getting to Paris, this time with the plain and simple colours of the Banesto jersey over his weary body.

Taking the peloton closer to the French capital was the 226.5-kilometre nineteenth stage from Hendaye to Bordeaux, as flat as the palm of your hand, and with the expectation that the sprinters would fight out a bunch finish. That was what happened, after a fast ride without incidents. There was a timid escape, 50 kilometres from the finish, by two riders way down the classification, Aubervilliers and Wauters, but this was engulfed by the peloton on the edge of Bordeaux, to enable the quickest of the sprinters, Frederic Moncassin, to win by centimetres.

Frankly, in Spain there was scarcely any interest in the Tour by this stage. With Olano having lost his chance of a podium finish and, above all, a sixth win beyond the reach of Induráin, the various Spanish commentators who sent back their daily reports had run out of anything to report, and lost the enthusiasm with which to report it. The newspapers were now devoting less space to the cycling race and were turning towards Atlanta, where the Olympic Games were due to begin that very night.

It was precisely about Atlanta that Miguel spoke at the finish in Bordeaux. Well, in actual fact, they dragged it out of him because it seemed as if the only thing that interested them now about Induráin was whether or not he had decided to go to the Olympics: 'The time trial tomorrow is going to be a test for me', he said. 'Depending on how I finish it, and how I feel, I will decide if I'm going to go to Atlanta or not. The time trial will be a tough race, over an undulating route; it will be particularly favourable for Riis who is finishing the Tour very strongly. Riis is my favourite for the time trial tomorrow.'

Echávarri corroborated this: 'Tomorrow's time trial is going to be the defining test for Miguel: it will let him know whether or not he is fit enough to go to Atlanta. The decision will be his alone; that is the least due to him. He'd very much like to go, he said that some while back, but only if he's in the right form. It's not going to be easy because he's not in good physical shape. We can only hope that his loss of form is a temporary thing.'

There would be 63.5 kilometres to ride in solitude, this time without worry, without any risks, without even having to fear any one on the undulating road through the vines from Bordeaux to Saint-Emilion. Miguel Induráin rode that final time trial in such a relaxed way that he almost brought back memories of the Induráin of better times. He rode with pride and with class, recording the second best time, 56 seconds down on Jan Ullrich – the surprise winner and the true revelation of this Tour – who only just failed to snatch the leadership away from his team leader. Bjarne Riis faltered somewhat, but after being in serious trouble, facing this unexpected scare, he came though to make the fourth-best time behind Ullrich, Induráin and Olano.

All that remained was the final journey of 139.5 kilometres from Palaiseau to the Champs Elysées where the podium was occupied by Riis, Ullrich on the second step and Virenque on the third. Induráin, in this impossible sixth Tour, finished in eleventh place, 14-14 down.

At least that day the supporters of the great cyclist from Navarra did receive a pleasant surprise: after analysing the results of Sabino Padilla's specialised medical tests, Miguel Induráin decided that he would definitely take part in the Atlanta Olympics which had begun that day. He didn't appear entirely convinced at the end of the stage when, in an improvised press conference, he evaded any clear statement about Atlanta, but, after appearing before the press, he went to the hotel where the medical and technical analysis of the time trial took place.

Later, while Induráin was quietly resting in his room, Echávarri explained: 'For the first time the pulse monitor has given data similar to that in the Dauphiné Libéré, breaking the 170 barrier and even reaching 185 pulses per minute.' Sabino Padilla confirmed this: 'Comparing Miguel's own feelings with the objective data and with other good periods in his career, we can be frankly optimistic about his prospects in the Games, after he's had ten days of rest.' Against all the forecasts, Miguel Induráin was once more finding his form and his decision to ride would give him a chance of an Olympic victory.

On Sunday 21st July the Tour reached Paris with a new star, Bjarne Riis, wearing the *maillot jaune*. In his honour the 129 survivors pedalled easily until they got on to the Champs Elysées circuit and ended with a brilliant exhibition of sprinting. MG's Italian, Fabio Baldato, took the last honours of the race, hitting the line millimetres in front of Moncassin, Abdoujaparov, Blijlevens and Zabel. Then came all the rest.

On the monitor in the Banesto van Miguel Induráin was able to witness someone else's glory on the podium. There was Riis, hugging his wife, Mette, who was crying with emotion, the Danish supporters hoisting their flags, the lap of honour. His supporters from Villava were also there on the Champs Elysées, and his family and friends, but it was not the same. They say that Induráin is a dispassionate man, with perfect control of his emotions, but when all the glorious paraphernalia of the Tour – which Induráin had enjoyed in the last five years, as if he had owned it – was being dedicated to someone else, nobody would seriously say that he couldn't be affected by it, even more so since the entire year's work had been aimed at repeating his triumph and establishing a new record.

After the end of the Tour Miguel was surrounded by cameras, microphones and reporters in the hotel, and in the Embassy where the habitual party was celebrated as if nothing had changed. Miguel knew how to conduct himself, initially giving the obvious replies and reiterating his sincere remarks about his lack of strength. Only when one little question insinuated something about his possible retirement did he bristle and, as usual, without any variation in his intonation, he hinted at future projects encompassing an Olympic medal in Atlanta, the San Sebastián Classic, other summer classics, and again aiming for the Tour in '97. He didn't even rule out the Vuelta for which he was already signed up. He alone knew his future and, from what it was possible to deduce after the bitter pill of the lost sixth Tour, it seemed as though we would have Miguel Induráin around for a while longer.

On 22nd July the Induráin family landed at Biarritz airport. At the very same time the Governor of Navarra was approving the award of the Gold Medal of the Community of Navarra to Miguel 'because since 1984 he has maintained a career which has no equal anywhere in present-day professional cycling. His personality goes beyond his impressive sporting performance; it is distinguished by such important qualities as intelligence, modesty, the value of team work and respect for his opponents which have increased his standing, and made him worthy of admiration everywhere.' At midday Miguel and his wife and son arrived at their home in Olatz to find the villagers crowded round the door to offer him their usual tribute. Though less well attended, it was every bit as warm hearted.

RESULTS

Tour of Alemtejo: first overall and two stage wins
Tour of Asturias: first overall and one stage win
Basque Bicycle: first overall and one stage win
Dauphiné Libéré: first overall and two stage wins
Tour de France: eleventh overall
Olympic Games (Atlanta): individual time trial gold medal

EPILOGUE

In the world of sport there's no point in resigning yourself to mediocrity and just settling for the second rate. There's no point, either, in relishing victory so much that at the least sign of your own weakness you become so frustrated or so jealous of the winner that you run off, and look for something else to do.

For decades Spanish cycling pedalled along that first, sad route, festooned with all the mediocre honours – successes in the mountains or colourful escapes which ended in stage wins. Bahamontes and Ocaña were the only exceptions: they were national heroes in the early years before the situation began to improve. Then, more recently, came Perico Delgado and, finally, Miguel Induráin.

Miguel Induráin got us accustomed to success and those given to hyperbole were coming up with excesses like 'Indurator', 'Robocop', 'God sitting on a black saddle', and other extravagances, scarcely before he had stepped off the podium. Then the myth was made man and Miguel Induráin was proved to be vulnerable – vulnerable to the wind, to the rain and to the cold which numbed him, to the treacherous *pájara* which paralysed him, to the unending pressure of the rival on the climbs where he was left to his own devices, to the ambition that surpasses the strength of the sportsman who cannot always win for the simple, forlorn reason that he is human.

It is then that the 'all or nothing' brigade start whispering about it being time for someone else to take over, and that, too, happened to Induráin, with some know-alls proclaiming that, with his arrival on the international stage, all that mattered was not the taking part, but the winning. Then, when Miguel Induráin showed himself to be human, their gut reaction was to demand explanations. Fortunately, and perhaps just to shut them up, Miguel Induráin left them confused: 'It has been a bad Tour, but I can still go on for a while longer.'

We will still see Miguel Induráin, as he indicated on the final night in Paris, in the Atlanta Olympic Games, perhaps in the Vuelta, perhaps again in full glory on the podium of his sixth and most ambitious Tour. And we will remember him as a natural phenomenon, but a human one.

We have seen, in this Tour of '96 when things went against him, how his most adoring supporters, his countrymen, chorused, at the end of the Pamplona stage, what has now become the hymn of the festival of San Fermín: 'Induráin–Induráin–Induráin'. It is sung to the tune of that triumphant American hymn which evokes the epics of the marines, mixed up with the circus chant of 'Now for the Most Difficult Yet'. This is the hymn which, for more than half a dozen years, has been deafening the fiestas throughout Navarra; it has its origins in the explosion of a lanky, ungainly kid into Spain's best-ever cyclist. 'He rides well,' they used to say of him in the Villava Cycling Club, 'but he cannot climb the Cuesta de Beloso.'

These pages recall the step-by-step progress of one of the most thrilling figures in competitive cycling, Miguel Induráin, who, for us, exemplified the transition from the happy-go-lucky sportsman into the dedicated athlete; from someone who had only the slightest, unnerving chance of success to someone who enjoyed repeated, expected triumphs. Then, just so we don't get carried away, it is appropriate that he, himself, should be the first to demystify the legend, through his simplicity, his perpetual sense of surprise, and guilt almost, at having won so much and with such ease.

Throughout these pages we have been able to show how the complete cyclist was constructed with the same concern for detail as in an experiment. Eusebio Unzué and José Miguel Echávarri, who discovered Induráin, understood that with his build, his sheer muscular strength, he could make a good time triallist, but they went beyond that. They carried on making an in-depth study of his anatomy and discovered that he had the making of much more than simply a magnificent domestique: he had a lung capacity of 8 litres – double that of a normal person; his heart diameter was 6.8 centimetres, as against the average 4.5 centimetres; his resting pulse rate was 30 beats per minute as opposed to the normal 60; his heart pumped between 40 and 50 litres of blood per minute instead of the normal 25 litres; his pulse returned from 190 to 100 in two minutes, while for most others it would take five minutes, and from 150 to 80 in 30 seconds, compared to the two or three minutes that others would need; on the turbo-trainer he was capable of driving a change of 500 watts when a normal person is capable of little more than 200 watts. Miguel's body, with all this physical potential, was theirs to develop, to draw out its competitive advantage, to use its energy wisely and to achieve the complete cyclist.

Equally, they studied Miguel's character, his temperament. They realised that he was extremely stable – he didn't allow himself to be affected by whatever happened in the race; he was calculating, his mind focused so that he would know when and how to act; he was very intuitive, and would make the crucial move at just the right moment. With these characteristics it was essential that he should develop the mentality of a winner, and they achieved this to such an extent that Miguel went to the very top in competitive cycling.

Stretching things to the point of hyperbole, one could say that Miguel Induráin was a cyclist made in the laboratory, through systematically developing both his physical and his psychological attributes. Eusebio Unzué discovered him; José Miguel Echávarri shaped him; the Italian doctor, Ferreri, honed every muscle of that machine to ensure maximum output; Sabino Padilla put all that together; and his team-mates always worked for him, unstintingly, and with total conviction.

For his own part, Miguel put in the necessary work, the strict discipline, and the austere way of life making the utmost of his own generous sacrifice. He knew from an early age that the bicycle was going to be his future and he dedicated himself to it totally. That gangling, ungainly youth, who went through agonies riding his bike up the Cuesta de Beloso, got where he did with hardly a change to that timid smile of his, an expression half-way between absence and surprise. Miguel Induráin does not have expressive features, nor has the marketing of him been able to alter them.

Without doubt, Miguel Induráin feels more comfortable when he is climbing the asphalt mountain roads than when he's put in front of the cameras and the microphones. God didn't give him the gift of eloquence and he looks upon the press conference as an unfortunate necessity, the toll that his popularity demands. From his first appearances Miguel monotonously referred to himself as 'we', which to some seemed impersonal and to others solemn: 'We have prepared thoroughly'; 'we saw the opportunity to break away';

'we have been there'; 'we are pleased with the win'. These are the phrases and the explanations which Induráin offers the press, ingenuously and without pride; the royal plural has much more to do with humility than with arrogance; it is a matter of timidity, and reticence.

In spite of his modesty, Miguel Induráin is the major cycling phenomenon in our history. Because of him, the love for the sport has spilled over beyond frontiers, beyond the barriers of ideas and social class. It is because of him that cycle racing has had such a remarkable expansion.

He is the total cyclist, made by hand and by computer. His example has spread throughout the world of international cycling, and now we are seeing the fruits of that same work and experiment: pure climbers who, without losing any of that ability, end up being able to fly against the clock; all-round riders who can still cut the air in a sprint finish, but also climb nimbly, even comfortably. These are the new cyclists of the modern age who, with fewer years behind them, and with smaller builds, are called upon to take over from Miguel Induráin. But they shouldn't be in too much of a hurry: they should wait their turn; it may not even happen.

Even as we speak he has just gone to Atlanta and carried off the gold medal, almost effortlessly, and that when, according to the merchants of gloom, he was at rock bottom. They say that he is obliged to ride the Vuelta '96 because Banesto insists upon it. What we know without any shadow of doubt is that, once there, he will fight for victory. They say, too, that he will retire next year. Perhaps those who say that say too much. There will still be days of glory for Miguel, and, for us, there will still be days to enjoy it.